SHATTERED
FAITH

SHATTERED FAITH

━━━━━

Sheila Rauch Kennedy

PANTHEON BOOKS

NEW YORK

Library of Congress Cataloging-in-Publication Data
Kennedy, Sheila Rauch.
Shattered faith / Sheila Rauch Kennedy.
p.   cm.
Includes index.
ISBN 0-679-43995-1
1. Marriage—Religious aspects—Catholic Church.   2. Marriage—
Annulment.   3. Catholic women.   4. Kennedy, Sheila Rauch.
I. Title.
BX2250.K39   1997
234′. 165—dc20   96–38523

2   4   6   8   9   7   5   3   1

Random House Web Address: http://www.randomhouse.com/

Book design by Chris Welch

Printed in the United States of America
First Edition

FOR OUR CHILDREN

Be not afraid.

His Holiness Pope John Paul II,
Crossing the Threshold of Hope
(1994)

Contents

AUTHOR'S NOTE

⊟⟿

The following is a true story. All of the characters are real. However, unless I was given permission to use the name of a major character, or unless his identity is obvious, I have used pseudonyms and in some instances changed identifying details.

Dialogues drawn from my conversations with the women who shared their stories and from conversations with their children are based upon my notes and verified by their recollections. In addition to interviews, my accounts of their annulments rely on their correspondence with the appropriate tribunal.

Descriptions of my meetings with the Boston tribunal, including dialogue, are based on my notes and written correspondence. Although I offered the tribunal opportunities to answer questions about my case as well as to give opposing points of view, the tribunal judge indicated that doing so could compromise confidentiality and declined to discuss these issues with me.

PROLOGUE

In 1993 my former husband asked the Catholic Church to annul
our marriage. For him an annulment was a simple matter and his
reasons for wanting one were straightforward. We had been divorced for over two years and he wanted to remarry. Since the only
way he could do so and remain in good standing within the Church
was to have our marriage declared invalid, he was prepared to testify
before a church court that in the eyes of God our marriage had never
existed. What's more, I was expected either to do the same or at least
not to impede the annulment process.

My first reaction to his request was emotional and personal. I was
appalled. My husband and I had known each other for nine years
before we married in a Catholic ceremony. We had been married for
twelve years before we divorced, and we had two wonderful children.
I could not understand how anyone could claim that our marriage
had never been valid. It seemed that if I were to agree to an annulment, I would be lying before God.

I knew that I would defend my marriage. Almost immediately, I
began searching for information to help me understand the annulment process and make some sense of the anguish I was feeling. I
read books on church law which traced the origins of annulment to

medieval times. I met with historians, priests, professors, and lawyers who were familiar with church courts.

After my initial research, I began to see annulment in a broader context. I grew to appreciate how difficult it was for the Church to remain loyal to its sacred principle that a marriage is forever while simultaneously showing compassion to its divorced members who wished to remarry. I saw too that there were times when an annulment might be justified, although most often these cases were childless unions of short duration.

My research did not, however, assuage my concern for my children. Nor did the reassurances of priests who explained that even if my former husband's petition were granted, our children would still be legitimate and full members of the Church. I was not worried about my children's legitimacy. I knew that American civil law would protect their legal rights. Nor had I presumed that the Church would discriminate against them.

My concern was for my children's moral development, a responsibility I felt the Church had shared with parents and the larger community for nearly two thousand years. To me, were the Church to declare my children the offspring of a marriage that had never existed, it would be abdicating its sacred and historical role to protect and promote their moral well-being.

My former husband's public statement that he was waiting for an annulment to set the date for his wedding sparked several news articles. When I responded to one such story, stating my opposition to the annulment, I discovered my views were shared by others. People I didn't even know offered me support. Men told me "to stick to my guns." Some mentioned children as their overriding concern. Others simply underscored the need for basic honesty in both our institutions and our daily lives.

But the vast majority of my supporters were women, many whose marriages had been annulled. Their letters told of their feelings of helplessness and betrayal. Many emphasized that the annulment had devastated their children. Moved by the eloquence and urgency of what these women said, I contacted some of them and asked if we could meet.

All of the women I spoke with were married for more than twenty years and each is the mother of least three children. Most were raised as traditional Catholics. The others were dedicated converts who joined the Church to share their husbands' faith. Largely because of their strong beliefs in the Church's teachings, they had forgone careers and defined themselves as wives and mothers. When the Church declared that the unions to which they had dedicated their lives had never existed, their faith in the institution and in themselves was shattered.

Listening to them talk of their marriages, I was at first struck by the sacrifices they had made for others. They spoke of family, community, and the ever-present Church. Most had been actively involved in their parishes. They taught religion classes, served on altar committees, and participated in Church-sponsored retreats. Sometimes it seemed as though they were speaking of a time long ago when the Church was the focus of community life.

As I listened more carefully, however, I realized that much of what they were saying was not about how things used to be but about their fears for the future. Many saw their church, the entity they had once trusted above all others, as one more institution that had abandoned traditional values for short-term gain and social convenience. They saw a future in which their children would be unable to rely on the Church either as a moral beacon within their communities or as a source of comfort in a family crisis. And they felt that without moral principle or truth, there would be no trust, and that without trust, a community and a family would break down.

There is an almost tragic irony in the annulment policy of the American Catholic Church. By all accounts as the next millennium draws near, more Americans are searching for truth and many are returning to organized religion to find it. Public speeches often sound similar to religious sermons with the emphasis on family values, commitment, community, and personal integrity. Politicians and community leaders now speak of individuals accepting responsibility for their actions as a prerequisite for successful social programs. Ethics is a common theme at business symposiums.

Ironically, as currently practiced in the United States, annulment undermines these same values many Americans are now celebrating. Those seeking annulments are not encouraged to accept responsibility for their failed marriages. Rather, the Church searches for a technicality in its laws that will render the marriage invalid. The person seeking an annulment is vindicated of responsibility for the breakup of the union on the grounds that there never was a true marriage in the first place. While the legitimacy of the children of annulled marriages remains intact, they nevertheless have become the offspring of unions that never existed. For some persons, annulment requires an even greater compromise in personal truth: lying before God.

Talking about their annulments was not easy for any of these women. Even in the one case in which the Church upheld the validity of the marriage, the investigative process proved to be cruel and morally flawed. Many women were afraid to speak, fearing that what few ties they had left to their church might be severed. Some were afraid that if they stood up to a former husband, he might withhold alimony or cause them and their children more hardship. And many were afraid to talk openly about their hurt and their feelings of loss, fearing that if they did it might be misconstrued as self-pity. In a very real sense, many of these women had been scared silent.

But as we came to know each other, the conspiracy of silence that had kept all of us quiet and powerless was broken. We saw that our concerns for the future would never be addressed unless we spoke now, and we saw that only by speaking would we be able to move forward, rebuild our lives, and again be productive members of our communities.

Today many of these women have a new faith, although sadly some have distanced themselves from the church that had been the center of their lives. Others are still searching for the meaning they lost, but all have begun to reconstruct their lives and are once again contributing to the common good.

As these women told me of their struggles, I couldn't help but think how sad it was that the Church had lost the trust of these most loyal followers. Americans of all faiths who seek a moral truth and a renewed nation may, as I did, learn much by listening to their stories.

SHATTERED
FAITH

1

GOBBLEDYGOOK

Easter had gone well. The thought kept going through my mind as I puttered around the kitchen drying the last of the hand-painted rabbit plates which had once belonged to my mother. I didn't have much need for special plates now, but I was still glad to have them. They were a link to my past, souvenirs of a more genteel lifestyle in a more predictable time when holidays meant gracious family gatherings at large, elegantly set tables with special seasonal plates.

For me, this Easter had been a turning point. It had been two years since Joe and I had divorced and four years since I had moved with our children from the Brighton section of Boston to the neighboring city of Cambridge. Though geographically adjacent, Brighton and Cambridge were in many ways worlds apart and each stirred memories of distinct times and circumstances of my own life.

In the late 1970s I worked in the housing office for the city of Boston. Often I spent weekends exploring the city's neighborhoods and admiring the older buildings. One afternoon, I discovered a charming but vacant three-bedroom bungalow in Brighton whose owner had recently died. With a wonderful view of distant fields, a very small woods complete with visiting pheasants, friendly neighbors, and off-street parking, the house was perfect for a couple planning to embark on a life together.

Shortly before Joe and I married in 1979, he bought the house and I set about making a home. I was very happy in our small urban oasis, and we were living there with our two dogs when our twin boys were born in October of 1980. Two dogs and twins called for more room and the next summer we moved to a rambling 1860s farmhouse on Boston's South Shore.

The farmhouse and the country life seemed to suit us well. With the boys' birth, I had cut back on my work for the city and now did much of it from home. The children acquired an abundance of pets: rabbits, chickens, kittens, a parrot, and even a pony. Joe, while busy with a nonprofit oil company he had recently founded, seemed genuinely thrilled with his growing family and always found time for us. But then in the summer of 1985, he decided to run for the congressional seat being vacated by Speaker O'Neill; and in order to live within the Speaker's congressional district, we moved back to Brighton.

Although we were able to find a spacious house on the same street where we had first lived, we were never able to recapture the magic we had shared in our first Brighton home. The pressures of the campaign and Joe's new congressional life began to take their toll and our marriage became trapped in a downward spiral. In March of 1989, the children and I moved across the river to Cambridge.

At the time of our move, I had no plans to divorce. It was simply clear that Joe and I needed time apart if we were to stabilize our lives. It was impossible for me to understand how our marriage, one that had started with such promise, had collapsed so completely. There are those who simply said that we were too different. Others said it was politics, still others our differing religions. I could accept none of these explanations.

Joe and I had always been different and, as is so often the case with relationships, our differences had been part of the reason we were attracted to each other. Joe is an extrovert. I tend to be shy.

Yes, it is hard to balance politics and family life, but the same can be said of most careers and I had supported Joe's political career. In fact, I liked politics and still believe strongly in public service. I had been a government major in college, and my graduate studies and subsequent work in housing and community planning were heavily grounded in politics. What is more, in 1980, shortly after our marriage, we had both worked on Ted Kennedy's presidential campaign. At the time, Joe had been my biggest supporter and offered me constant praise and encouragement. Why everything fell apart when he became a candidate and then a congressman is a question I still ask myself.

True, we have different religions: he is Catholic and I am Episcopalian, but we had married with a clear and mutual understanding that our differing religions would be a source of strength, not of division, for our family. Our wedding was a Catholic ceremony in a Catholic church, but my family's Episcopal minister was also present at the altar.

I never promised to raise the children Catholic. Rather, it was understood that our children would be the beneficiaries of both faiths and at the appropriate time, each would be allowed to choose his own religion. With this understanding, I joyfully participated at the boys' baptism, which we held at the Catholic parish in Brighton. Godparents were represented equally between the two religions; Catholic and Episcopal priests were present and both churches recognized the service as valid.

I never saw our religious difference as a competition. I happily worked with a Catholic priest to prepare the boys for their First Holy Communion. I admired this priest, whom I knew from my housing work, and welcomed his help in my children's religious development. Whatever had caused our marriage to unravel, I doubted its roots were religious.

Partly because the fate of our marriage was still uncertain when we left Brighton, I chose to live in a community which, although very different from our prior home, is also part of what had become Joe's congressional district. Economically and ethnically diverse and politically liberal, Cambridge is an independent city and probably best known as home to Harvard University and the Massachusetts Institute of Technology. While I had lived here fifteen years earlier as a student, many of Cambridge's neighborhoods as well as my own circumstances had changed.

There were no longer any bargain homes in Cambridge; and had it not been for a generous loan from my parents, I would not have been able to purchase the house I chose. There were more professional families with children in the vicinity than had been the case in my student years, some of which were headed by former school friends whom I had not seen since graduation. Now a single mother rather than a carefree student, I needed and welcomed the support and friendship of both my new neighbors and my old school chums.

So it was here in Cambridge that the boys and I, along with our three dogs, two cats, a parrot, and assorted fish, were trying to make a home. And it was here that as a family we set out to plan and cook Easter dinner, our first holiday meal without Joe. The boys provided the main course, a striped bass caught with their father off Nantucket. Like any fishermen, they were justly proud of their fish, and as twelve-year-olds, they particularly enjoyed telling the story of the catch to our ten or so guests.

Assembled on our small porch, which served as the dining room, our friends proved a willing if captive audience. The boys had set the dining room table with the rabbit plates and transformed the small space into a fitting site for a holiday meal. The plates quickly began to work their magic. When not listening to fish stories, our friends began to compare rabbits, and a warm spirit began to fill the room.

After the guests left, I decided to postpone most of the cleanup. I was proud of how hard the boys had worked, and I was enjoying the closeness the meal had created. I didn't want to lose its warmth to a pile of dirty dishes. Times of true intimacy with one's children are too few and far between.

And it was Easter. It was the first holiday that we really felt like a family again, although admittedly, there were three of us now, not four. The boys still missed their father and looked forward to their times together; but the three of us were now able to create our own emotional center. In keeping with the season, it seemed as if life were truly beginning again.

I was still enjoying this warm Easter spirit on Tuesday morning as I finished drying the last rabbit plate. Looking at my watch, I saw I would have time to do some of my own work before picking the children up at school. I had enjoyed the extra time with the boys. Usually their father picked them up on Mondays, but this week he had decided to stay in the Caribbean on vacation and return directly to Washington. I knew the boys were disappointed and a little jealous that they weren't on a fishing trip off a tropical island, but I was delighted to enjoy the entire week with them.

My thoughts were interrupted by the mailman at the door, who had a certified letter. Glancing at the envelope as I signed the receipt, I saw the words *The Metropolitan Tribunal, Archdiocese of Boston* and a church seal in the left-hand corner.

CITATION OF RESPONDENT [the letter began]:
I the undersigned by these present, respectfully cite: Sheila R. Kennedy (née Rauch), . . . , to respond in writing to me for the purpose of joining the issues and settlement of the question to be resolved in the case in which Joseph P. Kennedy II contends that his marriage to you is null under the provisions of ecclesiastical law on the grounds of: Lack of Due Discretion of Judgment.

The letter was signed by a church judge and accompanied by a brochure, entitled "An Ecclesiastical Declaration of Nullity," that outlined procedures I should follow to support my own beliefs "in regard to the validity of the marriage." But I was unable to read any further. As I rushed to the bathroom, I tried to remember when I had last actually vomited.

My stomach is one of the stronger parts of my body. Even when pregnant with twins I had been spared the bouts of morning sickness, but there was no denying what was happening now. I don't know how long I stayed in the bathroom, but I remember thinking Joe must simply be out of his mind. How could he possibly believe that the marriage that produced our children had never been valid? We had known each other for nine years before our wedding and we had been married close to thirteen. I could not go along with him on this.

Although I had no way of reaching Joe, I assumed his office did. After all, if there had been an emergency with the children, he would want to be notified. But strangely his staff in neither the Boston nor the Washington office claimed to know how to contact him. At first I thought they were just being obstinate, and then it occurred to me that they might think they were protecting me. The staff didn't know that I knew that Joe was in the Caribbean with Beth and that their relationship didn't bother me. For a long time I had assumed Joe and his assistant Beth Kelly would marry, and I wished them well. I had known Beth since she began working for him in the early 1980s. Long before Joe and I separated, she had been a frequent guest at our house and we at hers. In fact, the last Thanksgiving we had celebrated as a family, we had shared with Beth.

I liked Beth, and she seemed able to give Joe the support he wanted now that his world was politics. The only aspect of the relationship that bothered me, as old-fashioned as it might sound, was the children visiting them as a couple in Brighton when they weren't married. For me the sooner Beth and Joe married the better; for what really mattered was that she was genuinely fond of our children and they of her. A parent cannot hope for more and I knew I was lucky.

As I paced around my kitchen, I wondered if his office would still claim he was unreachable if I called back and said, "It's the White House calling. The President would like to speak to Congressman Kennedy, please." But I decided just to wait. I like the people who work for Joe and I didn't want to involve them.

Besides, if Joe was of the mind to claim our marriage was invalid, he probably would be less than amused to have his Caribbean holiday interrupted by a ruse. I told one trusted staff member why I needed to reach him, and then I tried to think of someone who could explain to me what was happening. I knew several priests from my work and I quickly called them.

When we spoke, they were sympathetic to my turmoil and each tried in his own way to minimize the significance of an annulment. All reiterated the Church's official position that an annulment is not "a Catholic divorce," but more than one admitted off the record that annulments are in essence the Church's way of "backing into one." There was a hesitation in their voices, though, which seemed to tell me more than their words did. No one wanted to say much and most suggested that I call the tribunal office directly.

When I did call, the receptionist put me through to Father O'Connor, who would be the judge in our case. Father O'Connor cautioned me that he could not say too much as doing so could compromise his position as judge, yet he assured me that even though I was not Catholic, I had a right to be heard. He also assured me that even if the stories I had heard about Joe's grandfather giving millions to the Church, one of his uncles receiving his First Holy Communion from a pope, and Joe himself being baptized by a cardinal were true, I would be treated fairly.

As had his fellow priests, he downplayed the significance of an annulment, assuring me my children would still be legitimate. He chose not to define "Lack of Due Discretion of Judgment," preferring to refer to it as the "usual grounds" under which petitioners seek annulments. Finally, he told me that an advocate who was an expert in canon law would be appointed to help me prepare my case, and that I should raise any additional questions with him.

I felt a little better after speaking with Father O'Connor. I stopped pacing around the kitchen and hung up the cordless phone that had been glued to my ear for the last two hours. It was almost pickup time at school. I vowed not to let the children know how upset I was. But once they were in the car, the boys seemed to sense that something was wrong. Children, particularly those who have experienced their parents' divorce, have a finely tuned radar for a parental mood change.

Dinner went slowly that night. I burned the chicken, and the boys asked more than once what was bothering me. Fortunately, they provided their own answer. My dog of fifteen years had only recently been put to sleep. A black-and-white cocker spaniel, he had been my companion before I married and had even been present at our wedding reception.

The children did not remember him in his heyday jumping into swimming pools or running behind their pony cart through the woods when we lived in the country. To the children, my dog had been elderly, blind, and in the end somewhat disoriented. Although they were sad at his passing, they were not as upset by the loss as they were concerned about how it might affect me. So they attributed my quietness to my dog's death, and while I was grateful for their assurances that he could "see again now that he was in heaven," I was far more appreciative that I did not have to invent some excuse for my black mood. That night we all went to bed early. The day that had begun with such warmth and happiness had turned cold and cruel, and I was glad it was over.

Early the next morning, even before I took the boys to school, Joe called. He had spoken with his office and had been told why I was trying to reach him. "You know," he began, "I'm sorry, but I don't believe those guys at the tribunal. They said it would take them at least three weeks to get that notice out. So I thought I would have time to talk to you about it before you got the letter. That's not a very nice way to find out about something like this. But don't you worry. You don't have to do anything about it. You don't even have to fill out the forms. They can take care of the rest."

I was stunned. "Joe," I replied, "do you realize that I'm opposed to this?" There was silence on the other end of the phone.

"How can you be opposed? What right do you have to be opposed? How can you prevent me from going on with my life?" he responded with a mixture of anger and disbelief.

"Joe, I have no problem with you going on with your life, and I wish you well. But an annulment is something very different from a divorce. An annulment says that there was never a true marriage in the eyes of God. I don't know about you, but I took our marriage very seriously. And I certainly took the conception and birth of our children seriously."

All my built-up anger had came to the surface. I remembered when the children had been conceived. Joe and I were working on his uncle's presidential campaign, and we were in Maine for the caucus. We had been married for a year and we were very happy. How dare Joe now imply otherwise. How dare he imply that the boys had been conceived outside of a true marriage. "I absolutely refuse to believe," I continued, "that our children are simply a result of some biochemical explosion that happened because you had fifteen minutes of unscheduled time during the Maine caucus."

"Now wait a minute," Joe interjected, "I'm not saying that."

"Oh yes you are," I replied.

"No I'm not," Joe repeated. "Look, Sheila, get yourself under control. Of course I took our marriage and the children seriously. And of course I think we had a true marriage. But that doesn't matter now. I don't believe this stuff. Nobody actually believes it. It's just Catholic gobbledygook, Sheila. But you just have to say it this way because, well, because that's the way the Church is."

"I'm sorry Joe, but I believe it," I replied, my entire body shaking with anger. I couldn't believe that he would ask for an annulment when even he didn't think our marriage was invalid.

"You *what*?" responded Joe. "Sheila, you can't be stupid enough to believe this. Jesus Christ! What's wrong with you?"

"Well," I said, "I guess He is part of the problem."

"Oh God, what are you talking about now?"

"Jesus Christ. I happen to believe in Him, too, you know."

"Oh God, you're not even Catholic," Joe added.

"No, but it's the same God. Episcopalians believe in Jesus Christ, too, Joe, and I already talked to the Church. They said it didn't matter that I'm not Catholic."

"You've got no right to believe this. This is my church, Sheila. You just can't let go. I don't know what your problem is. You're the one who wanted the divorce."

I caught myself, before I said something I might have regretted. "We both wanted the divorce, Joe," I tried to answer more calmly. "Our marriage became unworkable and intolerable, not just for us, but even for the kids. We certainly had irreconcilable differences. But there is a big difference between saying that the marriage doesn't work anymore and saying that, in the eyes of God, it never existed."

"Well," Joe answered, his anger rising at my unwillingness to yield. "Look, you can go ahead and fight this if you want. You may win or you may lose. But you're going to be spending an awful lot of time wallowing in ecclesiastical law." Before I could answer, he had hung up the phone.

Soon after my conversation with Joe, I notified the tribunal by phone that I planned to contest the annulment. Almost immediately, I sensed that the Church had not anticipated my opposition.

"You want option two," a gentle feminine voice from the tribunal office coached me over the phone. "That means you'll cooperate with our study."

"No," I answered. "I mean yes and no. I'll cooperate, but I'm strongly opposed to an annulment."

"No," she answered, "I don't think you mean that . . ."

"Oh yes I do. I'm strongly, strongly opposed," I insisted.

"Really—then you want option three," she continued. "We don't get many of those so I just wanted to be sure."

"I'm sure," I assured her.

Shortly after registering my opposition, I received a four-page blue questionnaire which asked about Joe's and my backgrounds, our courtship, wedding day, honeymoon, early marriage, and the breakup. I had no idea how to respond to the questions, particularly in the minuscule space the form provided. Staring at the same questions over and over, it didn't take me long to decide I needed to gather some information about annulment and meet with my advocate before attempting to tackle what I already thought of as the "dreaded blue folder."

After a little research, I learned to my surprise that annulments are common in the United States. The American Catholic Church annually grants over sixty thousand of them, three-quarters of the total granted throughout the world. In roughly 90 percent of all cases that come before American church councils, or tribunals, officials rule that "in the eyes of God the marriage never truly existed." As more than one observer of religion has noted, "The United States has become the Nevada of the annulment world." Another expert in canon law has boasted, "There isn't a marriage in America that we can't annul." In fact, foreigners who are likely to be denied annulments in their own countries are sometimes advised to obtain an American domicile and petition for one here.

I was equally surprised to learn that many people, particularly those who work for the American Catholic Church, consider that the ease with which it now grants annulments is a positive step, reconciling the traditional Catholic belief in the permanence of marriage with the modern reality that half of all American marriages end in divorce. Because Catholicism steadfastly defends its belief that a true marriage ends only in death, the Church maintains that even members who have been divorced in civil courts are still married to their first spouse and cannot therefore remarry in the Church. Those who do remarry, usually in civil ceremonies, are considered to be living in sin and are generally barred from sacraments, including confession and communion.

Annulments, I was told, are the solution to this bleak situation. For church officials they offer an easy way out of a seemingly impossible dilemma, and for divorced Catholics a way back into the Church. By annulling the first marriage, church officials in essence say that the couple was never truly married. The divorced parishioner is therefore free to marry for what the Church now views as the first time and to partake of the sacraments. Church officials stress that an annulment "heals" and enables parishioners to go on with their lives.

Without too much effort, I found a 1990 *Boston Globe* article in which Father Robert O'Connor, the judicial vicar of the Boston tribunal, the judge in my own case and the man who had assured me over the phone that I would be fairly treated, spoke of the Church's commitment to annulment. Assisted by ten full- and part-time judges who in turn were supported by a full-time staff of another ten people and approximately twenty consultants, Father O'Connor clearly viewed the granting of annulments as a positive trend. Upon referring to his annual 1990 budget of $255,604 and the purpose of annulments, he remarked, "Obviously, this represents a large financial commitment on the part of the Archdiocese to reconcile people to the Church."

The Church has made other commitments to reconcile its people through annulment. In 1992 the Boston archdiocese launched a special project to attract lapsed Catholics back to the fold. Financed by $150,000 received from a special collection and the donated services of the city's largest advertising agency, the Church ran commercials in newspapers and on the radio encouraging wayward parishioners to return to a more forgiving Catholic Church.

"For centuries," one notice began, "God has spoken to His people through Burning Bushes, Voices from the Clouds and Blinding Light. Could He possibly be speaking to you through this ad?" At one parish, eight people responded to the call. Four were divorced Catholics who had found the Church's tough stand against their marital status less than welcoming. Each was assured that if he sought an annulment, all would be well again.

The calm and detached way in which the Church presented annulment was in marked contrast to the confusion and anger I was feeling. To me, the Church was telling only part of the story. It neglected to mention, for example, that by reconciling "persons to full

sacramental participation" in its community, the same church was
also nullifying another sacrament—that of marriage.

More confusing to me was that the Church now seemed to be con-
tradicting its own teachings on the importance of a sanctified marriage. In the prenuptial counseling my former husband and I had
attended together, the importance of such a union as prerequisite for
conceiving and bearing children was the Church's predominant
theme. Now the same church was implying that sanctity didn't really
matter. In fact, the Church seemed to be sidestepping the issue en-
tirely by explaining that the children would still be legitimate despite
an annulment.

I am not a lawyer, but I remembered enough American history
from school to know that legitimacy, at least in the United States, is a
civil not a church issue. American law protects its citizens from religious regulation, and the separation of church and state is a cornerstone of our legal system. My concern about an annulment and its
effect on my children was spiritual, not legal. To me, the spiritual
domain was clearly a church responsibility and one which its priests
had stressed repeatedly before I married.

The same church that had so eloquently discussed with Joe and
me the importance of sanctity for our soon-to-be-conceived children
now wanted to declare that the union that had produced them was
flawed from the beginning and had never been sanctified at all. I now
saw this church as not only abandoning my children but, by hiding
behind civil law and an irrelevant legitimacy issue, as failing to address the spiritual issues that had been its rightful domain and responsibility for almost two thousand years.

In truth, rather than helping me prepare for my meeting, my research was making me think I was taking on a lost cause. I was nervous about meeting my advocate and my nervousness made daily
tasks seem as if they were insurmountable problems. For starters, I
didn't know what to wear. I thought since it was a somber occasion I
should wear something serious—probably black. My friends laughed
and asked if I was trying to convince the Church I was a widow. "Too
bad you don't still have the pony," one of them remarked. "You could
lead her along Lake Street, wrapping yourself in a long black robe,
and they wouldn't know what to make of you."

"I think the Church is trying to prove I was crazy when I got married in 1979," I replied, trying to camouflage my nervousness with a pathetic attempt at humor. "If that is the case, I don't want to show them that I'm a complete nut case in 1993."

My friends agreed. "Just wear an ordinary suit—not black. Get some stockings without runs, leave your sneakers at home, and put on grown-up shoes. Oh, and do something about your hair," was the consensus.

The tribunal office is a large, stately stone building located on the archdiocese's grounds in Brighton, a stone's throw from the house where Joe and I had lived and where Joe still resides when in the Boston area. For years I had admired the manicured grounds and the grand structure that had once been the cardinal's summer residence. Situated on a hill, the building commands a superb view of downtown Boston. As a city planner I had coveted the site as a park and I had envisioned children sledding as the highest and best use of its hill.

That morning, however, I didn't envision children engaged in winter games. Spring comes late and quickly to New England and usually leaves with equal alacrity. True spring days are few and highly prized, but such was the glorious day in mid-May when I arrived at the tribunal for my first meeting. The estate was resplendent in blooming lilacs and azaleas. While the sheer natural beauty somewhat calmed my trembling nerves, I was quickly reminded whose turf it was.

As I turned into the curving driveway off Lake Street, I was blocked by an empty beat-up car with its emergency blinkers flashing. Its bumper sticker read JOE KENNEDY, CONGRESS. Oh God, I thought, they've infiltrated the place already. I'm doomed before I start. But as I navigated around the vehicle, I assured myself it was a mere coincidence.

The tribunal offices are in a large, austere stone building with high ceilings and a grand staircase. Its atmosphere would be intimidating were it not for the graciousness of the receptionist who radiates kindness and compassion. She knew who I was before I told her and asked me to take a seat, explaining that my advocate would be right with me. As I waited I glanced at editions of *The Pilot*, a Catholic newspaper placed on the table beside me. One story pictured about twenty priests in individual photographs. All were white men. I wondered if there was a boardroom of a publicly traded company in America that was still all white male. Then I laughed to myself, wondering how many private clubs even looked like this anymore. My advocate arrived before I finished reading the story, but the pictures had been engraved in my mind as another reminder that this was not my turf.

My advocate, Father Lory, ushered me into his office, where he sat behind a desk and I on a chair in front of him, rather like a teacher and student. He seemed kind and intelligent and tried to put me at ease by telling me he had been to school at Villanova University outside of Philadelphia where my family lived. In truth, I felt sorry for him having me as a client, and I wondered if in the Church's eyes being assigned to me was a punishment for some wrong he had done. I doubted many former spouses contested requests for annulment and I suspected most advocates merely helped their charges fill out the forms and coaxed them along the road. I, however, planned to contest and with everything I had. If he was really going to be on my side, he'd have his work cut out for him.

We spoke of my marriage and the annulment process in general terms, and he assured me that the burden of proof that the union was invalid was on Joe. I mentioned a phone conversation I had had with Father O'Connor in which he had expressed concern that I was spending too much time answering the questionnaire and suggested that he simply take my testimony orally.

While I was grateful for the judge's concern, I told Father Lory that I preferred answering the questions in writing as the process helped me organize my thoughts. I felt that an annulment was an issue far more serious than my time was important. I was, however, concerned that I could not possibly respond fully to the questions in the blue folder in either the space provided or within the thirty-day time limit. So I asked if I could type my answers on a word processor and send them to him as I completed portions of the questionnaire. Father Lory graciously agreed and assured me that I could have additional time if needed.

Next, our discussion turned to the annulment process itself. Not surprisingly, my advocate's views paralleled those in the Church's brochure "An Ecclesiastical Declaration of Nullity" that I had been sent along with the official notification at Easter. "The purpose of the annulment procedure," the brochure and Father Lory explained, "is to serve one's conscience and spirit and to reconcile persons to full sacramental participation in the community of the Church."

Indeed, the process as described by both the brochure and my advocate seemed benevolent. Father Lory began by explaining how an annulment is possible. For those who have been baptized, the Church regards a valid marriage as a sacrament and consummated marriages as indissoluble. Yet while the validity of marriage is presumed, the presumption may not necessarily be true. Thus, if the Church can prove that a marriage was invalid, never consummated, or not a sacrament, then the union may be dissolved.

A tribunal, the judicial branch of an archdiocese, is entrusted to investigate marriages in which at least one spouse contends that the marriage is invalid. Such an investigation, the brochure continues, takes place only after a civil divorce and is based on the gospel and church law. To begin the process, a petitioner, the person seeking an annulment, meets with a priest, deacon, or pastoral associate and completes a form called "request for tribunal study." This form asks for biographical data and personal as well as marital history.

Once completed and signed by a parish representative, the petition is forwarded to the tribunal. Within thirty days the tribunal decides either to accept or deny the petitioner's request for an investigation. Assuming the case is accepted, the tribunal forwards formal notification to the petitioner stating the grounds for the study.

The tribunal then assigns an expert from its staff to assist the petitioner in preparing the case. All cases are assigned a name and a protocol number. Petitioners are told to refer to these codes in future correspondence or when calling the tribunal office. Once the Church formally notifies the petitioner that it is proceeding, it also notifies the former spouse in writing of the pending investigation. In most cases, a letter that states the grounds for the study is sent by certified mail.

At this point, I interrupted my advocate to point out that although my letter listed "lack of due discretion" at the end of the first paragraph as the basis of the investigation, I was left to my own devices to find out what the term meant. What I had learned was not comforting. The term refers to the provision in canon law known as "grave lack of discretionary judgment." If it could be shown that at the time of our marriage either Joe or I suffered from a grave lack of judgment, then we would have been incapable of assuming the "essential matrimonial rights and obligations." In essence, if one or both of us were incapable of marriage at the time we said our vows, they didn't really count: no sacramental bond was ever formed and, in the eyes of the Church, we were never married.

To me, the closest parallel in civil law seemed the defense of "temporary insanity." In such pleas, defendants claim they are not accountable for their actions because they were temporarily incapable either of controlling their behavior or of judging its consequences. In our case, my former husband apparently contended that as at least one of us had lacked sufficient judgment to marry, neither of us should be held accountable for our decision to do so. However, since Joe now wanted to marry again, any lack of discretion on his part must have magically disappeared. "Is it surprising," I asked my advocate, "that I find this reasoning or lack of it hard to believe?"

Father Lory did not take issue with my concerns. He merely cautioned me not to draw parallels between church and civil law. Canon or church law, he explained, has very different origins and a much longer history than civil law. I replied that as I was not a lawyer of any type, it was not the law but simply the logic that I could not grasp. "Well, don't feel badly about that," he reassured me. He had studied canon law for years and even he still found it difficult to understand.

"But that's not all," I continued. "That's just the tip of the iceberg." From what I'd found out so far, the American Catholic Church has interpreted "lack of due discretion" far more liberally then its counterparts in other parts of the world. In this country, the provision can refer to any number of psychological factors. While it can apply to emotional or personality disorders such as manic depression, the term may also refer simply to circumstances such as bad temper, overdependence, an inability to treat one's partner as an equal, difficulty in accepting adult responsibilities, addiction, or growing up in a dysfunctional family.

These are only some of the characteristics which the articles I had found cited as sufficiently grave to warrant an American annulment.

In fact, according to church scholars, 98 percent of annulments in the United States are granted on the basis of these types of so-called psychological factors. No wonder canon lawyers can boast, "There isn't a marriage in America that we can't annul."

"My God," I added, "I don't think Joe knows how to turn on a washing machine, and now that can be the basis for an annulment. If the world knew that every marriage where the laundry isn't split fifty-fifty means God never sanctified the union, everyone is in trouble."

"Now hold on," Father Lory cautioned. "It has to be a grave lack of due discretion. We don't annul marriages because husbands don't do the laundry. The burden of proof is on Joe, and remember, it [the lack of discretion] has to be grave. Don't believe everything you read about annulments. Efforts to make the issue sound simple can lead to a lot of misinformation and may only confuse you more."

I took a deep breath and we began to talk about "witnesses." Again, our discussion drew heavily from the Church's brochure. "Marriage," as the brochure explained, "is never a totally private relationship." It creates "profound effects on the family, society, and Church." To gain a broader understanding of this complex relationship, the tribunal asks both the petitioner and the former spouse to have friends and family respond in writing to a prepared set of questions.

These questions ask about the friend's or family member's relationship with the couple, his or her view of their backgrounds, the marriage, and why they think the marriage failed. The tribunal refers to these family members and friends as "witnesses" and asks them to send their responses directly to the tribunal to uphold confidentiality.

I told Father Lory that I didn't know whom to ask to be my witnesses. I thought it would be unfair to ask Joe's and my mutual friends as many of them either worked for Joe or might want to in the future. Others might someday want to seek his help, and being a witness for me could well jeopardize their friendship with him. I would have to think about whom I might ask and send him their names and addresses at a later date. He said that would be fine. I left the tribunal office thinking that even though 90 percent of annulments heard by American tribunals are granted, if the burden of proof was really to be Joe's, then it was not a done deal.

2

A More Meaningful Life

◆━━━━◆

The tribunal questionnaire is a four-page blue folder divided into four parts: background of both parties, courtship, wedding and honeymoon, and married life. Each of the four parts has either additional subheadings or questions within that category. Many are intended to uncover physiological or emotional conditions or circumstances that existed at the time of the wedding which would have made it impossible for the couple to form a sanctified bond.

Writing about Joe's and my relationship before, during, and shortly after our wedding was far more difficult for me than explaining why I thought it had failed. The more I thought and wrote about our backgrounds and early relationship, the more convinced I was of the original strength and sanctity of our marriage.

Both Joe and I had what in today's world is called a "privileged" childhood. Joe's family has, of course, been so constantly photographed and written about that I felt foolish adding my amateur observations. Writing about my own background made me realize how much I had to be thankful for: a close-knit traditional family of five children held together by two strong and caring parents, who, as I was facing my own divorce, had celebrated their fiftieth wedding anniversary.

My mother worked with a number of charities, but as was typical
of many women of her time, her primary role during our childhood
was that of supportive wife and parent. Later, when confronted with
the empty nest, she returned to graduate school so that she could
better assist young people with learning disabilities.

My father was a prominent citizen of Philadelphia, president of a
major bank, director of numerous corporations, and a civic leader. In
recognition of his service to the community, he received the Philadelphia Award, one of the city's highest honors. We were practicing
Episcopalians and shared an active family life through sports and love
of the outdoors. My parents provided me with both emotional and financial support through eighteen years of school, including graduate
studies, family vacations, and travel.

Joe and I were introduced by a mutual friend in the fall of 1970
during my senior year in college. Since we had known each other so
long before we married, it seemed odd to refer to this stage of our relationship as a "courtship." We had shared a lot during those years:
work and travel in close quarters in Africa, months when we had
been on separate continents, a brief period when he had been held
hostage in the Middle East after a plane on which he was a passenger
was hijacked, my years in graduate school, and perhaps the most difficult of all, his Jeep accident that left a young woman permanently
paralyzed.

We had attended large events together, including the opening of
the Kennedy Center in Washington, as well as numerous weekends
at our families' respective homes. I had been a frequent guest at
Hyannis Port, and he in turn had often visited my family's farm in
Pennsylvania as well as our summer camp in upstate New York.

By 1979, the year of our marriage, both of us were working and
financially independent. What is more, our relationship had been
tested more than some marriages are during a lifetime. Whatever
mistakes we were to make, they were not because we didn't know
each other. The reaction of most of our friends and family when we
announced our engagement was "It's about time."

Several weeks after mailing the first sections of my answers back
to my advocate, I met with him again. I gave him the names and addresses of possible witnesses: family members, my family's Episcopal

minister who had assisted at our wedding, and one brave friend willing to risk her friendship with Joe to be a witness on my behalf.

Next, we discussed what I was soon to refer to as simply "the letters" and "the picture frame." In 1971, shortly after Joe and I had
begun seeing each other, he went to Africa where I was soon to join
him. During the four- or five-month period before I joined him there,
he wrote me about sixty pages of letters, all with the same fond message of how much he missed and loved me. Considering we were still
seven years away from marriage at that time, I thought the letters
were clear indications that our relationship had not only generated
strong positive feelings on Joe's part, but that it had also evolved and
matured over time.

I had other handwritten notes that Joe's mother, his uncle, and
other members of his family had sent to me and my parents at the
time of our wedding. All referred to the strength and quality of our
love and how happy they were to have me as part of their family. With
such an abundance of written material from Joe and his family indicating how strong and positive our love had been, I wondered how
either he or his church could now claim there had never been a true
marriage.

The most moving of all the letters, however, was one that Joe had
written me from Paris so soon after we learned that I was pregnant
that we still assumed we were only having one baby. He referred to
being the father of my child as the greatest thing that "ever could
happen in my life" and stressed that "by itself that is more important
to me than anything that had ever happened." He went on to explain
that since our marriage, he had "just a happier and more meaningful
life because I have you to love and look forward to . . . I just love you
so much."

I still cannot think of words which could better set the stage for a
loving Christian family. I was happy to welcome children into such a
marriage. Joe's words captured the essence of our prenuptial counseling; indeed, no priest had ever spoken more eloquently. How could
the Church now say that the man who wrote those words did not understand what marriage was about or was incapable of meeting its
demands?

When Joe and I separated, I saved this and the other letters in case the children wondered if there had been love between their parents when they were conceived and born. If they should ever ask, my answer not only would be yes, but I'd have their father's letters to share with them and they would always know that they brought the greatest happiness to both their parents. I never dreamed I would be sitting in a church office trying to disprove their father's claim that they were not children of a true marriage. Nor had I ever thought that I would be using their father's own words as the basis of my case.

Finally, there was "the picture frame," sterling silver and engraved in my former husband's handwriting with the words *To the girl who made the proudest dad in the world. Merry Christmas 1980. Love, Joe.* It held an enlarged baby picture of our twin sons. My eyes welled as I handed the frame to Father Lory. I asked, "How can he claim there was no bond? These are his words, not mine, and his writing, not mine. So are the letters."

"They are nice children," my advocate responded gently. "You better hold on to the frame. The letters, I assume, are copies. I can keep them?"

"Yes," I assured him, replacing the picture in my bag.

We then returned to discussing how the tribunal completes its investigation. In addition to friends and family members who may be called as witnesses, the tribunal may also ask for testimony from those it refers to as "special witnesses." It is particularly interested in the views of persons who may have worked with the couple in a counseling capacity: doctors, psychiatrists, psychologists, professional counselors, priests, ministers, or rabbis may be called upon as special witnesses.

In order to have legal access to this confidential information, the tribunal may ask both the petitioner and the former spouse to sign release forms. In some instances, particularly if the marriage has been a long one, the Church may also ask the petitioner and/or the former spouse to submit to an evaluation by one of its own staff counselors. After all available information has been gathered, the staff meets to decide if the case should proceed to a formal hearing. If so, the petitioner's advocate and a judge, or if the case is considered complex, three judges, meet with the defender of the bond. The defender of the bond is an expert in canon law who argues for the sanctity of the marriage and protects the rights of "all parties." He along with the petitioner's advocate and the judges constitute the members of the court. In our case, since I was opposing the annulment, the defender of the bond would presumably represent my point of view.

As soon as possible after the members of the court meet, a date is set for a formal hearing with the petitioner. The petitioner is also permitted to read the testimony of his or her former spouse describing their marriage. Most often the petitioner meets alone with the judge, but sometimes the petitioner's advocate and the defender of the bond are present as well. Should the tribunal wish to meet with any willing witnesses, individual meetings are arranged. Likewise, should the former spouse wish to read the petitioner's testimony or choose to participate in a formal hearing, individual meetings are also arranged.

After the formal hearing, the defender of the bond and the petitioner's advocate present their views and after reviewing all the material, the judge or judges make a decision. Should the defender of the bond or either party disagree with the decision, an appeal is possible. Affirmative decisions are automatically reviewed by the appellate court. The tribunal of the Boston province, also located at the tribunal, is the appellate court for Boston cases. The entire process takes about a year and, as the tribunal's informational brochure explains, petitioners to the Boston tribunal pay a fifty-dollar application fee and an additional three hundred at the conclusion of the study.

Then, almost as a footnote to our discussion and in response to a question I raised, Father Lory told me that he anticipated that not only would our case require a complete process, but also that my attempt to prevent an annulment would be an uphill fight. "Why," I asked, "with all this written information, the letters, and the picture frame?"

"Because," he responded, "you haven't proven that there was a bond."

"But," I answered slowly, amazed at his response, "I thought you said the burden of proof was on Joe."

"Well, that's true. But your marriage didn't last."

"I know it didn't last. But I thought the issue was whether it existed or not in the first place. Whether it lasts or not is what a civil divorce is about, not an annulment."

"Yes. That's true, but we never even look at marriages that last. Many of them might not make it either."

"By that you mean you would have annulled them?"

"Not me, but the tribunal's process might have found them not to be true marriages; but because they lasted the question never came up."

"Sure sounds strange to me," was all I could mumble in reply.

That day I left the tribunal office perplexed and a little depressed. For the first time, I thought the Church was simply setting me up. Those guys can annul anything they want, I said to myself. I knew I could and would have friends and family respond as witnesses on my behalf and I would force myself to meet with the judge. But I also knew enough about statistics to realize that if tribunals rule in favor of those seeking an annulment 90 percent of the time, and that if Father Lory believed I still had an uphill fight even with all the evidence I had presented, then I had little hope of prevailing.

I was, after all, a Protestant in one of the nation's largest Catholic archdioceses. My former husband was powerful and popular. I was, as he so often reminded me, a nobody; and nobody in his town would be on my side. I fully anticipated that this second meeting with my advocate would be the end of my story.

The story, however, was just beginning. Power and even popularity can have their drawbacks. Shortly after I met with my advocate for the second time, Joe and Beth announced their engagement. Their announcement and Joe's public comments that he was waiting for an annulment to set the date provoked national though superficial press coverage of what I considered to be the serious issue of our marriage and its implications for our children.

In August of 1993, I decided to respond publicly to one of the articles. *Time* magazine published a slightly edited version of my remarks in its Letters section on September 6th.

Your article "Till Annulment Do Us Part," [which] the editors quoted, erroneously states that Joseph P. Kennedy II divorced me. In fact, I was the plaintiff in our 1990 civil divorce case, which became final in January of 1991. Second, while you note that we have twin sons, you fail to mention the impact of the possible ruling on them or on children of annulment in general. If our marriage were deemed never to have existed in the eyes of the Church, then our children, like others of annulled marriages, would have been neither conceived nor born to a sanctified union. I find this contention untrue, abhorrent, and contrary to the Church's teachings that such a union is a desirable prerequisite for bearing children. I am, of course, grateful the U.S. law will continue to protect my children's legal rights. But should an annulment be granted, such protection does nothing to fill the spiritual void left by the claim that my sons are "issue" of an unsanctified union. Thus, even though the odds of my prevailing in resisting an annulment are bleak, I will continue to defend the bond that brought my children into the world. I know of few mothers who would do any less.

Sheila Kennedy
Cambridge, MA

Predictably, the reactions to my letter varied. Many of my friends, although agreeing with my views, thought that my speaking publicly was simply out of character. Some wondered why I had so explicitly noted that I, not Joe, had been the plaintiff in our divorce case. The Church, while never denying that my statements were true, simply ignored the points I raised. Rather, it responded by claiming that since children of these marriages remained full members of the Church with their legitimacy intact, they were not affected.

My friends, of course, were right. My public response *was* out of character, or at least what had then been presumed to be my character. The truth was that my opposition to the annulment was beginning to change my personality, a change that I think was attributable to two factors. Until I received notice of the annulment, I had rarely stood up to Joe. Even though we had never signed a prenuptial agreement, I did not ask the court for alimony. When we separated, I moved out of the house and borrowed money from my parents to set up a new household for me and our children. I stayed in Massachusetts to facilitate his visiting the boys, and perhaps most important for someone such as Joe with political ambitions, I kept quiet.

For me, a marriage, even one that was over, remained a sacred bond. Though divorced, I remained loyal to it. Now by denying the sanctity of our marriage, Joe had broken that bond. He had in essence drawn a line in the sand and by opposing him, I had crossed it. Neither of us would ever be able to go back. I could not back down and face either myself or my children.

The second factor was my own tendency to hide behind my children's needs so I wouldn't have to confront their father. I know in retrospect there were other times when I should have faced up to Joe, but I had always been able to rationalize my giving in as being "understanding of his difficult schedule" or the boys' "need to see their father." I had never faced the truth that by the end of our marriage I had simply become afraid of him.

Now the shield of the children's "best interest" had been exposed. No one, least of all myself, could convince me that it was in my children's best interest to annul the union that had conceived them. Now protecting them required that I be active, not passive. It required that I face my own fears and if it also meant publicly speaking out, then so be it. I was prepared to lose, but I was not prepared to quit.

My reasons for noting that I had been the plaintiff in our divorce case were more complex. Many of my former husband's supporters, and to a certain extent Joe himself, simply wrote off my opposition to an annulment as evidence that I was either unwilling or incapable of facing the fact that our marriage was over. In fact, the opposite was true. I, far earlier than Joe, had accepted the painful truth that our marriage had irrevocably broken down; and I, not Joe, had taken the steps to end it.

But an annulment is not a divorce. Unlike a divorce, an annulment does not say something has either broken down or ended. It says the marriage never truly existed in the first place. This distinction, which no one seemed willing to confront, was at the root of my rage. To me, those who either minimized or denied it were the ones not facing the truth.

The Church addressed this distinction as it had my concern for my children: by sidestepping. When I asked for clarification, neither my advocate nor Father O'Connor would deny that what I said was true. Rather, they would simply repeat that an annulment is only an option after a civil divorce.

While Joe and the Church may have been comfortable with this blurred distinction between annulment and divorce, to my surprise the public understood my concerns. Boston may still have been his town, but many of those in the press, even some who were long-time Kennedy friends and supporters, were understanding and supportive of my position.

Equally surprising was the support I received from people directly. Many stopped me on the street when I was walking the dog. Others wrote to the papers themselves applauding my efforts. People I had never met wrote me letters and thanked me for speaking out. Not only was I overwhelmed with gratitude by this show of support, but for the first time since my ordeal had begun during the Easter holiday, I began to think I wasn't crazy after all.

3

TO HAVE HIS CAKE

I will always remember the first letter I received. It was from Deirdre, who explained that she had been urged by a large group of Catholic friends to tell me how grateful they were for my public opposition to Joe's request for an annulment. She emphasized that she represented neither nominal Catholics nor those seeking to find fault with the Church. Rather, she spoke for loyal long-time supporters who were increasingly frustrated by the scandal of the Church's annulling so many marriages for what seemed to be social convenience. Deirdre urged me to be wary and to presume nothing in my dealings with the Metropolitan Tribunal. She indicated that my concern for my children was wise and warned me that she had been unprepared for the anguish that the annulment of her own marriage had caused her daughters.

Then she offered to help me with my own case and said she was confident that others would gain from my brave stand. Her letter concluded with the assurance that the people she represented were only a small sample of those who she suspected shared our feelings.

I noticed from the return address that Deirdre lived less than twenty minutes from my house. I thought it would help us both if we talked about our experiences, and when I telephoned her, she told me that she had grown up in Ireland where the Church "is everything" and had come to the United States in the early 1970s with her husband and young daughters.

Deirdre was clearly deeply committed to Catholicism and I was eager to learn more about her experiences in the Church. A few days later, I set off to discuss religion, divorce, annulment, pain, and betrayal with a woman I had never met.

She greeted me at her front door. Deirdre is an immaculate housekeeper. Her home has an orderly, almost Victorian quality. The furniture and curtains are formal but inviting, and a friendly cat's constant purring made me feel at ease right away. We gravitated to her kitchen where we enjoyed a cup of tea and homemade muffins.

In response to her questions, I told her that my divorce had been finalized three years earlier and that until the annulment "exploded," I had thought things were going pretty well. I had begun to rebuild my life and the children seemed more settled and happier.

She was surprisingly open about the devastation of her own divorce, which became final in 1992. "I was so emotionally and physically wrought," she explained, "that at times death would have been preferable, had it not been for the fact that I had children for whom I felt a great responsibility. They were certainly the innocent victims. I don't think I will ever fully recover."

Remarkably, Deirdre seems to bear no ill will toward her former husband. After the divorce, she said, "I wished him well and hoped he would find the happiness he was seeking apart from me. After all, it was natural." She continued, "This was a man I had been on the road with, so to speak, for thirty years. There had been wonderfully happy times. Many of the great experiences I had would possibly never have happened had I not been married to him, and last but not least he was the father of my children. I have a mental picture of being on a long journey with a friend who insisted on taking a wrong turn, and for my own survival and the children's, I had to go ahead without him. I hoped he would find a safe haven."

As I listened to Deirdre describe the end of her marriage and the beginning of her life as a divorced mother, I was in awe of her lack of bitterness, her capacity to forgive, and her ability to reestablish a new life, qualities due I suspect in part to her Catholic faith. Yet there was an irony in her words that gave them an even greater impact. Deirdre and I both knew that just as she had regained her footing a new and more powerful threat was about to present itself.

"It was a beautiful May morning," she continued. "As I stood in line at the post office waiting to pick up a certified letter, an elderly lady in front of me was happily telling any and all who would listen of the flowers that had recently sprouted in her garden."

As the postal worker handed her the letter, Deirdre noticed that the sender was the Metropolitan Tribunal, an organization she had never heard of. "It looked litigious," she recalled, "which was enough to put a shudder through me after what I'd just gone through. I waited until I got into the car before I tore open the envelope. The first thing I noticed was the seal of the Archdiocese of Boston and I relaxed. I had always felt protected by the Church."

Deirdre's letter was essentially identical to the one I had received. The notice stated that her former spouse had asked the tribunal to review their marriage to determine if an annulment could be granted. As in my case, the grounds cited were "lack of due discretion." Deirdre's reaction, however, was markedly different from mine. She did not become sick to her stomach. Rather, she said, "I laughed out loud, . . . and mused as I drove home as to what priest he found who was so gullible as to present his case for consideration. Probably either one of these New Age guitar-playing types, or else one so incredibly holy that he would not doubt a word anyone told him. In any case, I wasn't terribly concerned. A twenty-six-year Catholic marriage that produced three children would not be so easily written off."

Looking back, Deirdre said that she now realizes that her faith in the Church actually worked against her in the annulment process. She trusted too much and never thought an annulment would be granted. "I was only familiar with the notion of annulment because of a similar case in Ireland a few years previously when a high-profile figure, with a marital history somewhat like ours, applied for an annulment on the same grounds. He was turned down, of course, but it hit the news and the whole country was laughing. There was some talk of a Frenchwoman and the general attitude was 'poor old John has lost it, but that's what happens when you get involved with foreign women.'"

Clearly, though Deirdre had lived in America for over twenty years she had not forgotten her Irish roots that had shaped so much of her character, and a smile enveloped her face as she told me of her childhood. "Oh, I suppose like most people of my generation I'm inclined to idealize my childhood," Deirdre recalled with her eyes twinkling. "We were too young to remember the terrors of World War Two and the deprivation of the Great Depression. By the time we were entering the work force we were the recipients of the great recovery of those times. The Irish weather couldn't have possibly been as good as I recall, but I remember the sunshine and long summer days.

"I loved life on the farm," Deirdre continued. "One of my earliest and fondest memories is of the lambing. I was only about eight years old and as I lay in bed I just knew that one of my favorite ewes had given birth overnight. I couldn't wait to meet the flock's newest arrival. Bounding out of bed, I rounded up five or so of my brothers and sisters and we ran to the shed."

There Deirdre found not one but three new faces cuddled with their mother in the warm straw. Deirdre and her brothers and sisters were overcome with excitement, for triplets almost surely meant that at least one of the lambs would have to be bottle fed, and bottle feeding almost invariably resulted in the lamb becoming a full-fledged member of the family. "Not that we needed another sibling," laughed Deirdre almost forty-five years later. "I was one of a large brood of children. Or, as my mother would say, 'the baker's dozen.'"

I had just met Deirdre and I didn't want to be rude, but I wondered how one woman could not only give birth to so many children, but also provide the love and nurturing they need to thrive. The look on my face must have said it all, for Deirdre laughed again and said, "Yes, one mother. But that wasn't unusual then in Ireland. We lived in the country. That was life and it was a good life. Those lambs actually followed us to school," she reminisced with a smile.

Financially speaking, Deirdre's family was not well off. But she explained that they didn't think of themselves as poor. "On the contrary, we considered ourselves very fortunate, for in addition to my father's income as a salesman we were able to live free in a house on my uncle's farm and while the farm principally raised sheep, it also produced enough vegetables for the large extended family. Other relatives worked in the retail trade, so most of the family's everyday clothes were bought at cost. One talented aunt made exquisite dresses for special occasions, and another knitted Christmas sweaters for the entire family. There was in fact almost a contempt for the material world throughout the community. Even our wealthier neighbors were frugal.

"The center of our lives was family, Church, and school. Since the schools were run by the Church, it's not an exaggeration to say that the Church was our lives. Catholicism was part of everything we were and did, and since at least ninety-five percent of the people we knew were also Catholic, the Church was the basis of our cultural identity as well as our religion."

Elementary school was coed, Deirdre told me, but at the secondary level girls went to schools run by nuns and the boys to ones run by male religious orders. Children from wealthier families usually boarded, but Deirdre and her siblings attended as day students. The Church was also the focus of Deirdre's family life, and the high point of her early childhood was undoubtedly her First Holy Communion.

"I was queen for the day. No question," she laughed. "But," she explained, "the priests were serious. I may have been only seven, but I understood penance and confession. My aunt made me a beautiful white dress with a matching bag and then there were those white buckskin shoes. Even with all the sisters in my family we each had our own dress for First Holy Communion. There were no hand-me-downs for such an important occasion. After the ceremony all the relatives came for a feast. I was clearly the center of attention, if only for that one day."

The family schedule was set by the liturgical calendar and as a small child, Deirdre noticed how well its rhythm of birth, growth, death, and regeneration blended with their agricultural life. Christmas was the highlight of the year. On Christmas morning, after a predawn check that Santa Claus had really come, it was off to the local church for six A.M. Mass. Deirdre's family usually arrived early to hear the carol singing and to greet neighbors, many of whom had relatives returning from abroad. "After Mass it was home to a full breakfast, appreciated all the more because," as Deirdre explained, "we fasted from midnight before receiving communion."

Lent and Easter were observed with equal fanfare and tradition. In fact, Deirdre admitted many of her friends thought Easter the more meaningful holiday, possibly because of spring and the sense of renewal, though her favorite was unquestionably Christmas. "Reflecting on the barbarism of the Crucifixion during Holy Week always put a damper on my spirits and I was never quite ready for the Easter Sunday festivities. However, those feelings always gave way to joy with the return of the birds, longer days, and all the lovely wildflowers, and perhaps most importantly the new lambs.

"Home life was good," Deirdre continued. "We were totally in step with our neighbors and with the people with whom we mixed. Everyone knew the rules and our values were reinforced almost by osmosis. Material success was admired insofar as it came as a natural consequence of hard work, but the measure of the person was how they treated others. It would be difficult to surpass the civility of the people amongst whom I grew up. Any penchant toward rigidity was balanced by my parents' personal philosophy—that compassion was the greatest virtue and self-absorption the greatest vice. The Church was our focus and my mother, who was in charge of our family's daily life, worked hard at being the best Catholic she could be. My childhood and particularly the Church gave me a strong sense of values that I have taken with me throughout my life regardless of where I lived."

When Deirdre was eighteen it was time to decide what she was going to do for a living. The choices, particularly for girls, were limited and the two that most appealed to her, teaching and nursing, required that she leave home. Her mother lobbied for teaching, stressing the more agreeable lifestyle, the civilized hours, and the long vacations. Her mother was unusual for her time in that she thought it was even more important for girls to be educated than boys. "Girls," her mother often explained, "will grow up to be their children's educators."

"As far as making a living was concerned," Deirdre continued, "I knew exactly what I wanted to do. I always wanted to be a nurse and midwife; all that time with the lambs had definitely left its imprint and even though my mother might have made a different decision, she supported mine. And so I went to London where an older sister was already in training." For Deirdre, London in the fifties and early sixties seemed to be one of the most exciting places in the world.

"We worked long hours, studied hard, and enjoyed ourselves when we were off-duty," she recalled. "Our teachers were exacting and the physical care of patients was paramount. We didn't spend hours writing up reports or noting things in triplicate. We didn't have all the electronic gear and so observation of the patient was critical to care. On the other hand, it never occurred to either the doctors or nurses that we would be sued, providing we were conscientious. I never thought of my job as work. It was too satisfying and rewarding in a very human way."

"But," I interrupted, "weren't you homesick? I mean, England isn't Catholic at all. Didn't you go through an enormous culture shock?"

Deirdre laughed. "Oh, no. I still had my Catholicism. The Catholic Church is still the Catholic Church wherever you go. I went to Mass every Sunday and on religious holidays. And really, there is very little difference theologically between the Anglican Church, particularly the High Anglican, and the Catholic Church. When I was in London a Catholic service would have still been in Latin and an Anglican in English, but that would have been about the only noticeable difference. Nowadays, since the Catholic service would also be in English, I'm not sure there would be any recognizable difference.

"I'm a traditional and, I think, devout Catholic but I've never been obsessive about my religion. Looking back it's true that most of my very close friends are Catholic. But that just happened. I didn't plan it to be that way. I had good friends and I loved my work. In short, it was a very happy time for me."

Deirdre met her future husband in 1961 when he came to visit a mutual friend who worked with her at the hospital. They were introduced by that friend and Deirdre cannot recall that either made any particular impression on the other. "I wasn't interested in any serious involvement or marriage." In fact, she and some of her colleagues, who were daughters of colonialists, were planning to finish their training and head for Africa for what was still regarded as "service" to an admittedly shrinking British empire.

Despite her African plans, Deirdre continued to see her new friend while she pursued a diploma in public health. After a three-year courtship they became engaged, and in 1965 they were married in Deirdre's home parish in Ireland. Both large families joyfully celebrated a union all assumed would last forever. Deirdre and her husband remained in Ireland until 1973, and during this time the marriage seemed not only sound but blessed. Deirdre saw marriage and family as her chosen career and, as had her mother, she lived it by being the best Catholic she could be.

She continued working for about three months before she learned that she was pregnant. Her husband, now in his early thirties, decided that with fatherhood approaching, he should have a profession with a more secure future than his current business. He chose medicine. Deirdre admitted that she might have preferred a less arduous career and perhaps one that would not have required additional schooling. However, she respected his decision and encouraged him in every way she could.

As in any good marriage, her love and support were acknowledged and reciprocated and the marriage flourished. Six weeks before her husband's graduation, Deirdre gave birth to their second daughter. Added to this excitement was the news that he had been accepted in an American fellowship program that would enable him to simultaneously complete his residency requirement.

Thus began the difficult process of deciding whether to leave Ireland, its memories, family, and friends, for America. "I remember us spending hours and days walking by the sea, discussing the pros and cons of the move. My husband was very concerned that it be the right move for me and the children. In the end we decided that since it would only be for five years, it was no great hardship and the children were still very young and would adjust."

In the summer of 1973, Deirdre and her family boarded a plane for the United States and while the Boston area would eventually become home, they spent the next five years in Minnesota. "Minnesota?" I repeated incredulously. I couldn't imagine a place less like Ireland in either climate or culture. While Deirdre admitted to being homesick in the beginning, she soon made many friends and even today fondly remembers the contrasting warmth of her neighbors to the cold of her first winter. Her neighbors were mostly either Jewish or Catholic.

"I was aware that Minnesota is more of a pluralistic society than Ireland where ninety-five percent of the people we knew were also Irish Catholic, but it wasn't difficult to adjust," Deirdre explained. "I enjoyed the mixture of people. The children adapted to their new life immediately and the school was very helpful."

The parochial school, in fact, more than the local parish, provided both a nucleus and a familiar cultural balance to their more heterogeneous neighborhood. Here other Catholic families of similar age and beliefs shared experiences as they raised their children. Soon Deirdre had another baby and even though her husband worked very hard, he always found time to spend with her and the children. Deirdre in turn found life as a full-time mom very rewarding.

On Sundays, Deirdre and her family attended Mass where the service was essentially the same as in Ireland. I asked Deirdre if the "universality" of the Roman Catholic Church that she had referred to earlier had been a source of comfort when she lived in Minnesota. She explained that she hadn't really thought much about it, but it probably made the transition from Ireland to the States easier. "I could go to church in Minnesota and have the same religious experience as I would have in Ireland. Because the Church is universal wherever you go, there's always a bit of home. It's a nice feeling. And Catholics are supposed to have the same beliefs throughout the world so in that sense Catholicism gives you a common bond."

When his residency was completed, Deirdre's husband had his pick of several prestigious job offers and he chose a Boston-based hospital. "We settled into life in Boston very quickly," she recalled. "My husband enjoyed his new position and his days now took on a much more orderly routine. He left for work at seven A.M. and apart from being on call every fourth week or so, we could expect him home each evening between five-thirty and six P.M. The family ate dinner together every night."

For Deirdre, life in Boston quickly settled into a routine similar to that in Minnesota. Again, the children's Catholic school provided the central focus. "I was very involved in the children's schooling," Deirdre explained, "and since it was very important to me that the children have a Catholic education, I selected the new family home because of its proximity to a private Catholic school. The school provided a close-knit, protective atmosphere. The mothers were very caring, mainly full-time homemakers who held the same values and beliefs, and we kept one another informed and alert to any potential pitfalls that we might perceive. It was a wonderful community of very caring parents and teachers." And of course, the family attended Mass at the local parish where the two older children prepared for First Holy Communion and Confirmation.

While the children's Catholic school provided a cultural as well as educational core and Mass a weekly reminder of the universality of the Roman Catholic Church, Deirdre and her husband also developed a new circle of friends, mainly in the medical and academic fields. "We would entertain frequently. I would prepare dinner and we would have lively evenings with friends, generally discussing the vagaries of Boston politics and so forth. The main difference between family life in Boston and Minnesota," she noted with a laugh, "is that in Boston religion and politics are so interwoven. Life could not have been more blessed." Indeed, after eighteen years, there was still no hint that this was a marriage that would not last forever.

Since under canon law, an annulment may only be granted if the Church determines that a sacramental marriage never existed, the reasons why a marriage eventually falls apart are only relevant insofar as they can help prove or disprove its original existence. From Deirdre's perspective, her twenty-six-year marriage met the criteria of a sacramental union: she and her former husband entered it freely and as mature adults. The service followed the rules of church law. Both knew, understood, and accepted the commitments inherent in a Catholic union. The marriage was obviously consummated and both she and her husband wanted children and accepted their roles as parents.

Equally important, Deirdre's marriage seemed to be sacramental in times of trouble. As Deirdre explained to me, Catholicism teaches that a sacramental marriage has a special and specific meaning. Historically, of course, men and women have married for eons. Their contract in most societies was usually a civil one. Christ changed that by elevating marriage to a sacrament. In essence, He took the marriage contract between a husband and wife and raised it to a supernatural level. By so doing He ensured the couple of God's special, sacramental grace. This sacramental grace, a true gift from God, is not only evidenced in times of joy but also in times of trouble. Jesus knew that even the best of marriages are never "cake walks" and He gave both husband and wife the right to call on God's special and supernatural grace to help their marriage survive such times.

During the last ten years of her marriage, Deirdre called upon God's grace many times. While it was hard to pinpoint when the marriage began its irreversible slide, Deirdre recalled that signs of stress began to emerge in 1983 after her husband accepted a promotion at another hospital. Although his new job was also located within the Boston area, the family moved to a larger house on ten acres in a nearby community. While her husband's work had always been demanding, he now seemed to withdraw more from family life. Sometimes he'd be home for dinner, sometimes not, but he no longer called to inform Deirdre of a change in plans.

In addition, as the older children became teenagers and young adults, they not surprisingly began to develop their own interests and were not as amenable to their father's schedule as they had been when they were younger. The youngest child, who had a history of learning disabilities, began to make progress, yet she still depended on her mother's conscientious attention and special classes to continue her education.

In 1986, at her husband's suggestion, Deirdre spent the summer in Ireland with the two younger children, soon to be joined by the eldest, who had been studying in Spain. Each day she and the children sent a card or letter detailing their activities and telling him how much they looked forward to his joining them. His arrival, however, kept being delayed. When he finally did come in August, the visit was only for two weeks.

Deirdre, in accord with her Catholic upbringing, responded to these stressful times by putting her trust in God and relying on His grace to see the family through. She continued to be the glue that held the family together and for almost another decade the strategy worked. But even though there were some pleasant plateaus during the last years of marriage, the relationship was clearly on a downward path. Eventually the marriage became unworkable and in 1992 Deirdre and her husband divorced.

Their civil divorce took place after twenty-six years of what appeared to be a normal sacramental marriage, and Deirdre knew from her years of Catholic education that under church law such a union could never be dissolved. So when she received the annulment notice, she thought she had no cause to worry.

But as one by one her Catholic friends came either to visit or to check in, as they were doing virtually daily during this difficult time, she told them of her letter; and each cautioned her not to place so much faith in the integrity of the tribunal. These women had known Deirdre for years, many since the time when their children had been schoolmates. Catholicism was the center of their lives and when Deirdre divorced, it was natural for them to provide both the understanding and support so critical to surviving a family crisis of such magnitude. Almost without exception, each of these women had personal knowledge of a situation like Deirdre's where middle-aged men were receiving annulments and remarrying in the Church. The general impression seemed to be that annulments were being handed out like candy.

Deirdre did not share their skepticism. "In the end, I decided just to write a letter to the tribunal stating the facts of the marriage and I decided to copy the letter to Cardinal Law of the Boston archdiocese. I'm well aware that he delegates the tribunal business to his staff there, but as a Catholic I'm entitled to write to the pope if I feel like it. I have great faith in Cardinal Law and I'm sure my action didn't upset him, but it certainly rattled the presiding judge. . . . It may even have sealed my fate for all I know."

A short time later, Deirdre received a letter from the tribunal acknowledging her opposition to the annulment, urging her to cooperate with their process, and informing her that an advocate would be appointed to assist her. As I had, she also received a copy of the blue questionnaire. She answered as concisely as she could their questions about her age and how long she had known her former husband. While some respondents find the tribunal's questions invasive, Deirdre thought they were straightforward. Contrary to the "hoary tales one hears," she explained, "they didn't show any great interest in one's sex life, apart from establishing that the marriage had been consummated. One could write as much as possible and attach as many sheets as necessary. My position was, what was there to say? If the Metropolitan Tribunal wished to engage in this charade, let it be on their heads."

It was not until the following May that Deirdre heard again from the tribunal. The presiding judge wrote to tell her that all information had been obtained and that a decree had been issued which granted both parties twenty-one days in which to present any further proofs or documents. The judge also mentioned the possibility of Deirdre's reviewing "some of the testimony submitted in this case": she had fifteen working days in which to do so. She did neither. "I obviously had no further testimony to offer and I didn't see the point of seeing 'some' of the testimony." As Deirdre explained, "How can one refute testimony one is not privy to? What if the testimony one doesn't see is the testimony on which the tribunal bases its decision? Even at that point I couldn't see how the tribunal could grant an annulment."

The judge's May letter was the last formal correspondence Deirdre would receive from the tribunal for some time. Sadly, one of her children inadvertently became the bearer of bad tidings. On a Sunday morning in July, her eldest daughter returned in a state of shock from visiting her father. With tears streaming down her face, she asked her mother if what her father had told her was true: had the Church annulled her parents' marriage? Deirdre calmed her daughter and told her that no decision had been reached. As far as she knew the case was still in progress, and she was sure "the Church would not make a decision of that magnitude and leave it for one of the parties to hear secondhand. And," she recalled, "I was firmly of that conviction until I called the tribunal the next morning."

The next day, when Deirdre explained over the phone what her daughter had told her, the secretary at the tribunal said that the judge in her case was in a meeting but another priest was available to speak with her. That priest confirmed her daughter's worst fears. The decision had been handed down a few weeks earlier, maybe even a month ago, and she would have been formally notified were it not for a typing backlog, a backlog which nevertheless had not prevented the tribunal from communicating with Deirdre's former husband. "I just fell apart on the phone," she recalled. "All I could think of was the implications for the children and how I would tell them."

Deirdre, still more forgiving than I could ever aspire to be, was quick to defend the priest with whom she spoke that day. She knew he was merely a messenger and she described him as kind and "very pastoral." Upon hearing her obviously distressed voice, he tried to be comforting. He regretted that she had found out in the way she had, and he tried to assure her that her children's status within the Church was not affected. But the damage had been done and as he had not been the presiding judge, he could provide little information. He would, however, leave a message with the judge to call her, and again he expressed sorrow for her pain.

But the judge did not call the next day, nor the day after that, even though Deirdre tried to reach him repeatedly. When he finally did return her call, he was anything but pastoral. As Deirdre recalled the conversation, "This is Father So-and-So." "Yes, Father," Deirdre answered, still obviously upset. "You called about your annulment," he continued. "Yes, Father," she responded. "You filed for the divorce, didn't you?" he asked. "I did," she answered. "And you wrote to the cardinal, didn't you?" "I did," answered Deirdre.

At this point, Deirdre explained, "I thought I had his drift." And when she asked if either of those actions had any bearing on their decision to grant the annulment, he said no, an answer which of course makes one wonder why he had asked those questions in the first place. Typically, Deirdre was more understanding of the tribunal's actions than it was sympathetic to her concerns for her family. "They are human," she rationalized, "and I'm sure the reason for my copying my letter to the cardinal was not lost on them. Conversely, I now couldn't escape the thought that perhaps an element of punishment for being 'uppity' didn't come into play in the decision to grant the annulment. I hope not, but if it did, I can take it."

As their conversation continued, Deirdre asked the judge to explain how the grounds of lack of due discretion had applied to their case, but he was unable or unwilling to do so. Rather, the judge told her that they had done the best with the information they had. Essentially, he had interviewed her former husband, two other judges had reviewed the information, and they all came to the same conclusion. When she asked about the possibility of an appeal, the judge told her, "It probably wouldn't do any good," and reiterated that the decision had been unanimous. So Deirdre did not appeal, although in hindsight she thinks she probably should have.

The annulment was ratified by the end of August, eight weeks before her former husband wed again with the full blessing of the Church. While Deirdre bears him no ill will for his wanting to go on with his life, not even her faith in Catholicism is sufficient for her to accept the tribunal's actions. According to the letter Deirdre received, her marriage was annulled on the grounds of her former husband's lack of due discretion of judgment, grounds whose meaning not even the presiding judge would explain to her.

Nevertheless, from her own research Deirdre managed to piece together an explanation. In September of 1965, this man, thirty-one years old, of above average intelligence, nonpsychotic, noncoerced, from a normal family background, suffered from some disorder that either made him unable to understand what marriage entailed or unable to fulfill its obligations. This disorder apparently continued undetected for twenty-eight years and unknowingly prevented them from ever experiencing a true marriage even though they became parents and raised three children, and he was a successful physician as well.

Additionally, the Metropolitan Tribunal of the Archdiocese of Boston has proven this to be true not only beyond a reasonable doubt but to a moral certainty. "Let us grant for a moment that they are correct," Deirdre observed. "Why then let a person of such defective judgment remarry eight weeks later in the Catholic Church?"

While a tribunal can impose restrictions on a person wishing to remarry even after an annulment is granted if it considers that individual incapable of marriage, it chose not to in this case. The presumption then can only be that her former husband was somehow healed of this terrible lack of judgment, although there is no indication of his undergoing any treatment to promote such healing.

Not even Deirdre's faith in Catholicism was sufficient to accept that presumption. Clearly the tribunal must have decided that Deirdre's husband was only incapable of marriage to her with whom he had lived for twenty or so years, not women in general. As she and I looked at each other, we couldn't help but laugh despite our obvious pain. But our laughter was neither humorous or joyful. "In a way Joe's right, you know," I said. "It is Catholic gobbledygook. But he's wrong when he tells me not to take it seriously. I still take it seriously and I don't think it's one bit funny."

"It certainly isn't funny," Deirdre agreed. "Probably the most dis-
turbing element of the whole matter is the reaction of our children to
the annulment. Somehow I will go on with my life, although I don't
know if I'll ever attend another Catholic service. But once I get the
children settled, I'll probably volunteer as a nurse. In a way I wish I
had done more with my life professionally, but I would have always
wanted to put my children ahead of any career, so I'm not sure how it
would have worked. Being alone in my fifties is not where I planned
to be, and for the Church to annul those twenty-six years is still very
hard for me to deal with sometimes.

"But I worry most for my children," Deirdre continued. "As they
correctly point out, it matters not how the Church tries to couch it.
They are not, according to the Church, children of a proper marriage.
I feel a certain culpability in that I did not avail myself of all the av-
enues available to me to oppose the annulment. What I would like to
come from my experience is a warning to others to leave nothing to
blind faith. I trusted the Church too much. I particularly regret my
lack of thought regarding the impact of the annulment on them emotionally, above all its impact on their faith. The Church offers no
counseling for them and they are just cut adrift, presumably to take
the news whatever way they can. How can I be expected to defend
the Church to them?"

As it turns out, Deirdre didn't have to. What her mother had
predicted so long ago in Ireland had proved to be true: Deirdre had
been her children's educator. Over the years she had taught them
many things that can't be learned from books and she had taught
them very well. Meagan is the eldest and the unofficial family
spokesperson. Though still in her twenties, she is a budding and talented entrepreneur.

We met in her new store, which offers a wide variety of children's
clothing. Just looking at the assortment made me want to turn the
clock back to the time when my own boys were infants. I recognized
Meagan immediately as Deirdre's daughter. Their eyes have the same
sparkle and remind me of a favorite tune of Joe's family, "When Irish
Eyes Are Smiling."

We introduced ourselves and headed across the street to talk and
grab a bite to eat. The atmosphere was so pleasant that I was reluc-

tant to bring up the subject of annulment, but I knew Meagan had a store to run and didn't want to spend the afternoon with me in idle chat. So I began, "How have you dealt with it?"

"What is the most upsetting is the way my mother was treated," Meagan answered. "I went to Catholic schools and even the university where I studied for three years in Spain was Catholic. The annulment would never have happened in Spain. I know what the Church is supposed to do in annulment cases. That's why when my mother got the notice, I told her not to worry. They had no case. We were a normal family. There was nothing strange about my parents or their marriage. What the archdiocese did was simply wrong."

Meagan went on to explain the way the tribunal misused the witnesses. "The witnesses are supposed to have known the couple throughout the marriage. Two of the witnesses in my parents' case hardly even knew my mother and might not even recognize her. The third was my aunt, and she didn't really know what was happening and feels awful about having participated in the process.

"The worst part was the way they spoke to my mother. I was in the room and I could hear her side of the conversation. They said that she hadn't received the notice because of a typing backlog, but clearly someone had told my father. Then they asked for her case number. Imagine, the Church has just annulled her twenty-six-year marriage and it wants her case number. NYNEX is more personal. Then I heard them ask if she had written the cardinal."

"Your mother told me that she hasn't been able to go back to a religious service, but that she sometimes goes to church and just prays."

"I know," Meagan answered. "She can't. It's too painful for her. My mother was brought up to follow the rules of the Church and she did. She believed them and more than anyone I know, she lived them completely. Catholicism tells you that if you follow their rules, then as far as the Church goes, things will work out. The Church simply betrayed her."

"And what about you? How do you view it for yourself?"

"They're saying we never existed as a family. Those twenty-six years were never real. I've only told one person about the annulment and that was someone I don't know very well. I can't talk about it with my friends. It's the same for my younger sister who's in college. She's pretty good at laughing things off. When she heard about the divorce, her attitude was 'big deal.' Half her class had divorced parents. She doesn't feel that way about the annulment. She doesn't talk about it either. Nor does my youngest sister, but she's a minor so I wouldn't speak for her other than to say she doesn't talk about it."

"What about your father? Have you been able to resolve it with him?" I asked.

"I haven't spoken to him since the day he told me. Maybe once on the phone, I can't remember. My younger sister doesn't speak to him either. We both refused to go to the wedding. We wouldn't have dreamed of going. It was a big Catholic wedding, eight weeks after the annulment, as if whatever supposedly had prevented him from having a true marriage to my mother for twenty-six years just disappeared. It's as if we were nothing. I honestly think my father knows what he did was wrong.

"But," Meagan elaborated, "he wanted to find a way to look good and still do what he wanted to do. The annulment basically let him have his cake and eat it, too. But it was wrong. I would have respected him more if he had just said that he didn't want to be married to my mother anymore. And then if he wanted to remarry in a civil ceremony, that would have been one thing. It still wouldn't have been okay, but it would have been better than saying he and my mother never had a true marriage.

"There is a stigma attached to annulment," Meagan continued. "The fact is that for an annulment to be granted there is supposed to be something inherently wrong with the marriage, and there wasn't. I was there those years. I know. And while the Church can say the children are legitimate, that's not the general perception. Even a priest who is a friend brought up the issue that we are no longer the children of a proper marriage. He tried to correct himself after he had said it, but it was clear how he felt. The Church can say what it wishes, but that is the truth of the situation."

"So how do you deal with this on a daily basis?" I asked. "I mean, you run your own business. You've been able to go on, take risks, and be a success."

"I'm pretty balanced," Meagan answered. "I don't go to church anymore. Basically, I know what the Church did here in Boston was wrong. As I said, it wouldn't have happened in Spain. And I don't think it would have happened in some other tribunals either. I don't believe what they said. I guess that's how I deal with it."

Meagan and I had been talking for well over an hour. It was time for her to get back to the store. It also seemed like a good place to stop our discussion. We said our good-byes but as I left, I couldn't help but think there was an almost tragic irony in her words *I don't believe what they said.*

There are no winners in situations such as these. I think the Church has lost far more than either of these women. Vatican spokesmen have, in fact, called American annulments an aberration from the teachings of the Holy Roman Catholic Church. This schism between Rome and America over annulment draws into question whether the Church still provides the universality that eased Deirdre's transitions between life in Ireland, England, and then America.

Both Deirdre and Meagan will carry on with their lives. Wherever Deirdre decides to volunteer will be lucky to have her, and Meagan's store is bustling with activity. More important, each has her own moral core to see her through hard times. But as a result of a process designed to bring Catholics back to the Church and heal families, two devout Catholics no longer attend services and two young women no longer speak to their father.

What Deirdre and Meagan told me touched me deeply. In the months ahead I was to call Deirdre many times for advice. Because of her warnings, I left nothing to chance. I became wary of the tribunal. I put all of my correspondence in writing, sent important letters by certified mail, and made copies of everything I sent. Additionally, while I felt somewhat cowardly at the time, I decided at least to postpone mailing a letter I wanted to send to Cardinal Law.

There were also times when I called Deirdre simply to talk, knowing that her views were always the result of sound thinking and solid values. For as much as Deirdre might question whether her life should have been more career oriented, I saw the values she passed on to Meagan as being the greatest gift a mother can give her children. If I can do half as well with my own boys, then my life will have meaning. Yet the most important lesson I learned from Deirdre was that if I wanted my own children to learn how to seek their own moral truth as adults, then by example if nothing else, I had to have the courage to do so myself. In short, I had to continue to defend the validity of my marriage to their father and with far more vigor than I had before.

4

A DETESTABLE OFFENSE

E ncouraged by Deirdre's support and reassured by the kind
words of strangers who had told me that I had not lost my
mind, I started to defend my marriage with a renewed energy.
I began by searching libraries for information on Catholic marriage, divorce, and annulment. I soon discovered that there were hundreds of
works on these topics, some more scholarly than others, some a combination of analysis and humor, and many written in foreign languages
that I could not begin to understand. Fortunately for me, religious
scholars, some of whom happened to live near me, proved to be more
than generous with their time and helped guide me through what at
first appeared to be a labyrinth of Catholic literature.

I learned that although Christ may have asserted that marriage
was for life, the Church has always permitted exceptions to its rule
against divorce. Saint Paul condoned divorce for converts. By this exception, Paul meant that if one party in a marriage became a Christian and the other refused to convert, the enlightened party should
first try to live a Christian life, but if that was impossible due to his
spouse's religious beliefs, he was permitted to leave. Upon remarriage
to a believer, his prior marriage was dissolved.

A variation on this principle, the "privilege of the faith," involved marriages in which only one party was baptized. Should such a couple divorce and the baptized spouse wish to remarry a Catholic, he or she might petition the pope for permission to do so.

This more tolerant view of divorce has deep historical roots and was not limited to marriage between nonbaptized people. As the historian James A. Brundage explains in his book *Law, Sex, and Christian Society in Medieval Europe,* in early Christian times Roman law and customs dominated much of European society. Marriages were often informal arrangements, and if a couple no longer wanted to be together, they simply went their separate ways. A formal divorce was seldom necessary.

After about A.D. 200, however, marriage began to be more formal and once a union was created, custom presumed that it would continue until ended by either death or divorce. The Church also stressed that marriage was binding, and by the early fourth century a church council had declared that in the absence of a reasonable fear of death, divorced and remarried Christians should be excluded from the sacraments.

For the most part, however, the Church's warning went unheeded. As marriage became more formal and binding, divorce became much more common. In fact, later in the fourth century Saint Jerome, one of the foremost Christian writers of the day and one of the earliest to stress that he thought marriage should be indissoluble, referred to two admittedly extreme cases. In the first a man had twenty wives, and in the second a woman was being buried by her twenty-second husband.

Reflecting the views of Saint Jerome and other fourth-century Christian thinkers, the emperor Constantine orchestrated many changes in both the Christian Church and the state government. Under his rule, Christianity became the state's favored religion and virtually another arm of his civil government. Christian bishops were entrusted with judicial powers that were enforced by civil authority. By the end of the fourth century even emperors placed themselves in peril if they ignored the policies and directives of the bishops.

Unlike Saint Jerome, however, Constantine did not view marriage as indissoluble. His constitution of A.D. 331 detailed the grounds on which divorce could be allowed. A husband could divorce his wife if she committed adultery, engaged in prostitution, or administered poisons. Wives could divorce their husbands for murder, poisoning, or grave robbing. The constitution also noted that wives could not divorce their husbands for drunkenness, gambling, or adultery.

As time passed, other grounds came to be acceptable for divorce. By the sixth century and the rule of Justinian, divorce by mutual consent was allowed but "reasonable cause" had to be shown in contested cases. A man could divorce his wife if she had a abortion, attempted marriage with another man, or "made a habit of bathing in the company of men other than her husband." Other justifications for either husbands or wives to divorce included an inability to engage in sexual relations, capture in battle, adultery, homicide, grave robbery, sorcery, a wife's spending the night away without the husband's permission, and "activities that endangered the life of the spouse."

The Church maintained its flexible attitude toward remarriage into the twelfth century, when Gratian, a jurist who most likely lived and taught law in Bologna, presented the first textbook on canon law. His work, entitled *A Harmony of Conflicting Canons,* came to be known as Gratian's *Decretum,* and established canon law as a discipline distinct from theology and Roman law, although admittedly influenced by both. Gratian made it very clear that once a person of sound mind willingly consented to marriage and the union was subsequently consummated, it was indissoluble. Adultery was grounds for separation, but the union remained valid and neither party was permitted to remarry.

In 1563 the Church reaffirmed this opposition to divorce at the Council of Trent. According to some historians, however, in 1563 the Church did not regard Trent as an opportunity to close the door forever on remarriage. Its primary goals were to reform the Church's internal organization and to determine how best to face the crisis of the Protestant Reformation.

It is understandable that church leaders saw clarifying marriage as one means to accomplish the council's goals. Despite the efforts of such leaders as Constantine, Justinian, and Gratian to delineate laws governing marriage, Christians had continued to marry throughout Europe under widely differing rules. An English king's remarriage, break with Rome, and subsequent alliance with the Protestants thirty years before were still causing havoc in Europe, and the Eastern Church permitted divorce and remarriage under certain circumstances.

There were two major points governing marriage that the church leaders sought to clarify: that the Church alone had the right to decide whether a marriage was valid; and that the Church had the right to regulate marriage without secular intervention. To address these concerns, the Church developed a form which required that in order to ensure the validity of their marriages, all Catholics must marry before a priest and two witnesses, a requirement which it was hoped would discourage them from marrying as they pleased without the Church's permission or involvement. This prescription was included in the decree *Tametsi,* and became applicable in most European countries almost immediately.

The church leaders also wanted to take a stand against divorce without causing a break with the Eastern Church, a break which would have been similar to that which the issue had already caused between Rome and the Church in England. To accomplish this tricky feat, the council adopted a decree which stated that the Church "did not err in teaching the indissolubility of marriage," meaning that the Church would not be doctrinally wrong if it taught a more conservative view of marriage rather than a more liberal one. The decree, more a masterpiece of diplomatic negotiation and compromise than a moral manifesto on marriage, was *not,* some historians maintain, intended to close the door forever on the issue of divorce.

Regardless of what the church leaders intended in 1563, there is little doubt that the Council of Trent became a watershed for Catholic marital law. From that time on, the Church steadfastly maintained its opposition to divorce and by so doing, spawned a virtual industry for the accommodation of those determined to find a way around the rule. As the authors Morris West and Robert Francis explain in their book *Scandal in the Assembly,* some of the ways by which people have obtained annulments range from the sublime to the ridiculous.

Sometimes it was impossible for me to read these accounts without laughing. At first I felt guilty making light of something as serious as religion and annulment, but I found that laughter helped ease the growing anguish associated with my own case. What is more, the authors went out of their way to point out that a sense of humor was a Christian virtue and laughter the appropriate response to what they had to say.

There was one woman, for example, who apparently could not have sex with her husband. However, after an affair with her neighbor, she found she was cured of her impotency and she and her husband consummated their marriage. Nevertheless, the marriage eventually failed and her husband sought an annulment. His canon lawyer maintained that the woman in question was "permanently relatively impotent." His reasoning went something like this: the sex she shared with her husband didn't really count because it was the result of adultery with her neighbor. Even though her adultery physically cured her of impotency, the act itself was a sin. Thus, she was not canonically cured. The Church granted the annulment.

One of my favorite stories could be an episode in one of the hospital shows currently popular on television. There was a Catholic woman who married outside the Church. For years, she and her husband lived happily and had three children. Then she was involved in a terrible car accident. All thought she would die and she was given the last rites. Miraculously, she held on and was able to communicate what some thought might be her dying wish—to be married in the Church. Church officials responded with both sensitivity and speed. She and her husband of many years were wed in a special church ceremony at the hospital.

After her wedding, she again beat the odds and instead of dying grew stronger. Soon it was apparent that she would pull through, and so began her lengthy recovery. But here her story took an odd twist. She decided that she no longer loved her husband. Rather, she wanted to marry one of her doctors. She divorced her husband and sought an annulment on the grounds that she and her husband had never consummated their marriage. She argued that even though she and her former husband had three children, those children had been conceived before she wed their father in a Catholic ceremony. The Church agreed. She was given her annulment and married her doctor.

Even with such imaginative approaches to annulment, there are times when either a person is unwilling to complete the process or one is unattainable. Such was apparently the case for one of the authors, Morris West. Faced with this situation and having already remarried outside the Church, Mr. West found a priest who was willing to hear his confession and grant him communion even though doing so was against official policy. Mr. West's solution is in fact so common that the practice has a name, the good-conscience solution, meaning that the parishioner has settled the issue with his conscience and has chosen to participate in the sacraments despite church policy. Some even do so without the knowledge of the priest simply by attending a service in a church where they are not known.

Another "answer" for those who have remarried and are therefore barred from confession and communion is far less common. In fact, the authors only knew of two couples who had attempted what the Church calls its brother-and-sister solution. The brother-and-sister solution allows those who have been together for some time to remain so and return to the sacraments provided they agree to live as brother and sister, meaning they promise not to engage in sexual relations.

One couple the authors interviewed who had opted for this solution found the sacrifice too great and soon returned to the pleasures of the flesh. The other had become addicted to alcohol. Apparently the Church thought that was permissible as long as they abstained from sexual activity.

Another book I found early in my search proved to be invaluable. In 1972, John T. Noonan, at the time a professor of law and chairman of religious studies at the University of California in Berkeley, described six annulment cases which had come before the Roman court, or Curia as it is sometimes called. Professor Noonan's analysis of these annulments highlights the difficulties inherent in relying on law as a guide in a religion based on the commandment of love. "The annulment is a fiction, obtained as an adjunct to a hoax. Annulments," Mr. Noonan continues, "are the magical product of an incomprehensible process in which legal reasons play no part and clerical discretion is absolute."

Indeed, some of the cases, while interwoven with serious legal analysis, show that for centuries the rationale behind annulment has often been incomprehensible, easily manipulated, and hurtful to many who tried to live their lives in accordance with church law.

In 1621, for example, Charles, age seventeen, married Nicole, age twelve. Charles wasn't all that happy with the idea, but he went along because it was what his parents and many family advisors wanted him to do. Nicole was also his first cousin and because of this relationship, the pope had to grant them a special dispensation to wed. His Holiness was happy to do so, however, because Nicole and Charles weren't just ordinary people. Their fathers were not only brothers but also sons of "le grand Henri," the duke of Lorraine. The marriage of Nicole and Charles was intended to stop warring between the brothers and ensure that the dukedom remained within the family.

Adhering to their parents' wishes, Charles and Nicole married but refrained from consummating the union for three weeks until the papal dispensation arrived. Then they celebrated their marriage again and set up house. Charles soon became bored with his twelve-year-old bride, although she apparently fell in love with him.

Then Grandpa Henri died. As planned, Charles and Nicole began ruling Lorraine jointly, but Charles was not happy with domesticity and soon picked a fight with the wrong man, Cardinal Richelieu. The cardinal, who was governing France, responded by invading Lorraine. Charles fled to a neighboring state to the south but Nicole became a virtual captive. She was taken to the French court and forbidden to leave.

From all reports and even his own letters, Charles truly missed Nicole; but shortly he fell for the charms of the great beauty Beatrice, whom he then wished to marry. Understandably, Beatrice's mother was less than thrilled that her prospective son-in-law already had a wife. Similarly, Charles's sister, fearful that Beatrice would not be a good match for her brother, arranged for the beauty to marry the prince of Cantecroix.

An undaunted Charles offered three thousand Masses for the timely death of Beatrice's new husband, and on February 15, 1637, his prayers were answered. The prince died. With her daughter pregnant, Beatrice's mother now supported her marrying Charles even though in the Church's eyes her future son-in-law was still married to Nicole and it was less than clear who was the biological father of the child.

In order to marry with the Church's blessing, Charles and Beatrice sought the help of a Jesuit priest and former professor of moral theology, Didier Cheminot. The professor found good reasons why Charles's marriage to Nicole was invalid: Charles's father had co-erced him into the marriage; the service was not performed by a priest nor his delegate as required by the Council of Trent; he and Nicole were first cousins. In addition, according to Cheminot, Nicole was not really a Christian, for she had been baptized by a priest who was subsequently convicted as a sorcerer. Four other local theologians concurred with Cheminot's analysis.

Now that the nullity of the first marriage was justified, Cheminot maintained that Charles had a duty to marry as soon as possible. He had to produce an heir, as any day his enemies might do him in. Speed was of the essence. Charles should not wait for a formal ruling by the church court. He must marry at once.

Cheminot's suggestion that Charles and Beatrice marry without a formal decree from the church court was very bold, for it meant that at least momentarily they were ignoring the Church's all-powerful judicial structure. Even within the couple's close circle of family, friends, and advisors, there were those who disagreed with the decision to move forward without a formal decree. Some worried about the couple's souls, some about the repercussions that would surely follow when the Church learned that its authority had been defied, and most worried about both, for foremost in the minds and hearts of men in those days was that the canonical system of justice had to be upheld.

For Charles, Beatrice, and her mother, however, Cheminot had provided the justification they needed to move forward without a formal decree. Mr. Noonan draws a parallel between their views and those of some modern taxpayers who will try almost anything to avoid paying a tax provided their lawyer tells them it's okay to withhold payment.

Charles and Beatrice married within a week of the funeral of Beatrice's deceased husband. The Church, however, refused to accept Cheminot's decision that Charles and Nicole's marriage was invalid and for the next seventeen years Charles continued to attempt to have this marriage annulled. The road was not easy.

At one point, Charles's brother Nicholas-François tried to orchestrate a reconciliation between Charles and Nicole, but Richelieu would not allow her to leave France. Soon Charles allowed Beatrice to ride with him publicly on campaigns. Upon hearing this news, Nicole decided that she'd had enough humiliation and heartbreak and appealed directly to the pope to save her marriage.

The pope had good reasons to heed Nicole's plea for help. He liked Nicholas-François, who on more than one occasion had locked horns with the French, a country which in the pope's view was too closely allied with the Protestants. The pope also wanted to uphold the decrees of the Council of Trent, decrees which solidified the Church's power over Catholics' right to marry.

By provisions of the council, a married man living with a concubine was to be warned three times and then excommunicated. The fact that Charles had taken Beatrice as his wife only made his predicament worse since the pope had previously referred to men who take second wives in the lifetime of their first as "sons in iniquity . . . condemned to the galleys in perpetuity."

Despite the high level of opposition, Cheminot continued to work on Charles's behalf and sought to have the case tried by a panel of judges rather than the pope. Nicole, however, questioned the objectivity of the judges and asked the pope to judge the case himself.

In 1639, the pope upheld Nicole's objections, but assured Charles that the case would be tried by a special commission provided he agreed to separate from Beatrice and that she entered a convent. Charles not only refused to agree, but he also cut a deal with Richelieu by which he regained Lorraine. Shortly thereafter he returned home with Beatrice as his duchess.

The pope was not amused at Charles's continued defiance. In 1642, he excommunicated both him and Beatrice and referred to their relationship as a "scandal" and "a detestable offense known to all the Christian Community." In 1654, the Church ruled for the final time that Charles and Nicole's marriage was valid. Soon Charles was arrested in Spain, probably because of the fear that his anger and frustration at the Church's denial of his annulment might entice him to join the Protestants.

Nicole, apparently feeling no bitterness toward the man who for seventeen years had tried to annul their marriage, worked to have him released and pledged him her continued and undying love. Charles, in turn, was moved by her efforts and gave her authority over both his land and troops. In his last correspondence, he wrote that he had been wishing for "a chance . . . to make you know that nothing could ever be so much yours as I am." Nicole died shortly thereafter. As Mr. Noonan points out, she was forty-eight, married for thirty-six years, and separated for twenty-three of them.

Charles, now virtually free to marry Beatrice, decided he didn't want to. He protested that he needed a dispensation because the law forbid marrying a former lover if the petitioner attempted to wed the paramour during the life of the former spouse. Beatrice understandably thought Charles was stalling. Only on her deathbed did Charles relent. An archbishop dispensed the couple from adultery and Charles, not a man to be inconvenienced, married by proxy. Two weeks later, Beatrice died, having married the father of her children and the husband she thought she had wed twenty-seven years earlier.

Many a man with such an eventful marital history might wish to spend his twilight years as a bachelor, or at least might be wary of young brides. But not Charles. A year after Beatrice's death Charles wed again. This time the Church blessed the union. He was sixty-two, his new wife thirteen.

No wonder I found annulment hard to understand. As far back as the 1600s, the process was easily manipulated for political purposes. John Noonan's work enabled me to see that my confusion was not as strange as the Church was leading me to believe, but rather consistent with learned observers dating back to medieval times. His stories also provided a defense mechanism that I needed to retain my emotional balance as I continued to fight the annulment of my marriage.

Sometimes stuck in Boston traffic, with Mr. Noonan's work fresh in my mind, I would envision these very serious, erudite men of long ago as they sat in the Vatican surrounded by great art. With underlings to care for their daily needs, they had little to do but decide the fate of others. These men, accountable only to the pope, played if not the original then certainly one of history's most powerful mind games. Today, while some such formidable minds are no doubt still at the Vatican, I'm sure others can be found working for think tanks, computer firms, or even toy companies.

I envisioned these great men transposed to a modern era, still dressed in their elaborate robes with Michelangelo's *Creation* looking down upon them, giving birth to Annulment Nintendo, or a board game for which a clue reads "Petitioner baptized with unclean water from Boston Harbor, advance three spaces." I would laugh to myself, totally oblivious to the traffic jam.

Then the traffic would ease, I'd pick up my children at school, and annulment didn't seem funny anymore. That was the problem. Mr. Noonan's people may have been tragic, but to me they weren't real. For the most part, they had lived fairy-tale lives, in far-off places long ago. Because I was separated from them by both time and distance, their troubles didn't bother me. In fact, I found their stories humorous. My children, however, were real and so were those whose mothers were then writing me painful letters. To us, annulment wasn't a joke.

My next correspondence with the tribunal wasn't funny either. While my response to the *Time* article had generated significant discussion within the press, the Church chose not to discuss it with me at all. Rather, in late September my advocate wrote me stating, "Upon reviewing your case I find you were involved in counseling. Professional testimony from your counselor would be very valuable to our study of your marriage." The letter instructed me to sign a release giving the tribunal legal access to the counselor's files.

I was aghast. While I knew from discussing the annulment process with my advocate that the tribunal might seek testimony from special witnesses, and I remembered that in response to one of their questions in the blue questionnaire, I had told the Church that Joe and I had met with counselors, I had not provided names. The Church, however, had learned, probably from Joe, the name of at least one of our counselors. More unsettling was the fact that the letter and accompanying release were both demanding and explicit but at the same time vague.

The Church did not "ask" me to sign the release form as my advocate and I had discussed: it told me. While a signed release form would waive all my legal rights of privacy "even if they pertain to drugs, alcohol, or sensitive material," the letter itself was unclear if the "you" to which it referred was simply me or a plural "you" referring to Joe and me jointly.

Months later, while reading Father Stephen Kelleher's book

Divorce and Remarriage for Catholics? I would learn that my experience was not unusual. Father Kelleher wrote in part: "Once a party seeks an annulment on the basis of the lack of discretion of the other party, all action on the part of the tribunal zeroes in on this point. There is little or no advertence to the possibility of lack of due discretion in the other party."

While the tribunal had always avoided answering my question as to whose discretion was at issue, mine, Joe's, or both, I suppose I should not have been surprised that the Church might choose not to label one of its more prominent members indiscreet. As I put the tribunal's letter aside, I felt a growing uneasiness that the Church was about to join forces with one of the country's most powerful political families and direct their combined and awesome power against me.

The request for medical records raised more than power and privacy issues. It raised a fundamental question as to whose side my advocate was on. If the burden of proof was really on Joe, then why was Father Lory trying to uncover information from someone Joe had referred to in his testimony? Should not a request for such information have been made by the expert in canon law assigned to Joe and should not Father Lory have discussed the implications of such a request with me before proceeding?

More important, while I had nothing to hide, I had serious reservations about the objectivity of the counselor in question. In the late 1980s, while still married, I had asked another highly respected psychiatrist if he thought our counseling was effectively addressing our family's needs. While finding no fault with the primary counselor as an individual, the second doctor pointed out that it was unclear if the primary counselor was representing me or Joe as individuals, our marriage, or the children. Nor was it clear if his duties were limited to family counseling.

At one point, for example, he had provided financial and budgetary advice. On another occasion, without even being asked, he had drafted a custody agreement outlining where, when, and with whom the children would live in the event of a divorce, an agreement which appeared to both me and my lawyer to be more favorable to Joe than one which both he and his civil attorney had previously accepted. In addition, this counselor had also made the largest legal contribution allowed to at least one of Joe's congressional campaigns.

The second counselor noted that no one individual, regardless of how gifted, could work professionally in such a confused setting with unclear allegiances, and he strongly advised me to have a neutral third party assume control. It was, however, the opinions of this first counselor that the Church wished to review in an effort to prove with "moral certainty" a lack of due discretion so severe as to render Joe's and my marriage invalid.

I felt that by signing a release to allow such a review, I would in essence be party to a clever hoax disguised as a quest for truth. I thought it was wrong to sign such a release, and I wrote Father Lory and told him so.

My letter explained that while I remained committed to working with the Church in its investigation, I thought relying on the opinion of the counselor in question would impede their efforts to find the truth. I also pointed out that the type of counseling I had participated in was not of sufficient depth to reveal any significant personality disorder that would have existed at the time of my wedding even if there had been one. Further, I noted that as I had never been counseled for drug or alcohol abuse, I was unclear as to the relevancy of the tribunal's inquiry into this issue.

Specifically, I was unclear as to what my condition in the late 1980s and early 1990s, the waning years of my marriage, had to do with my emotional state in 1979, the year of my wedding. If, however, the Church still thought consultation with medical professionals would help their investigation, I would authorize the doctor who advised me to amend the counseling structure to speak with them. However, I cautioned, the tribunal should understand that this doctor's advisory arrangement with me never constituted a professional doctor-client relationship.

Finally, if the tribunal still had questions regarding a dependence on drugs or alcohol, I reminded Father Lory that in 1988 I had been hospitalized for severe pneumonia. During this time, I had undergone a myriad of tests. A dependence on drugs or alcohol would more than likely have been revealed during my hospitalization. Should the tribunal be concerned with this issue, I would authorize my primary-care physician to discuss my medical history with them and allow them to review my hospital records.

By providing access to both a second professional, my primary

doctor, and detailed medical records, I thought I was more than continuing to cooperate with the tribunal's investigation. Father Lory responded to my letter by writing that he understood and accepted my
reasons for declining to sign the original release. He then asked me to
sign another one identical in substance to the first except that it
named the consulting psychiatrist as my physician. Once again I explained in writing to the tribunal that as I had not had a doctor-client
relationship with this psychiatrist, I doubted he had any medical
records. Nevertheless, the Church had my permission to discuss my
health with him or to inquire in writing if the tribunal preferred.

My correspondence with the tribunal over the issue of counseling
made me even more sensitive to the psychological power of the
Church and to the anguish of the women who continued to write to
me. I was deeply moved by what they told me, and I realized that my
anger and hurt paled in comparison to theirs.

I was not Catholic. I still had my faith. While my relationship with
Joe had dominated roughly twenty-five years of my life, only about
thirteen of those had been spent in marriage. While my children
were and would remain the center of my life, I did have a profession I
might be able to return to and my family had both the resources and
the willingness to help me.

Many of the women who wrote to me had led very different lives.
Largely because they had believed so strongly in the Catholic
Church, most had embraced the role of wife and mother as life itself.
Some had spent well over twenty-five years solely caring for husbands
and children. Others had forgone educational opportunities and only
a few had a career they could pick up again. Facing divorce under
these circumstances is difficult enough; but when the Church, which
is supposed to offer comfort in times of family crisis, declares that
the marriages to which these women had given their lives had never
been true ones, it's a marvel they could put their lives back together
at all. I felt a deep compassion for these women; but except for writing them back and telling them so, I was at a loss what to do.

Help came from a most unexpected source. I received a letter from
ABC News in New York. Chris Wallace, a senior correspondent for
Prime Time Live, a weekly news program, had read my letter to Time
and was interested in doing a segment on annulments. I was sur-

prised. Knowing Mr. Wallace's reputation as an effective and probing political correspondent who at times covered the White House, I couldn't imagine why he would want to talk with me about annulments. Furthermore, while some of the letters I had received had been from men, the majority had been written by women. Annulment seemed to strike a chord for women and they spoke of it differently than men.

While the women wrote openly about the turmoil that annulment caused in their and their children's lives, the men by and large were struck by the intellectual hypocrisy. For these men, annulment made no sense to a rational mind. They themselves, however, did not offer insights as to how annulment might have affected them emotionally. Either they had not experienced this emotional devastation, or they chose not to reveal it to me. While they were just as supportive of my opposition as their female counterparts, when they spoke of the pain, they almost invariably referred to a woman whom they were close to, usually their mother or sister.

Curious, I called Chris in New York. He explained that he too was intrigued by what he referred to as the apparent "disconnect" between the obvious reality of marriages that had lasted many years and often produced children with the Church's position that these same marriages had never existed. The show's producers wanted to create an informative program that would explain modern annulment to a general audience.

When I told Chris about the letters I had received, he agreed to try to contact these women with hopes of incorporating some of their stories into the show. Women who for so long had been unable to find anyone to listen to them would finally be heard on national television. I was excited and I eagerly agreed to participate. My own journey was about to enter a new realm.

5

AUNT LAURA

Even though I was excited that the women who had written to me would have an opportunity to tell their stories on national television and my instincts told me that Chris Wallace would present a balanced discussion about annulment, I was worried about participating myself. I had been raised in a family that avoided publicity. Now by agreeing to cooperate with *Prime Time,* I was in a way working with the media. I began to second-guess myself. What if I sounded like a complete idiot? I wasn't Catholic. What if I was asked in-depth questions about Catholicism? Other than a few short comments I had made about housing policy and homelessness, I had never spoken on television. Would I compromise the children's privacy? I was opposed to their father's annulling our marriage because of the impact I feared it might have on them, but thus far I had been able to fight the annulment without drawing the boys into the battle. What if they were to return home from school and find television reporters in our living room asking questions about my marriage to their father?

Since I thought it was important for me to address these concerns before the taping began, I telephoned Chris in New York. Of course he could do nothing about my not being Catholic or my inexperience on television, but he did assuage my concerns about the boys. We agreed that the children would not be filmed, and that the interview would be completed and the house returned to its normal state before the boys returned from school. In addition, any photographs that the network used of the children would be ones that had been made public before the divorce or were already accessible to the press.

My fears of sounding like an idiot prompted me to continue my research. I was confused by an apparent inconsistency. Most of the material I had read discussed annulments that had occurred at least thirty years ago and had been judged primarily on the basis of a couple's sexual relationship. For example, all of the cases I had read in *Scandal in the Assembly* focused on questions such as whether someone was impotent and if so, when and with whom? Was the couple married when their children were conceived? It seemed as if the essence of marriage was sexual intercourse.

Yet despite the apparent sexual obsession discussed in much of the annulment literature I had read, my advocate and others continually referred to "modern" church policy, interpersonal relationships, and partnerships when talking about Catholic marriages. Their unmistakable implication was that there had been substantial changes in how the Church viewed marriage. Before I talked publicly about annulment, I thought I had better learn more about these changes and what had brought them about.

I soon learned that most of these changes occurred as the result of the Second Vatican Council, a council of church representatives who gathered at the Vatican from 1963 to 1965 to discuss Catholic teachings and formulate modern church policy on a wide range of subjects. For many modern Catholics, the Second Vatican Council, or "Vatican II," as the assembly came to be known, is one of the most important religious events of their time. Some Catholics think that policies the council generated were too liberal. Others don't think they went far enough.

Marriage, divorce, and annulment were major topics at Vatican II. After careful study and deliberation, the council determined that there was indeed more to marriage than procreation and they set out to modernize the concept of a Catholic union. No longer was marriage solely for the purpose of begetting children. Rather, in addition to procreation, the Church now emphasized that modern marriage also required a personal component and the mutual self-giving of husband and wife. The union is a covenant, a "community of life and love" rather than merely a contract. As such, it required modern themes such as a partnership between spouses.

The choice of the word *covenant* rather than *contract* to refer to marriage is itself indicative of how carefully the council introduced change into church teaching. Covenant and contract both mean a binding agreement, a bargain. The difference between the two is more one of connotation than denotation. Covenant brings to mind God's promise to the human race. The connotation is one of love and caring. Contract, on the other hand, connotes a written legal agreement that can be the basis of a court suit. By referring to the marriage as a covenant, church leaders sought to broaden and soften the concept of marriage more than to change it. Marriage was still a contract, but by referring to it as a covenant after Vatican II, the Church emphasized sharing and interpersonal commitment rather than the mere exchange of sex for children that had dominated much of its earlier teachings.

Following Vatican II, the Church began many initiatives to promote a better understanding of Catholic marriage. One such effort was the New Committee on Marriage. Under the chairmanship of an American priest, Father Thomas Doyle, and based on research in the United States, the committee examined a broad range of issues that affect marriage, including the disintegration of the extended family, mobility, lack of stability within the nuclear family, and a lack of support for marriage within society in general. Marriage, Father Doyle noted, had become more of a "rite of cultural passage of family significance as opposed to an act of faith and a sign of commitment to a Christian community."

The committee set out to change that, and from 1980 to 1990 the Canon Law Society of America published its findings in a series entitled *Marriage Studies*. Early in its endeavor, the committee found that in the United States preparation for marriage was often woefully inadequate. Not only was a 40 percent divorce rate among Catholics in 1975 roughly the same as the divorce rate among the general population, but 30 percent of these civilly dissolved marriages failed within the first year.

To help stem the divorce epidemic, the committee stressed the importance of broader and more serious prenuptial counseling. It suggested that clergy work with couples to determine not only if they were ready for a serious commitment to a Christian marriage but also whether they were psychologically compatible with each other. The studies reiterated the well-known but often ignored fact that happy marriages require far more than an undefined love. They require commitment, communication, and conflict resolution, an ability to deal with differences and share personal vulnerabilities with a spouse, daily stroking, and a mature and complete knowledge of self.

Few would argue that the Church's attempts not only to promote a better understanding of marriage but also to assist Catholics in preparation for the sacrament are time well spent. However, despite these efforts the divorce rate remained high, prompting many church leaders to seek new ways to help divorced Catholics, particularly those who wished to remarry and yet remain in good standing within their church. Here, however, there was far less consensus on what constituted wise and prudent policy. Rather, as evidenced in *Marriage Studies,* a collection of papers based on the committee's findings and published in several editions by the Canon Law Society of America, opinions varied and new approaches have continued to evolve.

For example, church scholars debated if and when the so-called good-conscience or internal solution could be used. As described in *Scandal in the Assembly,* the good-conscience or internal solution allows divorced and remarried Catholics seeking reconciliation with their church but unable to obtain an annulment to partake of the sacraments if they themselves feel doing so is justified and provided their actions do not bring "scandal" upon the Church.

Some scholars such as Morris West, who relied on the internal solution to restore himself to the sacraments, view it as a way to provide reconciliation without annulling a marriage. Others think it makes a mockery of the Church's strong stance against divorce. To make matters more confusing, the Church in Rome does not approve of the internal solution although the practice continues to be used in the United States, even if unofficially.

Similarly, even some scholars who agree that liberalized annulment offers the best hope for divorced Catholics disagree about the grounds upon which a marriage should be judged. Can an annulment be granted if one of the parties has "relative" as opposed to "absolute" incapacity? Relative incapacity means that the person was only incapable of having a marriage with the person to whom he was presumed married. Absolute incapacity means he was incapable of marriage in general.

Relative incapacity is not only easier to prove, but it also enables the Church to circumvent the thorny issue of how it can grant an annulment because someone is incapable of marriage while at the same time allowing that same person to marry again. Rome, however, does not approve of using relative incapacity as a basis for annulment, and even in the United States some scholars are opposed to its use. What is at issue, they assert, is the capacity to live a Christian marriage, not simply whether two people can get along.

Rome adheres more strictly to canon law, the church law on which annulments have always been judged and a basis of many of the Vatican II reforms. Canon law is complex, with roots that date back to the twelfth century if not earlier. What is more surprising, at least to someone untrained in law such as myself, is that it is virtually impossible to understand modern annulment without at least a general understanding of the history of canon law and how it still affects much of church policy.

As Professor Charles Donahue, currently of the Harvard Law School, explained in a 1976 article for the *Michigan Law Review,* in medieval times church courts heard a broad range of cases: contracts, will administrations, property claims, as well as marriage. All were argued on the basis of canon law. Today in the West, and particularly in America with our constitutional separation between church and state, such issues are brought before civil courts. However, as far as the Catholic Church is concerned, secular courts have no authority over the marital status of its members. Catholics who are divorced in civil court and wish to remarry yet remain in favor with their church must take their case before a church tribunal.

While this requirement may seem to be insignificant, it is noteworthy that marriage is virtually the only issue that affects a Catholic layperson over which church courts have retained jurisdiction. Other issues of personal behavior such as adultery, stealing, or even presumably the more serious sin of murder are not addressed by church courts. Rather, these issues are dealt with through the Church's moral as opposed to legal code. Because these other "sins" fall under the Church's moral code, a Catholic discusses these problems with his priest privately in confession. It is in confession that he seeks forgiveness and clears his conscience.

Unless a person is familiar with canon law, he is unlikely to appreciate how difficult it is for a priest to help a divorced Catholic who wants to remarry. In civil law, except in cases that carry mandatory sentences, the court has more options than a church tribunal. Civil courts may usually determine not only the guilt or innocence of the accused, but also the punishment if the person is found guilty. Allowing the court to adjust the sentence enables it to be more understanding about the circumstances under which a crime was committed.

Such, however, is not true for tribunals. The penalty for disobeying church law is mandatory. Divorced Catholics may not remarry in the Church. Those who remarry outside the Church may take neither confession nor communion. Tribunals do not have an option of saying, Well, you were married and you blew it. But it wasn't all your fault and we know you're sorry for your mistakes. So we'll give you another chance. You may remarry in the Church.

Nor can a tribunal adjust its punishment to fit the extent of the petitioner's crime or sin. Even if the Church thinks that the person seeking to remarry was innocent of all wrongdoing and a model Catholic in her first marriage, its hands are tied. A tribunal cannot say, No one in her right mind would have stayed married, considering how your husband behaved at the end of the marriage. You were right to divorce and we wish you only the best in your new marriage. Rather, church law states that "a valid marriage ratified and consummated can be dissolved by no human power and for no good cause save death." In short, if you were married, unless the church council formally annuls your marriage, you're stuck.

Today's tribunal assumes, although not always correctly, that even if something could have been done to save the petitioner's prior marriage, either before or at the time of its collapse, it is too late to do so by the time it hears the case. Given the stiffness of the penalties, the high divorce rate, and the assumption that nothing can now be done to save the prior marriage, it is easy to understand why tribunals bend over backward to grant annulments. Furthermore, since few people really know how the Church decides annulment cases, there is little accountability and a tribunal can do virtually as it pleases.

That is not to say that the Church has not established a logical basis for the frequency with which it grants annulments. Quite the contrary: it has established a broad rationale to justify annulments. This rationale is based upon the Catholic principle that insanity, or *amentia* as it was called in medieval times, in either the husband or the wife at the time of the wedding vitiates marital consent and renders the marriage invalid. The Church has expanded this principle to cover "lack of due discretion, emotional immaturity, psychic or moral incapacity, and psychic or moral impotence." Based on these conditions it has created three separate but overlapping grounds for granting annulments: insanity, lack of due discretion, and psychic incapacity.

The simple insanity plea is usually limited to cases where, in the opinion of psychological consultants, either husband or wife suffered from a total incapacity to consent to marriage because of sickness or "disturbance of the mind by which the use of reason is impeded." This definition is very close to the historical concept of *amentia*, but in today's tribunal such a judgment at least theoretically must rest on the opinion of psychological or psychiatric experts.

Lack of due discretion is the ground upon which my case and that of every other woman who spoke with me was brought before the tribunal. This category, and the third of psychic incapacity, are harder to define and often overlap. They include people who did not understand what marriage was about at the time they married, people who did not really want to be married although they said they did, and people who suffered from a personality disorder so severe that it made it impossible for them to assume their marital obligations.

While it may be plausible for one of these conditions to exist undetected for a short time and thus prevent a couple from attaining a true marriage, it is far more difficult to believe that a party in a long-term marriage, particularly one that produced and raised children, suffered from such a severe yet undetected defect. What is more, for a tribunal to prove with moral certainty that such a defect existed at the time of a marriage that may have taken place literally a decade or more before it began its investigation constitutes an even greater challenge.

The Church has approached this challenge by calling on the mental health profession to provide such proof. There is a problem in this approach, however, because the more is learned about mental illness, the more medically complex it becomes and the less it fits any clear definition of what has historically been referred to as insanity or *amentia*. Rather, modern medical evidence supports the assertion that there is no set definition of mental illness.

There is also a variety of opinions among mental health professionals as to the degree to which physical factors, such as a defective gene, environmental components, or a combination, affect what has traditionally been referred to as "mental illness." While individual doctors constructively debate the relative importance of these various factors, the profession increasingly views health as a combination of physical, mental, and even spiritual components, all of which affect a person's well-being.

Similarly, as professionals debate the definition of mental illness, they also have a variety of opinions about cures. Modern drugs have proven so effective in combatting or controlling some types of illnesses that were previously categorized as "mental" that the profession itself is unclear when, for how long, and in combination with what other treatments they should be prescribed. Nor is it even clear what constitutes "cured." Is a person who must take medication to control a mental disease cured?

Another potential problem with the Church's growing reliance on mental health professionals for annulment is that psychology and psychiatry rest on a very different premise than Catholic teachings. At least in America, most therapists work toward helping clients understand and resolve personal and interpersonal conflicts that adversely affect their feelings or behavior. The therapist is careful to refrain from passing judgment on what his client tells him and hopes that by providing a safe and nonjudgmental way for his client to face his problems, he will enable him to live a happier and more productive life.

In traditional Catholicism, however, a troubled parishioner seeks counsel from a priest who is unlikely to explain either unhappiness or unacceptable behavior in terms of an inability to understand or to process feelings, but rather as a failure to follow church teachings. The emphasis is more on how others, the Church, or society views the petitioner's difficulty rather than on how he perceives it. In many instances, the priest passes judgment on what the parishioner confides. The parishioner may subsequently feel both guilt and shame, after which the priest may recommend penance as a cure.

Yet when a mental health expert is called to give testimony to a tribunal, he must often put Catholicism aside and suggest that at least one of the parties could not consent to marriage because of a preexisting psychological condition over which he or she had no control. It is this preexisting condition, an indication that the marriage was invalid from the beginning, not a failure to follow Catholic teachings or even the spouse's actions, that is responsible for the breakup of the union. Thus, neither party should feel guilt or shame or even responsibility.

In certain cases, the expert may even be expected to overlook the fact that he is not following standard professional procedures when he makes his evaluation. Even though the expert's profession stresses the importance of working with a client, he may be asked to render an opinion concerning a marriage that took place decades before and sometimes without ever meeting the person he is supposed to be evaluating. As it is usually the tribunal that retains and pays for his services, the expert is well aware that only if he finds a condition that existed at the time of the marriage, a condition the tribunal can subsequently interpret as sufficiently serious to have prevented a true union from ever being achieved, will the petitioner be allowed to remarry in his church.

The expert also knows that since the evaluation will be locked away in the church archives, no one will ever find out what he really said. Nor does he have to say that anyone suffered from a severe mental disorder. An opinion of immaturity or stress will be sufficient. It will be the tribunal itself that interprets the expert's opinion as grounds to annul the marriage. The professional is not asked to make such a judgment.

Given this context, it should not be surprising that many experts' testimony stems more from heartfelt sympathy for the petitioner than from medical evidence. It may also help explain why in over 90 percent of the cases that come before it, a tribunal rules in favor of annulment. Often the experts and the tribunal are trying to find justification for allowing a divorced Catholic to remarry in the Church, and in cases in which he has already remarried civilly, to restore him to the sacraments as well. To them, the ends may well justify the means.

Indeed, it is hard to understand why the Church still insists that marriage remain the only lay issue over which its courts retain jurisdiction. The days when the Church's ruling on the validity of a marriage was of legal consequence, as it was for Charles and Nicole, have long since vanished in most parts of the globe. In today's world, the Church's relegating marriage to its courts has the negative effect of limiting a priest's ability to serve as a pastor for his parishioners. Murder is presumably a greater sin than divorce. Yet even a murderer can seek penance from a priest through confession and be forgiven for his sin. However, a divorced Catholic who has remarried outside the Church cannot even attend confession. Rather, he must go before a court where in many cases he is forced to stretch the truth in order to be allowed to confess. That first confession after an annulment must go something like this: Forgive me, Father, for I have sinned, and I lied about my marriage so I could come here and tell you about it.

The Church's new definition of marriage and subsequent changes in policy and law were only partly responsible for the large increase in annulments that have been granted since Vatican II. A new administrative structure has allowed the Catholic Church throughout the world to restructure its judicial system and create a decentralized system of tribunals. Designed to enable the Church to respond more compassionately to the diverse needs of its universal community, an entity of nations and individuals who sometimes had little in common but religion, the decentralized system also enabled the national churches to grant far more annulments than would have been the case had the Vatican merely modernized its concept of marriage and revised its policy.

No other country created a more elaborate, expensive, and effective system of tribunals than the United States. Within this well-funded and decentralized system, the American bishops gave its tribunals broad latitude to render judgments and a mandate to provide compassion to divorced Catholics while continuing to respect the Church's historical opposition to divorce—a tricky balancing act if not an impossible task.

How American tribunals went about their task and at what cost to the sacrament of marriage and church teachings is a case in point. While most people supported broadening the concept of marriage, annulment proponents quickly embraced the new concept as justification to annul almost any marriage. Many asserted that rather than an invalid marriage being a rare occurrence, many existing unions did not measure up to the revised concept. However, unless the couple divorced and one spouse asked for an annulment, no one would ever know.

Even though couples who married before Vatican II signed up for a different kind of marriage, if they should divorce and one spouse asks for an annulment, their marriage will be judged by the new criteria. In cases where only one spouse wants an annulment, new rules for decades-old marriages cannot help but cause anger, hurt, and confusion for the party who believes the marriage was valid. As one woman put it, "When I married I promised to love, honor, and obey my husband. Now I'm being told I was never married because he didn't treat me as an equal."

While some church scholars have noted that annulments of long-term marriages, particularly those with children, raise additional issues and require special sensitivity, the American annulment process does not reflect these concerns. In fact, many tribunals appear reluctant to recognize any inherent differences between a marriage that lasted less than a year and one that lasted more than a decade, even if the latter gave birth to and nurtured children. As one mother told me, "It seems as if some American tribunals are willing to quite literally throw the baby out with the bathwater."

Many former spouses are also hurt and confused by the fact that the same high standards for marriage that are used when someone wants an annulment tend to disappear when a person remarries. More than one woman, for example, told me that her former husband had had a vasectomy before remarrying, a clear indication that he was less than open to the idea of having children with his new wife, even though such openness is considered a cornerstone of Catholic marriage. Others told me that their former mates insisted that the new bride sign a prenuptial agreement before they married, plainly indicating that the second marriage was conditional, another violation of church policy.

Although I felt somewhat more knowledgeable about annulment than when I began my research, I now wondered how anyone could produce a twenty-minute television program that could explain it. But then I realized there was a lot I was leaving to chance by cooperating with *Prime Time*. I really knew very little about how the show was going to be put together or who other than myself was going to be interviewed. Basically, I was trusting Chris Wallace to treat me and the other participants fairly.

On the morning of the interview, I got up a bit early to straighten the house and take the boys to school. Then I came home, changed from jeans into a suit, and set out coffee and doughnuts for my expected guests. Soon the film crew began to arrive. So many people and so much equipment came to the door that I had no idea how everything would fit into our small living room. But the crew knew exactly what it was doing. My single contribution was to move our parrot into the back of the house so that any remarks he had to add would not be picked up on tape. While the crew worked, I calmed my nerves by eating doughnuts. Soon they transformed our living room into a set, complete with devices that prevented the circuits from blowing should the lights and cameras overdraw the electricity.

Several hours after the crew began setting up, Chris and Dave Kelley, the producer, arrived. Perhaps sensing I was a bit nervous, Chris told me just to talk as if the cameras weren't even there. At first that seemed impossible with the lights surrounding me, but after a while I did indeed forget about the cameras and simply talked.

The interview lasted about three hours. Chris asked me how I found out that Joe wanted an annulment and I told him about receiving the notice over the Easter holiday. We discussed Joe's and my telephone conversation in which Joe had referred to annulment as "Catholic gobbledygook" and had told me not to take it seriously. Chris ended the interview by asking why I didn't just go along with the annulment. After all, I wasn't Catholic and it wasn't even my church. I thought for a moment even though I had answered this question for myself many times before. "It's the same God," I answered, "and you are lying before God, and you are lying before God about the birth and conception of your children. And to me, that's just unacceptable."

After the interview, Chris and Dave left for the airport and the crew simply reversed the process it had begun in the morning. Less than an hour after the interview was over, the crew and their equipment had vanished without a trace. In fact, the only telltale sign that anyone had been there at all was that the living room looked cleaner than it had that morning.

Prime Time repeated this process to varying degrees at various locations with two other women whose former husbands had requested annulments, with one of their former husbands, and with church spokespeople. Then in a New York studio, editors spliced and taped the film, added some historical background, and explained how a person obtained an annulment. Presto, a television program was born.

The show was televised January 6, 1994. It began with co-anchor Diane Sawyer noting that Joe had requested an annulment of our marriage and then continued to present a variety of views on the topic. Three priests, Fathers Curran, Cogan, and Sharfenberger, Pat Cadigan, a woman who had successfully fought an annulment petition, and Barbara Zimmerman, a respondent who had not been as fortunate as Pat, spoke on camera. The program concluded with footage of Joe and Beth's wedding, which had taken place the previous October in a civil ceremony at Joe's house in Brighton.

The first priest, Father Curran, was an expert on canon law. He referred to annulment as a "loophole" that the Church found and then "drove a Mack truck through it." He added that canon lawyers sometimes boast that there isn't a Catholic marriage in the United States that they couldn't annul.

Then Father Cogan, a leading canon law expert, expressed an opposing opinion. He explained that because an annulment "says there never was a marriage from the very beginning," it enables the Church to "hold on to a higher principle," in this case the permanance of marriage, while at the same time showing compassion to divorced Catholics who wish to remarry.

Next, Father Sharfenberger, a judge from a New York tribunal, explained that even though the annulment process could cause pain to
some, pain was not always bad, particularly when enduring it helped
uncover the truth. Father Sharfenberger then demonstrated how a
tribunal operates.

In his mock trial the petitioner was a woman. The couple had been
together eleven months before the marriage fell apart and the reason
the marriage failed was that her husband "came home drunk." Expert
witnesses were on hand presumably to corroborate the testimony.
Indeed, in this hypothetical case, an annulment seemed a reasonable
and compassionate solution. The judge also explained that annulment was not just for the rich. The Church, he noted, subsidizes the
cost for those who cannot afford to pay and in fact he didn't know of
a "tribunal in the United States where the cost is more than the cost
of a camcorder."

Pat Cadigan, veteran of a twenty-three-year marriage and mother
of four children, also gave her views on annulment. A bright, educated woman who is now a professional writer, Pat had been divorced
fifteen years when her former spouse sought to annul their marriage.
As was true for most of the women I spoke with, her case was based
on the contention that her former husband lacked due discretion at
the time they married. Unlike the other women, however, Pat successfully defended her marriage at both the tribunal and the appeal
levels.

Pat views annulment as one example of the Church's bias against
women, a bias which encourages them to be wives and mothers and
then negates the choices they make. "I felt as though it was about to
negate a twenty-three-year career to which I had devoted myself exclusively," Pat told Chris. "The cost of this kind of process is disillu-
sionment. It's hard to believe in a church that can be hypocritical
about this. . . . It's a bunch of celibate old guys deciding what the rest
of us are going to do."

Barbara Zimmerman, the second woman Chris Wallace spoke with
about the annulment of her marriage, had been married twenty-
seven years and was the mother of five when she and her husband divorced in 1989. Two years later, true devastation struck when he
convinced the St. Petersburg tribunal in Florida that their marriage
had never existed. Shortly thereafter, Barbara's employer transferred

her to northern Minnesota not far from the Canadian border, and it was here that she and Chris first spoke.

"I felt like I didn't matter, like all that effort and all that time that I spent didn't matter," Barbara told Chris. "He wanted me to say that there was never a marriage, and there was a marriage. It failed, but there *was* a marriage."

Like many viewers who saw the broadcast that evening, I was moved not only by the depth of Barbara's pain but also by its raw quality. While most of the women who spoke with me had been deeply wounded by their annulments, there was an added and more elusive dimension to Barbara's anguish. Later, after I learned more about Barbara's case and met her in person, I understood why she felt as she did.

I watched the broadcast at home alone. Even though I had been careful not to speak disparagingly of Joe during the interview, I thought it best if the children didn't see me on television talking about my marriage to their father and I was grateful that they were in bed by the ten o'clock broadcast. Afterward, several members of my family and a few friends called to say they thought my interview had gone well. I never heard from Joe.

I was pleased with the show and I thought Chris had lived up to his part of the bargain. The program was fair and the Church had ample opportunity to present its point of view. Most important, I thought the show had focused on the topic of annulment and had not tried to take advantage of Joe's last name, or worse, scandalize our marriage. Chris had assured me he would not allow that to happen, but still, by going on television, I had taken an enormous leap of faith with only a reporter's word to depend on. The irony was both obvious and unsettling. It could be safer to trust a newsman than the Church.

I was nevertheless a little disappointed that because of scheduling problems some of the women who had written to me and whom *Prime Time* had contacted were not interviewed. Others had decided that they were not comfortable speaking on television and declined to participate. Yet I had a premonition that I would become friends with Pat and Barbara, and indeed after the show we began to correspond. Pat and I had several conversations in which she told me that despite her success, she had no idea why her efforts to prevent an annulment had succeeded and so many others had failed. She recalled a tribunal letter that she read at the chancery office where she was allowed to review some of the material submitted in her case. Because she was not permitted to Xerox any of the tribunal's "evidence," she copied it in shorthand. The letter noted that Pat had refused to participate in the annulment process although she was "quite free in her opinions regarding the tribunal and the process in general."

The letter also observed that "in order for the Church to declare a marriage invalid, a tribunal must be morally certain that an allegation against the validity of marriage has been proven. While there exists the possibility that the petitioner lacked discretionary judgment in this particular case, this court is far from certain that this [is] true . . . there is no reason to believe, based on the evidence submitted in this investigation, that the petitioner lacked sufficient discretionary judgment to choose marriage with Patricia. . . ."

There were other factors that Pat thinks might have made the judge more reluctant to annul her marriage than others. Pat had previously interviewed this same judge for an article that she hoped to have published in *Newsweek*. As it turned out, Pat's article was not published, but in a civil court a judge who had been previously interviewed by a defendant would most likely be replaced with one whose objectivity was less questionable. Pat informed the tribunal of the possible conflict of interest; it seemed unconcerned. Even now, Pat is uncertain if her interview was relevant to the judge's decision, and in retrospect other issues also unrelated to canon law may have come into play. Shortly after upholding the validity of Pat's marriage, the judge left the priesthood and subsequently married.

Regardless of whether Pat's article influenced the judge, she chose not to respond to the seventy-one questions she received from the St. Louis tribunal. Among other requests, the letter told her to forward to the tribunal any medical records she might have of either her own treatment or that of her former spouse. Of course, sending the tribunal her former husband's records without his permission would have been unethical if not a violation of civil law, as would her husband's sending her records without her permission. Instead of responding to the Church's specific questions, Pat addressed the issues she considered relevant to annulment on her own terms and in her own words.

"I seriously object," Pat wrote, "to this administrative body entering a finding that I was never married. The marriage was irretrievably broken after twenty-three years and four living children. It was, however, entered into with hope, commitment, and maturity *at the time,* after the requisite premarital counseling and with the blessings of the Church. For a tribunal to hold that this marriage did not take place is demeaning to the concept of matrimony as a sacrament.

"I have refused to take part in this annulment procedure because I do not believe in the validity of the annulment process. When the Church grants 65,000 to 70,000 petitions each year, it admits that it has been wrong all along in inviting couples to make lifelong commitments in good faith; it weakens marriage with double-talk. . . .

"I'd like to remind this tribunal that the pregnancies mentioned so often in the questionnaire eventually became people," her letter continued. "Four surviving children of this marriage are affected by this annulment proceeding. They deserve to have names and faces in this file. . . ."

Reflecting the closings of several letters she had received from a nun at the St. Louis tribunal, Pat concluded her letter: "It is my prayer, too, that the proceedings of the tribunal will reflect the teaching of Christ regarding marriage."

I came to realize that Pat has a refreshing, at times almost dry sense of humor about the Church. It's a humor that sometimes camouflages the seriousness and hurt associated with what she has to say, a defense mechanism which has helped her overcome some of what she regards as the negative aspects of Catholicism. In one of our early conversations, Pat gave me an example that illustrates what she regards as "the arbitrary, authoritarian, small-minded, and uncaring attitude of the men who make up the Catholic Church."

During the time that the appeal of Pat's former husband's request for an annulment was under consideration, her favorite aunt died at the age of ninety-one. Aunt Laura had instructed that her body be cremated, and since the Church has permitted the practice for some time, the family adhered to her request. But the local bishop did not approve. When Pat and her family arrived with the ashes at the steps of the church, they were told that Aunt Laura's remains would not be permitted inside. Poor Aunt Laura was forced to miss the service. "I wouldn't have stood still for this decision," Pat told me, "except for the fact that I knew how Aunt Laura would have laughed about having to wait in the car during her own funeral.

"I can no longer take the Church seriously," Pat summarizes. Yet even beneath this seemingly straightforward statement, there is ambivalence. Quickly she adds, "That's not quite true. To paraphrase Miss Jean Brody, if you give a child to the Catholic Church when she is seven, she is theirs forever. You never quite forget the 'shall nots' and the 'musts' and the 'if you don'ts' inculcated by nuns and others who teach the doctrine of the Church. I call myself a recovering Catholic. Like alcoholism, you get over it one day at a time."

In the summer of 1994, Pat published a one-page article, "The Never Wife," in the Hers column of the *New York Times Magazine*. The article gave a concise, moving, and at times amusing account of her experiences with annulment. She told how one of her now-grown daughters phoned and asked if an annulment would make her a bastard and Pat an unwed mother. She was kidding, Pat adds, "Sort of."

When Pat asked a priest about the pain that women with annulled marriages and their children must endure, he answered that pain "can be a good thing." In response, Pat took a tranquilizer. Later Pat sought comfort in an old friend who was both a lawyer and a successful petitioner, having obtained his own annulment after a twelve-year marriage and five children. He assured her that annulment is a lot of "mumbo jumbo" and she wouldn't even "know it happened." Then they both laughed as he told her that he thought she had "one hell of a palimony suit."

Several months later, I met Pat. From the way she looked on television as well as our conversations, I had assumed she would be roughly my contemporary. It wasn't until she reminded me that she had been divorced fifteen years before her former husband requested an annulment and that she began college four years before I was born that I realized she couldn't be. She is in fact in her sixties, and when we met she made it clear that she had no interest in rehashing a marriage that was over a long time ago.

Pat and her sister grew up in northern Wisconsin and were raised by her widowed mother, a supportive extended family, all of whom strictly adhered to church rules. They went to Mass every Sunday and on Holydays of Obligation. No one ate meat on Fridays. They fasted and abstained during Lent, received the sacraments regularly, and in general abided by the Ten Commandments and the Six Precepts of the Church. Pat firmly believed that unless a person were Catholic, he or she would not go to heaven. "We were baptized Catholic," Pat explained. "We received the appropriate sacraments and left the world protected by the Extreme Unction, now the Sacrament of the Sick."

The Sacrament of the Sick was more than a phrase for Pat. Her father, a prominent attorney, had died a "lingering and heroic death" from stomach cancer, and she herself suffered from earaches so severe that the family spent her second-grade year in Tucson, Arizona, in an attempt to cure them. Yet despite her year in the southwestern sun, Pat's earaches resumed when the family returned to Wisconsin, and the bishop gave her mother special permission for Pat to attend the public junior high school rather than the more drafty parochial one, a permission needed in their diocese, Pat explains, because parents who enrolled their children in the public school without it were denied absolution in confession, a threat "taken seriously by my conscientious mother."

Pat's Catholic education did not end when she left parochial school. Her mother sent her to Christian Doctrine classes and month-long church schools each summer. "I can still recite the answers to many of the questions in the old Baltimore Catechism," Pat said. "I know the Seven Deadly Sins, the Sins Crying to Heaven for Vengeance, the Ten Commandments, the Six Precepts of the Church. We memorized these things as some children memorize poetry. Questions brought up at high school religion classes included: When a doctor must choose between a mother and baby, must he choose to save the baby? Did Japanese kamikaze pilots go to hell? Was necking a mortal or a venial sin?"

Pat always did very well in school. Not only did she win a scholarship to Vassar, at the time one of the most prestigious all-women's colleges in the country, but she also completed its program in three years. "My mother cautioned me against philosophy courses which might test my faith," she recalls. "I accepted this caution without thinking. Although I didn't yet question the rules by which I was supposed to live, neither did I have a deep religious fervor. Catholicism was simply a fact of life. I didn't give it much thought."

After Pat graduated with a degree in political science, she moved to New York City to work for a private foundation. "It was 1948 and my job was basically secretarial. All of the women in the secretarial pool were graduates of eastern women's colleges," Pat remembers. "There were few opportunities for us in professional positions then, even though the men who held them were no better educated than we were."

Pat, however, always thought her foundation work would only be short-term. As had her father before her, Pat was going to follow the family tradition and attend law school. Yet as much as Pat wanted to be a lawyer, a counterpull was drawing her in another direction. "It was always important to my mother that I marry a Catholic. Is he Catholic? was her first question about everyone I dated. All of us knew about how the Catholic rules on birth control could make what we called mixed marriage, or marriage to a non-Catholic, miserable."

Pat met her future husband at a summer wedding in the Midwest. He was Catholic and the son of a physician. As had Pat, he had grown up in Wisconsin, and even though the two had never met, their families knew one another. World War II was raging when he graduated from high school and he postponed college to serve in the armed forces. When he and Pat met after the war, he was attending college at the state university. They dated as often as they could, even after Pat returned to her job in New York. The following summer, he, too, took a job in New York. Soon Pat had to make a decision: marriage and a family or law school and a career.

In the 1950s, for most women the choice of career as opposed to marriage and family was almost always an either/or proposition. Combining the two was rarely an option. For Pat, raised as a true Catholic, marriage and motherhood were as natural as breathing, or as she put it, "enshrined in the canon and assumption of the Catholic faith." There really was no choice. That summer she became engaged and about a year and a half after she met her future husband, they married.

The newlyweds moved to southern Illinois. Pat admitted she found her years there tough. Her husband worked nights for a newspaper. "It wasn't New York," she explained. "I missed the city and the excitement."

Five years later, they moved to St. Louis, and for Pat life changed dramatically for the better. St. Louis was a city. "It had a symphony, an art museum, and a great newspaper, And we had a four-bedroom house in the suburbs complete with green grass," she added with characteristic humor.

They also had four children within five years and Pat fully embraced her new role as a mother. In fact, even the idea of law school remained dormant until she and her husband divorced seventeen years later. "The two eldest children attended parochial school for their early education. Later they transferred to public schools, but I was very careful to ensure that they were all baptized, made their First Communions, and were confirmed in our local parish where we attended Mass. We were a typical Catholic family."

As do most marriages that ultimately fail, Pat's eroded in stages. In these early phases, when she began to question where her life was heading, she often turned to the Church for answers. While the women's movement caused many, including Pat, to question the role of a full-time homemaker, Pat saw Pope John and Vatican II as evidence that the Church, too, was seeking to be more relevant to people's daily lives. Later, when she felt that Catholicism was too rigid, she joined the Catholic Pentecostal movement.

Though many Pentecostals leave their institutional churches, the group whose meetings Pat attended retained its Catholicism, hence their name Catholic Pentecostals. Similar to most Pentecostal groups, Pat's defined itself through experiences as much as through written doctrine. It believed in the baptism and in the Holy Spirit. The group also participated in ecstatic worship and speaking in tongues.

Just to be sure she wasn't drawn too far away from her Catholic roots by such an untraditional even if Catholic service, Pat attended the Pentecostal prayer meetings with a Benedictine monk. He provided what she referred to as the "cautionary intellectual component to what was essentially a totally emotional experience," and the Pentecostal prayer groups provided the support and comfort she needed at the time. Clearly, Pat wasn't ready to cut the cord from her church.

Pat isn't clear what ultimately drove her away from the Church. Part of the reason was the women's movement. Slowly, she began to feel that she had bought into a system dominated by men and a male point of view and that she had to rebel against it or risk her own mental health. Meanwhile, the marriage was experiencing what the civil court later acknowledged to be "irreconcilable differences." As difficult as the decision was, Pat felt she would be happier and healthier if she separated from both her husband and her church.

Pat is clear, however, that even before her former husband requested an annulment she had begun to distance herself from Catholicism. For Pat, the annulment request was another confirmation that her new attitude toward the Church was valid. Yet even with her purported rejection of Catholicism and even after being divorced fifteen years, the request for an annulment hit her hard.

Part of her hurt was due to her view that an annulment belittled her choice of marriage and motherhood as her exclusive career. Yet perhaps equally devastating was her own awareness that despite her efforts to let go of her Catholicism, she hadn't really succeeded. In fact, the Church still had an enormous hold on her.

Indeed, Liz, one of Pat's daughters, described this hold to me when I asked about her thoughts on her father's requested annulment. Liz explained that in some respects the timing of the request couldn't have been worse. For the first time since her parents' divorce, the entire family was going to be together for Christmas at the Utah home of the eldest daughter. Both parents, all four children, and their respective families had made travel plans and the necessary reservations to meet there and share the holiday.

Then her father told her mother that he was seeking an annulment. "We went ahead with the reunion," Pat's daughter explained. "But it was awful. No one spoke of the annulment, but it ruined the holiday. Clearly it was too much for my mother. Even certain songs upset her. It wasn't rational. My father's request had simply undone her."

"In a funny way, though, I think the annulment proceedings turned out okay for my mother," Liz continued. "She is very bright and she's right when she says that she followed the Church's teaching by giving up a career for marriage and family. When anyone gives up that much for something, it has to hurt when people say that your sacrifices weren't for anything real."

For Pat, in fact, there was almost a poetic justice in how the annulment proceedings turned out. While the Church's power over Pat may have caused her to forgo a career by encouraging her to become exclusively a wife and mother, the Church also inadvertently enabled her to obtain some of the recognition that she might have enjoyed had she pursued a career outside the home. Although her writings had been widely published in St. Louis newspapers and magazines, the publication of an article in the *New York Times* gave an added impetus to her writing career. As her daughter observed, being published in the *Times* would make any writer feel better.

The annulment proceedings were not as beneficial for Pat's former husband. While his requesting an annulment immediately before the family's Christmas reunion may have been bad timing, Liz doesn't think he realized that his request would bother her mother as much as it did. "He just wanted to get married again and needed an annulment to do it," she told me. "It's sad for him in a way, because since he didn't get an annulment, he hasn't remarried."

Like many children whose parents have been through the annulment process, Liz wishes one weren't necessary to enable divorced Catholics to remarry in their church. On the other hand, the Church's annulment policy hasn't driven her from Catholicism. "Annulment is an issue for my parents and I respect that," Liz explained. "But it really isn't for me. Catholicism isn't as much a part of my life as it was for my parents. I haven't been to confession since I was thirteen. To be honest, I was afraid of it then and I used to make up things that I hadn't really done, just to get it over with. I don't know if I'd still be afraid now or not. When my parents divorced and my father didn't live with us anymore, I stopped going to church."

Like many younger American Catholics, Liz picks and chooses certain aspects of Catholicism and rejects others. She plans to marry in a Catholic service. She and her fiancé just completed their focus test, a list of about two hundred questions that are designed to help the priest determine if the couple will be compatible as husband and wife. "We will be married by a Franciscan monk whom I really like," Liz added. "He tells wonderful stories about faith and hope, the things religion should be about."

What if what is now unthinkable for Liz should happen? What if her marriage should end in divorce? "I can't think I'd ever even want to marry in the Catholic Church again," she answered. "I can't see how annulment would ever be an issue for me."

Pat's son John is a husband, father, public relations practitioner with a master's degree in mass communications, and a practicing Catholic. He quotes from the book *Joshua* by Joseph F. Girzone to illustrate his views on annulment. Joshua, a modern-day Christ figure, is called to Rome to explain his views which the Church considers heresy. During his address, Joshua discusses annulment and asks the church elders: ". . . what is the benefit of priests monitoring the intimate details of people's lives? That's what the Pharisees did to maintain control over people and make them answerable to them for their behavior. . . . And how can you hope to maintain control over so many millions of relationships and commit so many thousands of people to this work of such doubtful values, when there are countless millions of Christians drifting away from God because of neglect? Is it not better to leave the judgment of the intimate details of people's lives to God and go about the work of bringing the message of Jesus to the millions who need to hear him?"

Even though Pat's children thought that annulment was wrong, all were quick to defend their father. Liz understood why her father wanted an annulment and expressed sadness that he feels he cannot remarry without one. John also expressed sympathy for his father's predicament. "I dearly love my father and my mother and want happiness for them both. If they wanted to remarry, I would rejoice for them. But I think that annulment is an unnecessary loophole, a way to make divorce somehow acceptable in the eyes of the Church."

Pat is an articulate spokeswoman for her views. Her comments on *Prime Time* conveyed not only her own feelings about annulment but also the hold the Church still has on her, despite years of trying to divorce herself from her Catholicism. Yet in a way, Pat seemed atypical of the women who had written to me. Being threatened with annulment did not cause Pat to lose her faith. The annulment process simply confirmed what she had already come to believe about the Church.

Even more unusual is the fact that Pat twice successfully defended her marriage. Perhaps her successes were due in part to her training as a writer or perhaps to the fact that her former husband initiated the process fifteen years after their divorce, enabling her to respond to the tribunal more rationally than others who faced the inquiry on the heels of divorce. But the fact is that Pat's marriage was not annulled. As Liz noted, "Because the annulment wasn't granted, no one is saying there wasn't a marriage."

6

HEART OF HEARTS

As I watched the *Prime Time* broadcast, I sensed that Barbara Zimmerman's annulment had been a very different experience from Pat's. Not only had the Church erased her twenty-seven-year marriage, but my instincts told me that her feelings, particularly her pain, were probably more typical of the women who had written to me. I wanted to talk with Barbara in person, learn more about her case, and understand why she felt as she did. Then, if my intuitions were right, I wanted to piece together a picture of how annulment affected women who steadfastly believed in the validity of their long-term marriages despite the Church's ruling. When I contacted Barbara in Minnesota, she told me that she planned to be in the East in several months, and we arranged to meet outside Philadelphia, not far from where I grew up.

Barbara, the eldest of three children, was born in Atlanta, Georgia. Her father was in the military and the family moved constantly. "We moved so much that I didn't go to Catholic schools," Barbara told me. "I think just one of my schools was Catholic. I got my religious training at the parish and from my mother and father. I remember playing tennis with the parish priest. I was brought up in a strict Catholic home. My parents were married fifty-four years and as far as I knew it was a solid marriage. I do not know how they handled their difficulties. At that time children were not privy to the personal lives of their parents and we never saw them fight or argue.

"From what I observed, my mother was the practical one but she always gave in to my father. They were very active in the community, both socially and charitably. My father," Barbara continued, "was basically a big fish in a little pond. My mother never worked outside the home. As a matter of fact, she never learned to drive until after I was married. She was a convert and very active in our local parish where she was a member of the altar society, which means she helped care for the altar and its flowers.

"It wasn't easy being Catholic in Florida in the 1950s. There weren't very many of us. In fact, when I took three days off from school to participate in my church's retreat, the school gave me zeros for each day that I missed. I could miss school for church, but we never missed Mass. My mother wouldn't allow it.

"Our home was very authoritarian," Barbara continued. "My parents' word was law. I wasn't allowed to date until I was sixteen, but I was never rebellious. My brother, who was eleven months younger than I, was the rebellious one. I was considerably older than my younger sister and was married when she was three years old. I am very fond of her."

Barbara and her future husband, Bob, met at a dinner of the Knights of Columbus, a society for American Catholic men founded in 1882 to "promote fraternity, benevolence, and civic loyalty" among its members. Above all, the society seeks to protect the interests of the Roman Catholic Church. Barbara was seventeen, Bob twenty-two, a flight cadet and soon to be a second lieutenant in the air force. "There was a turkey dinner," Barbara recalls. "Bob seemed intelligent and polite. He didn't make a pass and that was a nice change, although he did spill coffee on me. I didn't think much about him. I was going out with other people. I was seventeen, and since my parents only allowed me to begin dating when I turned sixteen, I was enjoying my new freedom and having a good time.

"About two weeks later Bob called and invited me to go deep-sea fishing. I told him that I had to be back early because I was planning to go to a party at a local fraternity later that evening. We worked it out so I did both. But after the party, I stopped going out with other people and Bob took me to my senior prom. I still have a picture. Bob looked dashing in his full air force regalia. I wore a white strapless gown. Bob had a shy, innocent quality that attracted me even though he was also somewhat uncommunicative. What I liked most about him was that he seemed respectful. He conveyed a feeling that I could depend on him, that he'd be there for me.

"Also," Barbara continued, "he was Catholic and there weren't many Catholics in Florida in those days. Because of our Catholicism we had the same values, particularly regarding family and children. Bob was even more devout than I. Later I found out that he had considered being a priest but had changed his mind. I'm still not sure why. All I know is that by the time we were involved, he wanted to marry a nice Catholic girl and have a family. It's funny in a way. From the beginning of our relationship, I knew we would be married. I think a large part of why I felt that way was his Catholicism. I would only marry a Catholic and he was the first one I ever dated."

"In the summer of 1955, the air force transferred Bob to Texas. When he went on a thirty-day leave around Christmas, he went home to his family in Detroit. I went to visit him there and stayed for about two weeks. During this time, Bob gave me a ring. He never really even had to propose. We both just knew we were going to be married. Bob returned to Texas and I went home to Florida. Bob joined me there about three days before the wedding. We met with the priest and made the final preparations for the service.

"Virtually all the priest talked about was the importance of children in a marriage. Since Bob and I already thought that raising children was the primary reason to marry, the priest didn't tell us anything we didn't already know. Both of us felt strongly that marriage was a sacred union and by committing ourselves to it we were promising to abide by the rules of the Church and raise a family under God's law. That belief was what gave meaning and purpose to our lives."

That April, Bob and Barbara married in a traditional Catholic ceremony in her home parish in Florida. "I even vowed to obey him," she remembered with a smile. Indeed, for Barbara her wedding was a rite of passage into her chosen career as wife and mother. Aside from summer and Christmas jobs, Barbara had never worked outside the home and despite her being a straight-A student, college was not an option. "My father wouldn't have allowed it," she told me. "He thought a college education was a waste for women. It was the 1950s. People married earlier in those days, particularly in the South. It was what girls were brought up to do, especially if you were Catholic. I was young, hopeful, in love, and looking forward to spending the rest of my life with the man I had married. We both wanted children and I expected a close, loving relationship with my husband."

After a brief honeymoon in the Bahamas, Barbara began to realize her goals. The newlyweds first settled at a military base in Texas, and Bob continued his service as an air force pilot. Very soon, in fact nine months and four days after they were married, a son arrived. Both Barbara and Bob were delighted to become parents and immediately arranged for their son's baptism. Bob's parents arrived for the service; and indeed it seemed to all as if Bob and Barbara were partners in a strong and meaningful marriage.

"We were happy," Barbara recalled. "We lived in a duplex and were members of the officers' club. It was a traditional life for a military family. I played bridge and was friendly with the other wives. Bob flew a lot and wasn't able to go to Mass every day, but he remained a scrupulous Catholic."

About a year and a half later, Bob left the service and the family moved to Detroit. Bob worked in his father's insurance business and for a while they lived with his parents. Barbara was frank that she found living with her in-laws difficult. "Bob's father never called me by name. He referred to housework as 'squaw work' and basically controlled our lives. One night I had made a cake and he asked if I had made it from scratch. When I replied that I had used a mix, he refused to eat it. He was constantly criticizing me."

After several months, Barbara decided she needed some advice on how to get along with her in-laws. Not surprisingly, she turned to the Church. A priest at the University of Detroit talked with both Barbara and Bob and convinced Bob of the need for greater independence from his parents. Shortly thereafter, with assistance from his father, Bob bought a house. Unfortunately for Barbara, it was only a few blocks away from her in-laws.

While Bob's parents continued to be a problem for Barbara, this did not inhibit her from nurturing her own growing brood. Because of her faith, Barbara did not use birth control, and within two and a half years she gave birth to three children and to five in just over six.

With each child Bob's parents became more difficult. "At one point," Barbara explained, "I went back to the Church for help. First, I met with another priest, but he told me he couldn't see me without my husband. I tried to explain that my husband refused to come and asked him just to work with me. At this point he told me to have a glass of wine at dinner and reiterated that he couldn't see me by myself because, as he put it, 'Women are occasions of sin.' Needless to say, I was flabbergasted. I hardly thought I was 'an occasion of sin.'

"Later, I did go by myself to Catholic Social Services. The counselor told me that I had three choices: live with it, change it, or walk away from it. I decided just to make the best of it. After all, nothing is perfect, and if Bob's parents were part of what God thought I should bear, then so be it. I had no dryer, no car, and three kids in diapers. You can imagine what the basement looked like. And you know what?" Barbara asked almost rhetorically, "I really enjoyed it. I absolutely loved being a mother. And I loved being married. After all, being a wife and a mother was my chosen career. I was still a very devout Catholic."

There was another aspect of Barbara's life that was growing in importance. About three years after she and Bob had married there had been another addition to the family. At the time it had seemed insignificant but in retrospect it altered Barbara's life. "As a child, I had read *Lassie* and all those books about collies by Albert Payson Terhune. I had always wanted a dog, but I had never been able to have one. At the point when I only had two kids, I bought a collie, Shannon."

At first Shannon was just a family pet, and as do many dog owners, Barbara took her to obedience school. Once enrolled, Barbara found she had a knack with dogs and she decided to try her luck at shows. Shannon, however, was not, as they say in the dog world, of "show quality," meaning she didn't win any prizes. Undaunted, Barbara bred her to a friend's champion and began showing one of the offspring.

Under Barbara's tutelage and before she was a year old, Shannon's daughter Ellen became a champion, a designation that meant she had earned a required number of points at various shows. Barbara, meanwhile, had become a licensed dog handler: she was now legally certified to show dogs for money and had proven herself qualified to do so. "You either have an eye for animals or you don't," Barbara explained. "If you do, you're born with it. You can't really learn it."

Barbara was born with the gift. She was very good at what she did and for the first time since high school her talent was acknowledged. Barbara was well on her way to a successful career in the dog-show world. Both children and pets kept coming. In 1964, Barbara and Bob bought a larger, five-bedroom house with two acres. It was home for their five children, cats, dogs, horses, rabbits, and goats. "Some of my friends," Barbara recalls fondly, "referred to it simply as 'the zoo.' "

While the menagerie made for a lot of work, it also provided a warm and active atmosphere in which to raise the children. And raising children was what mattered most to both Bob and Barbara. Because there weren't any parochial schools where they lived, their children attended public school and received religious instruction at home and at the local parish. First Communions and Confirmations were always cause for celebrations and the family attended Mass together.

Although Bob did not participate in caring for the animals or in the housework, he held the fort when Barbara went off to dog shows, which was sometimes as often as every other weekend. "I would put the meals in the freezer before I left on Friday night. Sometimes some of the children came with me," Barbara recalled. "When I returned on Sunday the place would be a mess, but that was okay. We had a traditional marriage. Bob made the money and I took care of the house and children. He was used to having his dinner on the table. I think he thought if he was nice enough to 'let me,' as he put it, go away for the weekend, then I could clean up when I got back. It was the price I paid for going."

There were other costs associated with Barbara's being away so much on weekends. Bob didn't mind all the animals and action at home. In fact, he rather enjoyed the environment because he didn't have to think of family activities. He also tolerated Barbara's absences, but her being away so many Sundays did cause problems. She usually missed Mass and they could not go as a family nearly so often. Church had been the family mainstay, at times the only activity that they did together. Missing church was a loss. As a couple, Barbara and Bob were growing apart.

After the fifth child was born, Barbara felt she had enough children. "I went to a Catholic doctor. I never would have gone to one that wasn't and asked for birth control." Barbara recalled, "He gave it to me. I didn't tell Bob, but of course he found out. He was such a devout Catholic. I think it really hurt him and it widened the wedge between us. It was as if we were living in the same house but the other person wasn't even there."

The wedge became larger. Seventeen years after they married, Bob and Barbara separated and then divorced. Looking back, Barbara isn't sure exactly what pushed the relationship over the edge. There had been the years of problems with Bob's parents. Barbara never got the support she truly needed. Bob had never been easy to communicate with and when she had turned to the Church for help, the priest told her to have a glass of wine with dinner. All of these factors undoubtedly contributed to the marriage's unraveling. Equally relevant was that as Barbara became more involved with dog shows, she began to experience a new side of herself. "I'm stubborn, I know," she admitted, "but I was good at something and I didn't want to quit. I still took care of the children. They loved coming to the shows. Bob could have come with me some, but he wouldn't."

A year or so after the divorce, another handler whom Barbara had known for a long time started to show up at the same shows as Barbara. "He lived in Nevada," Barbara explained. "Michigan wasn't exactly close. I finally figured out that he was coming to see me."

They began dating, and a couple of years later they married in a Methodist service. "I would not have dreamed of asking for an annulment," Barbara said. "I never questioned the fact that Bob's and my marriage had been valid. After my second husband and I were married we drove out to Nevada. The children stayed with their father to finish the school year and then joined us in June. My new husband and I shared an enormous interest in dogs and I thought we'd be this wonderful team. I fell for him.

"That summer the children went to shows with us. We all enjoyed the show life and it was a fun summer. But my second husband was jealous of my children. I'm very close to them and he didn't like it. He also had a temper and things didn't work out. We were only married eight and a half months when I packed up and drove back to Michigan."

Once back in Michigan, Barbara faced new challenges. Since Bob was living in the family home, the children lived with him and Barbara moved into a nearby apartment. She no longer had a kennel, nor did she have enough money to live. "I had to find a job," Barbara remembered. "I began at $2.40 an hour selling women's designer clothing at the mall. After about six months, I was the assistant manager and after a year, I was running one of the stores. But then I found out that the shoe manager, who was a man, was making more than I was even though I was his boss. The chain that owned the store where I worked wouldn't change its policy. They said he had a family to support. I quit along with two other people.

"Then I worked for a wholesale company that sold sporting merchandise to college bookstores. I did that for about two years. I had to travel a lot. Being responsible for my own finances was a change for me, but I liked the independence."

Bob, too, had gone on with his life after the divorce and was involved in another relationship. "It was sort of strange," Barbara recalled. "Our divorce was very amicable. Bob and I would attend the children's Little League games and family reunions together. I sat with him and the children at his mother's funeral. His girlfriend sat somewhere else and she didn't like that much. It was as if Bob and I were still married. After a while, I realized that reconciliation was inevitable. Our marriage had never really ended. Even now, I feel as if I'm still married to Bob.

"There were five years between our two civil marriages," Barbara continued. "Bob agreed to work on our marriage with me. I felt that he now understood that I wanted to be an equal partner. In the Church's eyes, our first marriage was still valid, so we just had a civil ceremony in Vegas. For a while things went better. I felt that Bob was including me more. Both of his parents were dead and our children were grown, so I stopped working and we moved to Florida for a fresh start.

"But soon after we moved, I learned that Bob had bought twelve houses as investments and used our Michigan home as collateral for the loans. He had never even told me, and I felt that by keeping me in the dark, he was betraying what he had promised when we remarried—that I would be treated as an equal. I can't see how you can be an equal and have no say in financial decisions, particularly ones of such magnitude. It was a control issue. He still wanted to run everything and I couldn't handle it. We separated again.

"We were living apart, although both of us were in Florida, when I invited Bob for Thanksgiving dinner. I was cooking for eighteen or so people. I like having people over for holidays, particularly people who have nowhere else to go. Well, Bob called and asked if he could bring someone with him. I said sure, and he arrived with a woman who was about twenty years older than he.

"I can still remember so vividly. Bob came into the kitchen where I was cooking and asked me what I thought of his guest. I said she seemed nice and that she reminded me of his aunt. He agreed and then told me that he wanted to marry her and that he wanted a divorce. I wasn't really surprised, and I wasn't upset. I felt he needed to be taken care of, though I did suggest that they just live together, as the age difference was noticeable. After the divorce was final, she and Bob married in a civil ceremony. None of the children went."

Barbara doesn't know exactly when Bob began annulment proceedings. She first learned of it when one of her sons contacted her in late February 1991. "He was upset," Barbara recalled, "because the Church had sent him a letter asking about our marriage. He didn't know what to do and I didn't know anything about it. I was furious that the Church would send my children such a letter. I immediately contacted a priest, and a short time later in early March I received a certified letter from the St. Petersburg tribunal."

Unlike the letter that I and most other recipients I spoke with received, Barbara's did not cite grounds for her former husband's inquiry but merely stated that he had requested an evaluation of their marriage. The letter also asked Barbara to indicate if she had anything to say regarding the evaluation by filling out an "option form" which had been "enclosed for her convenience." The tribunal gave her twenty working days in which to respond. As had I, Barbara filled out the form indicating that she was opposed to the annulment and mailed it back.

About three weeks later, the tribunal wrote Barbara again and informed her that it was ready to begin its study on the grounds that "the in-depth and due discretion necessary for . . . a sacramental marriage might have been lacking." In addition, the tribunal enclosed a questionnaire for Barbara to fill out and asked her to send the names of other persons who might help it "understand her former marriage."

Barbara was given a month to answer the questionnaire. If the tribunal did not hear from her within that time, it would proceed with the case and presume that she had decided not to participate further. The letter made no offer to answer questions that Barbara might have. Nor did the Church appoint an advocate to help her prepare her case.

Barbara answered the questions as best she could. She told the tribunal that her marriage was valid and that she strongly objected to the annulment. She explained that although she had friends who would be willing to speak on her behalf, they had only known Bob and her since their last separation and divorce. Thus, she was unclear if what they had to say would be of any use to the tribunal's study, a study which, after all, was purported to be concerned with the parties' condition at the time of their marriage. If, however, the tribunal wanted their views, Barbara asked it to let her know and she would then contact her friends.

Then for the second time, Barbara asked about the letter her son had received. She carefully explained that Bob had apparently not only submitted their children's names to be witnesses without consulting them, but had also neglected even to inform the children that he was requesting an annulment. The letters from the tribunal had, in fact, caught the children by complete surprise.

Apparently, their father and the Church wanted them to be witnesses to help determine if in fact their parents had ever been married, a judgment based largely on the condition of the couple at the time they wed. But how could these grown children comment on their parents' condition at the time of the wedding, when these same children had not yet even been conceived? The tribunal did not respond to Barbara's letter or to her concerns about her children. The children understandably refused to be witnesses.

Then in August, almost six months since Barbara had first written to the Church, some of her children again began to contact her about the annulment. They had received identical letters from their father indicating that the annulment was to be granted. Barbara's reaction was not unlike that of Deirdre, who had learned of her annulment from her daughter. At first she couldn't believe it.

Barbara immediately wrote both the judicial vicar at the tribunal and the bishop of the Diocese of St. Petersburg explaining what her children had told her. She also pointed out that the tribunal had not been in touch with her since she had responded to its March questionnaire and that as far as she knew none of the people who had offered to be witnesses on her behalf had been contacted.

Barbara's letters also raised some very specific questions: "Do you just decide that there was no marriage on the basis of the questionnaire we answered? Am I allowed no voice in this at all? This is my marriage you are talking about! Are the sacraments no longer safe? Is this how the Church works in these matters?

"We had a valid marriage," Barbara continued. "It failed. There is no way around that. If the Church allows a long marriage to be dissolved on flimsy grounds, then why not just allow divorce? I do not know the grounds used. I don't know anything and I would respectfully request some information before the Church tells me that I was never in a marriage I tried so hard to save."

The reactions of the St. Petersburg tribunal were not unlike those in Deirdre's case. There the Boston tribunal had explained that a "typing backlog" had prevented it from notifying Deirdre by mail that the annulment had been granted, even though it had been able to inform her former husband quickly. In Barbara's case, the tribunal insisted it had sent the letter of notification, enclosed a copy, and expressed regret that she had not received notification at the appropriate time. Both tribunals failed to grasp how sons and daughters must feel when they tell their mothers that the Church has declared their parents' marriage void.

It was not Barbara's fault that she was unaware of the grounds upon which the tribunal had made its decision. Not even the official notification stated grounds. Rather, in addition to the official notification, the tribunal sent Barbara a cover letter, which was not signed by the vicar to whom she had written but by another judge. Although this letter also failed to cite grounds, it did attempt to explain why the Church had annulled the marriage. The judge stated that the tribunal had based its case on "her testimony" in which Barbara had indicated a "total lack of partnership" in the marriage. He noted that an "interpersonal partnership" is an essential right and obligation of marriage.

The judge then added that he was "confused" that Barbara was insisting on the "validity" of the marriage when it was, after all, she who had testified that her former husband did not fulfill this "right so essential to a valid sacramental marriage." The letter concluded by telling Barbara that if she had anything to add she should contact them within fifteen days.

Six days later, Barbara again wrote the tribunal explaining that she still did not understand the grounds upon which it was granting the annulment. She also asked the judge several direct questions: "If Bob could or would not fulfill the right to an interpersonal partnership in our marriage, what makes the tribunal think that he will be able to do this in his current [second] marriage?

"It is interesting that you say the annulment was decided on the basis of my 'testimony,'" Barbara continued. "The questionnaire I answered was presented by the tribunal to me as part of a study of the marriage. In no way was it indicated that it was 'testimony.' If I had refused to answer the questionnaire, would his petition have been granted? I think I am entitled to know the answers to these questions. . . . I wish to state my strong objection to this annulment and the way it was handled. . . . This action is driving six Catholics [Barbara and her five children] away from the Church.

"I would also like to know," Barbara's letter concluded, "if I had an advocate to plead for my side and if I have any recourse in this matter. . . . I was born a Catholic and I will die a Catholic and I try to live my life in accordance to God's will, but I will publicly object to the Church using the annulment process to allow my husband to remarry in the Church when our marriage was valid. The Church did nothing to help save the marriage. This whole farce gives scandal to the Church and I will not hesitate to say so."

A little over a week later, while Barbara was waiting for the tribunal to respond to her letter, she received one from the bishop. His letter was in response to her inquiry written at the end of August, the same day that she had asked the tribunal to explain its actions. Ironically, the bishop's letter suggested she do what she had already done—contact the tribunal. The bishop thoughtfully included the tribunal's phone number and assured Barbara that one of the priests would be "happy" to see her and hopefully answer some of her questions.

Barbara, however, lived two hours from the tribunal office and had a full-time job. Better to wait, she thought, until she heard from the judge before asking for time off and scheduling an appointment. But the judge never responded to her letter. Rather, in December she received a standard notice that the annulment had been upheld on routine appeal. One of the judges to whom she had written signed the official decree, the other the accompanying cover letter.

Barbara was shocked by the Church's ruling. What it now claimed was her testimony was in fact her answers to its questionnaire, and they were answers which indicated neither a "total lack of partnership" nor the absence of an "interpersonal" one as the judge stated, but rather the lack of a full partnership and an equal relationship, particularly regarding family finances.

When the Church asked, "To what extent did you like him/her as a person? Could you accept him/her without having to change all of his/her faults?" Barbara answered that Bob was basically a good person, but that he had shut her out of decisions about how they lived. "I never saw a tax return. I knew nothing about our finances . . ." she wrote. "I had no right to know how much money he made or how it was spent."

When the Church asked, "Was there any particular factor which led to the final separation?" Barbara answered, "I found out about the decisions he had made without my knowledge—the rental property, the borrowed money that I was responsible for as well as he, and confronted him. He would not discuss it."

When the Church asked, "Why do you personally feel this marriage failed?" Barbara answered, "My inability to accept less than full partnership."

Essentially, the judge equated what Barbara considered an "unequal relationship" with "a total lack of partnership." Then he claimed that because Barbara "testified" that her marriage was unequal, it lacked any degree of partnership. Since an "interpersonal partnership" is one of the components of a sacramental marriage, he concluded that her marriage was invalid.

But clearly Barbara and Bob had a partnership, and clearly it had been interpersonal. They had been together twenty-seven years, endured a divorce, worked through a reconciliation, divorced again, and had given birth to and raised five children. What kind of a partnership could such a relationship have been, if not interpersonal?

It is difficult to believe that the judge did not recognize Barbara and Bob's twenty-seven-year marriage as a traditional Catholic one centered upon raising a family. It is far more plausible that he used Barbara's statements about their marriage's lack of equality particularly on financial matters as the basis for his decision. After all, the "last straw" for Barbara had been Bob's failing to include her in financial decisions. Yet few Americans and probably even fewer Catholics would say that many marriages are truly equal partnerships, particularly regarding finances.

As Barbara and I continued to discuss the meaning of "partnership" and "equality" in marriage, I started to laugh. I wasn't meaning to be rude or to make light of her pain, but my mind kept going back to a session from Joe's and my prenuptial counseling.

We were meeting with Joe's family priest in his mother's large living room in her house in Virginia. We were surrounded by family memorabilia and the American flag stood stately in the corner. The priest had given me a small book of short sayings that reflected the Catholic view of marriage, and we were hoping to select at least one to include in our ceremony. When I held the book, it kept opening to a selection based on a passage from Sirach: "Blessed is the quiet woman in the well-kept house."

"Father," I remember saying only somewhat jokingly, "I have real trouble with this one."

The priest assured me that there were about two hundred others to chose from and suggested that I pick another.

"I'm looking for 'Blessed is the husband who cares for the children and cleans the house so his wife can go to night school,' but I can't find it," I replied.

The priest and even Joe, who has never been exactly an advocate for equality between the sexes, laughed, adding, "I don't think you'll find that."

Needless to say, the priest and Joe were right. I never did. Nor did I expect to, but the priest was also right when he said there were other passages that would appeal to me more. We chose the well-known passage from Corinthians that describes the attributes of love and a less well-known selection from Colossians on the importance of compassion, kindness, humility, gentleness, patience, and forgiveness. Given the Church's view on a woman's place when Joe and I married in 1979, it is almost impossible to believe that the Church regarded marriage as an equal partnership when Barbara and Bob wed in 1956, twenty-three years before we did.

Fortunately for me, Barbara thought my story was funny, too. When she started to laugh as well, I felt better and we began talking about how Catholic marriage had changed between the times she and I had married. She and Bob had not chosen passages for their service. I certainly never promised to obey Joe. Barbara's marriage in 1956 was before Vatican II and mine in 1979 was after.

Nevertheless, even taking into account the Church's post–Vatican II views on annulment, I couldn't understand how the judge could have granted one in Barbara's case. I needed to see for myself what current church law really says. Later when I had returned to Boston, I consulted my copy of *Code of Canon Law*, a book which had been a gift from Deirdre. These codes, compiled by the Canon Law Society of America, are written in both English and Latin and my version, published in 1983, incorporates the teachings of Vatican II. As I suspected, the codes tell a different story about the issues of equality and partnership than the judge had conveyed to Barbara.

There are 133 canons covering thirty-five pages that relate either to marriage or the celebration of the wedding. Of these, 107 discuss why marriage is important and how to prepare for receiving its sacrament. The remaining 26 explain what to do when something in the marriage goes wrong.

Nowhere, however, in its thirty-five-page discussion on the laws of marriage is there one reference to equality. Yes, the codes refer to marriage as a covenant by which men and women "establish a partnership," but it is for "their own good" (the couple's) and for the "procreation and education of offspring," not for equality. In fact, there is nothing in the codes themselves that even suggests that a more liberal use of annulment is justified. Indeed, even the experts who favor more liberalized annulment admit it's the interpretation of the canons rather than the canons themselves that provides justification.

There is little doubt that there are as many opinions about annulment among those within the Church as there are among those who seek to follow its teachings, and the Church is also aware that few of its followers are going to spend much time studying canon law. In 1994, as part of an effort to enlighten mainstream Catholics about many of the post–Vatican II reforms, the United States Catholic Conference released an English translation of the *Catechism of the Catholic Church*.

The new Catechism, an eight-hundred-page volume, outlines how Catholics should interpret God's word in the modern world and face controversial issues such as artificial insemination, euthanasia, birth control, masturbation, and sex abuse. The monumental work, the first Catechism to speak for the universal Church since the Roman Catechism was released after the Council of Trent in 1566, became an instant best-seller in the United States, a fact which seems to indicate that rather than retreating from their church, many American Catholics are trying very hard to understand its teachings.

Despite my best efforts, nowhere in its eight hundred pages could I find a reference to equality or equal partnership as even a desirable goal for marriage. Given the level of discussion on other sensitive issues, particularly those relating to intimacy, it's hard to believe the writers would not have discussed equality as Barbara's judge had interpreted it had they considered it relevent to marriage. Rather, the Catechism notes that "men and women have equal dignity though in a different way. . . . The woman, 'flesh of his flesh,' i.e., his counterpart, his equal, his nearest in all things, is given to him [the husband] by God as a 'helpmate.' "

The new Catechism did not change the purpose of marriage. In fact, it notes that it is as the Creator willed it from the beginning: for husband and wife to "renounce themselves and take up their crosses so that they will be able to receive God's grace and live according to His laws." Barbara's view that marriage is a sacramental union in which husband and wife commit themselves to raising a family under God's law followed these teachings. It was through their children that Bob and Barbara's "interpersonal partnership," a partnership the judge correctly observed is a "right and an obligation of marriage," blossomed.

Indeed, rather than being out of step with the modern Church, Barbara seemed to have a far better understanding of marriage than the priest who judged her case. While he seemed to ignore the importance of children in her marriage, the Catechism refers to children as "the supreme gift to marriage" that "contribute greatly to the good of the parents themselves."

Barbara lived her Catholic beliefs as she raised her family. Even when their marriage failed, both she and Bob remained true to their marital vow to raise their children together and in "accordance with God's law." Although divorced, Bob and Barbara attended their children's functions as a couple.

Finances had always been Bob's domain, and even though his unwillingness to loosen control of the purse strings may have widened the rift between him and Barbara, he nevertheless remained consistent in fulfilling his financial obligations to his children. Bob made most of the family money, and paid for his children's college education. It was a partnership.

By the fall of 1993, the Church's ruling had been festering within Barbara for almost two years. "I promised to obey my husband when we married." Well aware of the paradox, she told me, "Now the Church has annulled our marriage because I supposedly claimed there was no partnership or I wasn't an equal. . . ."

Barbara knew the Church was wrong. She knew she had been deceived, but she only began to learn how badly when she told her story to Chris Wallace. During her interview, Barbara learned that the Church had given Bob a completely different reason to justify its granting his request for an annulment.

Chris justifiably, although mistakenly, assumed that Barbara was aware of Bob's explanation. According to what Bob had told him in a separate interview, the Church's decision had nothing to do with a lack of equality or partnership in the marriage. Rather, it was based on Bob's testimony which stated in part that Barbara had been a victim of abuse as a child. Because of this, the Church decided Barbara was somehow psychologically impaired and unable to fulfill the obligations of marriage. Thus, a true marriage had never existed.

The Church had no evidence to corroborate Bob's testimony, and because Barbara was unaware of the allegations, she was unable to offer any explanation of her own. While she confirms that she had confided to Bob that as a child she had been a victim of abuse, Barbara firmly believes that it was not of major significance to their marriage.

"No one has a perfect childhood," Barbara said to me, "but that shouldn't be used as a way for people to escape responsibility for a failed marriage. Both Bob and I made mistakes. Both of us should accept responsibility for our actions and go on from there, not pretend that we were never married."

The Church is supposed to have either medical evidence or a professional evaluation before making a serious judgment such as the impact of alleged child abuse upon a marriage. Barbara was not told of the allegations, nor evaluated by a mental health professional. The Church's decision to annul her marriage based upon uncorroborated evidence that lacked a medical basis raises several other questions that should be particularly sensitive for the Church. Are marriages in which one party was abused by a priest as a child invalid? Many of these cases have been both medically and legally proven and have had devastating and sometimes permanent emotional effects on the victims.

If Barbara was incapable of marriage because she was an alleged victim of abuse, what about the perpetrators of extensive and documented abuse? Priests take a vow similar to that of marriage when they enter the priesthood. If they turn out to be child abusers, is it not logical to assume that they suffered from some psychological defect at the time they took their vows? Is it not also reasonable to assume that this defect prevented them from bonding with the Church in much the same way that a victim of abuse might be inhibited from bonding in marriage?

But the Church does not annul the priesthood of child abusers. Why are the victims of abuse assumed less capable of forming sanctified bonds than these perpetrators? These questions were not discussed in a counseling session nor even in the privacy of Barbara's home, places that could have offered a safety zone in which Barbara might have dealt effectively with her pain. The Church, in fact, never raised them at all, perhaps assuming that because she would not learn the real reason for her annulment, neither she nor church personnel would have to deal with the emotional wreckage these issues would surely raise.

But when Chris told Barbara that Bob had said abuse was the reason for the annulment, the truth was out. As cameras rolled, the related questions rapidly sank in. "Chris Wallace didn't ask anything about the implications of the abuse," Barbara explained. "But I knew and they kept going through my mind. I felt that the Church had completely betrayed me. It was as if I was being gunned down by an automatic machine gun."

Displaying a sensitivity many viewers find lacking in television today, the *Prime Time* camera crew stopped filming until Barbara regained her composure. "Looking back," Barbara said to me thoughtfully, "I'm glad I know the truth. A part of me always knew they hadn't annulled my marriage because it wasn't equal.

"But" she continued, "the abuse wasn't why my marriage failed either. Basically the Church didn't have a case, so they lied. Either they lied to Bob or to me. Or maybe they lied to both of us. That's a lot of lying just so someone may remarry in the Church. And to think they do it all in the name of God."

There is evidence to support Barbara's claim. The Church did not impose a restriction upon her remarrying, an action it is supposed to take if a spouse is presumed to suffer from a condition that is both sufficiently grave to render the marriage invalid and transferable to another union. While Bob admitted that he told the Church Barbara had been a victim of child abuse, he never indicated that she had been treated for its effects.

Barbara's ordeal was not yet over. Several weeks after the *Prime Time* broadcast, she was at a public function. "I was trying to make some sense of it all and work through some of my feelings," Barbara recollected. "A priest was there and he must have recognized me because he told me I should be ashamed of myself. Then he added that I had caused 'scandal to the Church.' 'Excuse me,' I said. And he repeated that I should be ashamed of myself because I had caused 'scandal to the Church.' Then he explained that he had seen the piece on *Prime Time*."

"Barbara," I blurted out, "you and I both know that where annulment is concerned the Church has brought scandal upon itself. It doesn't need any help from the likes of you and me."

Barbara's life has gone on. After her second divorce and a stint in real estate, she answered an ad in the newspaper to help a new mother run an office. Once hired, she learned new computer systems and basically took over most of the office management. "Best of all," she said, "I really hit it off with the owner's wife, who was the new mother referred to in the ad. Right away we became friends. Now I'd say she and her husband are my best friends."

There are still the dogs. In fact, when I met Barbara she and a dozen or so of her colleagues had just finished judging 2,500 dogs. When I asked if that's not roughly the number of contestants entered in Westminster, America's most prestigious dog show, Barbara answered modestly and with a smile, "This show doesn't have the prestige of Westminster. But I love what I do and I'm good at it."

Even though Barbara now has her own life, it is her children and grandchildren and the importance she attaches to family that give her life its meaning. Long before her children were born, she believed that the purpose of her marriage and indeed her life was to raise children under God's law. Despite all she has been through, she has remained loyal to this belief. It is her rock.

Knowing the strength of Barbara's beliefs, I wasn't surprised to find that not only are her children extraordinary in their own ways but they also have a special relationship with their mother. "She showed us by example to be kind and the difference between right and wrong. She also taught us to think for ourselves," said her daughter Jenny.

Barbara's children live very different lives from one another, yet each has found what is important to them. A son, Stephen, has degrees in both psychology and sociology. He is also a master cabinetmaker. Jenny, a mother of four children under the age of ten, including three-year-old twins, is taking a break from working in her husband's meat-packing business to raise their children.

Stephen and Jenny spoke with me as unofficial family representatives. Stephen is in his mid-thirties, married, and the father of a seven-year-old son. "I was raised a Catholic. Catholicism was very important to my parents, but I have moved away from the Church," he explained. "Its hypocrisy turned me off to religion.

"To me, annulment is just typical of so much that is going on in the Church today. The Church is such a male-dominated institution. I don't know why someone doesn't point out the gender bias in the annulment proceedings. I was the one who told my mother it was happening. The Church never helped her. Rather, it helped my father through the whole process and left my mother in the dark. I doubt the tribunal would have even sent her the notice if she hadn't contacted them and complained."

Stephen doesn't think of the Church as a moral indicator anymore. "Morals," he says, "are about right and wrong and that's about how you act and how you treat other people."

Stephen thinks that the Church has abandoned its role as a moral leader and has allowed the evangelists to take over. "Some people think evangelism is silly," he explained, "but they miss the point. Evangelism is responding to a real need that people have for something to believe in. The power of that belief can be scary."

I asked Stephen how as a father and as someone who has obviously thought a lot about morals and right and wrong he plans to pass these values on to his child, particularly since he is raising his son outside the Church. From my question it's clear to Stephen, who has a degree in psychology, that my interest is more than theoretical.

"I wonder and I worry," I explained, "for my own children. Before I became involved in the annulment process, I had never really thought much about how my children would learn to distinguish right from wrong. Somehow I thought moral development would just happen, almost by osmosis. I assumed that when my children became young adults their beliefs would be based on religion, perhaps a hybrid of Catholic and Episcopalian doctrines, but ostensibly Catholic. Now, I just don't know. How can my children be expected to believe in a church so hypocritical that it annuls valid marriages that it previously blessed, including perhaps the one into which they were born?"

While Stephen didn't answer my questions directly, he did point out that as someone who had moved away from the Church because of this same hypocrisy, he was teaching his own son moral development through mythology and by example. He explained that there are many stories in Greek and Roman mythology that teach right from wrong. Many of the stories in the Bible do the same. "They help children develop a sense of right and wrong.

"Mostly though, children learn by example. Of course, when they are young their parents are the example they see most. As parents it's important that we act and treat other people in a way that we want our children to emulate. Teaching by example," Stephen emphasized, "is what I try to do for my own son. The importance of example makes annulment even harder to justify. I have to admit, I think less of my father for doing it."

Jenny shares her brother's beliefs about God and the Church. "I believe in God, but I've left the Church. The annulment was the last straw. We were a family. We did everything together. I know that my parents had a valid marriage. The annulment was wrong and it's hypocritical.

"I have tried to stay open to both my parents. I'm sort of the family communicator. We all laugh about that sometimes. I've just had to let go of what my father did," Jenny continued. "He wanted the annulment for his new wife, so he just made the rest up. He may have even convinced himself that he and my mother were never married."

Jenny recalled a conversation between Chris Wallace and her father that was part of the *Prime Time* broadcast. Chris asked him, "In your heart of hearts, do you think you were divorced or that you were never married?"

Her father answered, "The way I look at it today is this: I never was truly married."

To which Chris added in a surprised tone, "Twenty-seven years, five children—"

Her father interrupted, "In my heart of hearts, I never was truly married."

"Well, he may believe that in his 'heart of hearts' he was never married to my mother," Jenny said, "but we all know that's not true."

Several months after I spoke with Jenny, her father wrote to me that while he was sorry for the pain the annulment had caused Barbara, he nevertheless feels the Church is justified in granting annulments on the basis of psychological impotence, particularly in light of its tradition of granting them on the basis of physical impotence. He also clarified what he meant by his statement that in his heart of hearts he and Barbara were never married.

"The question of whether or not a marriage ever existed," he began, "is one that I would personally be willing to let God decide. . . . I obviously felt that there was an impediment to my marriage due to the torment and insecurity brought by my bride from her childhood. I own up to my contribution by my own failure to be the answer to her problems. However, I had nothing to do with the cause of her problems, and it was just those problems which she admits to that I feel had a direct bearing and impediment to a true marital relationship. This was what I had in mind [when] stating that in my heart of hearts, I did not feel a true marriage ever existed."

Bob and his new wife, Helen, were together for four years until she died in the spring of 1995. Barbara freely admits that Helen brought him happiness, and neither she nor her children begrudge him that joy. They just don't think the annulment was justified.

Jenny is also honest and strong enough to admit that family relations might be easier now that her stepmother has passed away. "This spring after she died," Jenny explained, "my father came and spent a week with us. It was the first time my four kids ever spent any time with him. They thought he was great. I think he'll be more a part of our family now that she's gone. I hope things get better between him and my mother now, too. My father is a good guy. I'd like people to know that. The annulment was wrong, but he's still a good guy."

"What are you doing about your children's religious training?" I asked. "Are you bringing them up Catholic?"

"No way," Jenny answered. "I just can't deal with the hypocrisy. It's a problem sometimes. We live in a very Catholic community and my mother-in-law asks about Confirmation for my nine-year-old. But I can't do it. I've told her that she can take him to church if she wants. But I just can't.

"My children will learn right and wrong by example. That's how my mother taught us. Morality is about how you treat people. The way the Church treated my mother was wrong. We have an honest family and my husband and I have a very honest relationship. My children see how that works, so I think they will be okay."

7

AMERICAN SOIL

Even though I was pleased with the *Prime Time* show, I was concerned about how the Boston tribunal would react to its broadcast. Would it hold my participation against me? I had heard nothing from the Church about the annulment since my September 1993 correspondence with Father Lory about my mental health. During the intervening months, I had waited to hear that the tribunal had begun reviewing my medical record, but it was not until February that Father Lory phoned me. To my surprise, however, he was not calling about a medical review, but to arrange a meeting with Father O'Connor, the judge.

When I questioned Father Lory as to the status of the medical inquiry, he told me he didn't know but he'd check with Father O'Connor. His answer made me suspicious. If he were in control of my case, why did he need to check with the judge? And if the judge had made a decision regarding the relevance of medical records, why didn't Father Lory know about it?

At this point, however, I thought it best to keep these concerns to myself, and I only asked if this were to be an informal meeting or my official testimony before the tribunal. Father Lory assured me that this would be an informal meeting and after a few rounds of calls, the date was set for March 1st.

March 1, 1994, was a very different day from the May morning when I had first visited the tribunal the previous spring. Boston had been enduring one of its coldest and snowiest winters in recorded history. Potholes and frozen slush made driving and even walking a challenge; and by March most Bostonians' moods had begun to reflect the weather.

I arrived at the tribunal office a little early and was grateful to find a plowed parking space along the driveway. Once I was inside, the coldness and austerity of the building combined with the weather sent a chill through my body, and I decided to keep my overcoat on while I waited for Father Lory.

Father Lory met me in the waiting area of the building's large foyer. We said our hellos and as if either of us could possibly have been unaware of the weather during the past three months, we started telling each other how cold the winter had been. Soon one of his colleagues walked by and they began conversing in a language I could not understand. I presumed it was Latin.

A short time later, Judge O'Connor approached. I had talked to the judge on the telephone, but this was the first time I had seen him in person. He looked like a judge. He was a tall, rather large man and even without judicial robes, he conveyed a sense of authority. We assured each other that we were glad to meet.

We both knew, however, that we held opposing views on an issue for which there would be no compromise. I also knew that as long as I was in this building, he was in control, another fact which made me nervous. The judge gestured toward his office and suggested that Father Lory and I wait there while he finished some other work. We did as we were told.

Even though I was now ensconced in the judge's office, I still assumed that as Father Lory had told me on the phone, I had been invited for an informal meeting. While we continued to wait for the judge, I began to discuss some of my general concerns about annulment. I explained that I was troubled by what women had told me about the negative effects of their own annulments on their children.

Father Lory answered by repeating the Church's position that annulment does not affect children. He then added that perhaps the mothers should be more careful and suggested that if I examined the cases more closely, I might find that the mother had cried in front of a young child and caused the child to become upset.

I felt a surge of disbelief at his response. With all of the pain associated with annulment, how could a priest think it would be either unusual or harmful for a mother to cry in front of her child? And how could a priest view a mother's expressing that pain as a "fault"? What's more, I felt sure that none of the women who had written or talked to me had cried in front of their children.

As I listened to Father Lory's explanation, Deirdre's story suddenly flashed through my mind. She had learned from her daughter Meagan that her former husband's petition had been granted. It had been Meagan's father, not Deirdre, who had told their child of the Church's decision. Meagan, educated in Catholic schools, was upset by the ruling and called her mother for comfort. Only when Deirdre phoned the tribunal for an explanation on the following day was she told that indeed the annulment had been granted and that a "typing backlog" was probably the reason she had not yet received her notice.

While I could not fathom how a typing backlog could have been Deirdre's fault, I kept that view to myself and simply told Father Lory that I didn't think any of these women had cried in front of their young children. Then I added that it didn't appear to be young children who were the most vulnerable but rather young adults, particularly daughters who had attended Catholic schools.

For these young women, who were by and large raised to accept the traditional Catholic role for women, annulment was very hard to understand. I then stressed that even though I wasn't Catholic, I could not understand how the Church could annul these unions. What was more, had I been raised in the Catholic Church, I, too, would be emotionally lost at the prospect of an annulment.

Further, in what seemed an odd paradox, these women had told me that the Church, which did not recognize divorce, offered support for divorced Catholics; yet it seemed to provide none for "annulled" Catholics and the family even though it recognized annulment. Father Lory assured me that I was mistaken and despite what I had heard, the Church did provide support for those affected by annulment.

He then added that he thought I was right not to involve my children, but cautioned me not to be so concerned with other cases. He then explained that my talking to these other women would confuse me and would not help my own case. I replied that while I appreciated his concern, I simply couldn't ignore what I had been told. These women were in great pain. Furthermore, my children would also grow up just as the children of these women had, and even though they were boys, if the Church did grant their father an annulment, they would need an explanation.

I then asked Father Lory to explain what appeared to be an inconsistency in the Church's presumption of validity. The Church based its annulment inquiry on one essential point: even though all marriages are presumed to be true, the possibility exists that this presumption may be false, and only if that presumption is proven incorrect can a marriage be declared invalid.

While the Church is willing to question the validity of the marriage, it does not question the validity of the petitioner's request. In my case, Joe had already told me privately that he believed we had a true marriage, but since he needed an annulment to remarry in the Church, he was willing to say we didn't. Furthermore, he reflected this same sentiment publicly when he told *Prime Time,* "I cannot remarry and remain a Catholic in good standing without an annulment. I deeply regret any pain this process may have caused my ex-wife."

At this point, Father O'Connor entered his office and answered that indeed the Church presumes the petitioner's request to be valid. Although his presence made me unsure whether I was supposed to be talking to him or to my advocate, I tried to explain that I was aware of the presumption but that what bothered me was that the Church didn't even question it. Rather, the Church questioned the presumed validity of marriage. And that question seemed much greater, because the Church also maintained that marriage was a sacrament. In other words, it seemed as if the Church was minimizing the importance of a sacrament at least relative to the validity of the petitioner's request for an annulment. Neither the judge nor my advocate offered to explain what appeared to me to be a flaw in the Church's inquiry.

Instead, the discussion switched to whether or not annulment undermined families. Still thinking I was having a general conversation with my advocate, I pointed out that although the Church maintains that the annulment doesn't negatively impact families, my experience indicated the opposite. I explained that as they must be aware, I had two thirteen-year-old sons. Before Joe and Beth married, the boys could visit them and everything was okay. The four of them could go to church and share the sacraments together. The trouble only started when Joe and Beth married in a civil ceremony.

Now only the boys could take communion and the only practical way out of this dilemma was to declare that the union that produced them was never a true one. I emphasized *practical* because it was my understanding that if Joe and Beth were to agree to live as "brother and sister," in other words agree not to have sex, they would all be allowed to share the sacraments. However, even though I didn't know Beth well enough to comment, I doubted that Joe would be willing to go along with such an arrangement.

I asked the judge and my advocate what kind of message they thought such a situation sends to two thirteen-year-old boys. It's okay with God to live together as long as you don't marry? Or where God is concerned, sneak and you shall find?

My advocate remained silent as Father O'Connor assumed control of the conversation. The judge answered that the Church certainly did not suggest that it was all right for people to live together without being married, but that the issue of cohabitation would be addressed with Joe "pastorally," not through the annulment process.

He then added almost parenthetically that *Prime Time* only gave one side of the annulment story. I quickly took issue with his view and added that I had only agreed to participate with *Prime Time*'s producers on the condition that the Church also be given a chance to present its views. A now somewhat indignant Father O'Connor answered that the tribunal would never discuss an annulment case publicly.

I answered that the Church didn't have to discuss our case, but it could have provided general information. It seemed, I said, that the Church wanted to have it both ways. It told people such as me that I didn't understand annulment. Yet it refused to provide any information that would explain all the contradictions. I noted that I had asked his office for books and other material to help me understand. But everything they offered was written for those who want an annulment, not those who don't. I said, "Then I found out about Father Kelleher's work and . . ."

Father O'Connor was clearly appalled that I had been reading Father Kelleher's writings. He interrupted me and explained that the Church does not approve of his views. Now, I, too, was angry—at the judge's implying that a fellow priest's work was off-limits, at his contention that *Prime Time* had only told one side of the annulment story, and most of all, at the Church's unwillingness to question the validity of Joe's petition.

Father Kelleher had run the New York City tribunal for more than a decade and he knew as much about annulment as anyone. As for the objectivity of the *Prime Time* broadcast, Chris Wallace had told me the show would relate both sides of annulment in a way that was understandable to a general audience. To me, they had lived up to their part of the bargain.

As far as the validity of Joe's petition was concerned, he had never denied even on television that we had anything but a true marriage. But the tribunal ignored what he said and went ahead with the annulment anyway. I told the judge that I felt sorry for someone whose church made them lie before God about the birth and conception of their children in order to remarry. But what they wanted to do was not good for my children and I could not go along with it.

The room was suddenly completely silent and it became clear that despite what I had been told, I had not been summoned to the tribunal for a general meeting. Clearly, both the judge and my advocate had an agenda and I felt both deceived and trapped. Determined not to lose what little self-control I had left nor to give these men the satisfaction of seeing me break down, I bit the inside of my mouth until I tasted blood. Then I swallowed hard and mumbled, "Whatever it is you want to do, let's get on with it. We're never going to agree."

Father O'Connor handed me a Kleenex and in a more gentle tone suggested that I sit in a chair beside his desk. As I approached the chair, I turned my face away from the desk, and hopefully out of his sight. Then I spat the accumulated blood into the Kleenex and stuffed it into the pocket of the overcoat I was still wearing. Turning back to face the desk, I saw a tape recorder beside Father O'Connor's papers. "Oh," I remarked, somewhat surprised, "you're going to tape this? Do I get a copy?"

Father O'Connor answered that he would give me a transcript. As I sat down, I said that a transcript would be fine. He looked at me, smiled, and added that he would only give me a copy if I promised never to tell anyone what was said in the room.

Again, utter silence prevailed and anger engulfed me. Didn't this man know that this was America? In this country, not even a priest is permitted to force someone to give up his constitutional right of free speech. How dare he use a copy of my own testimony as a bribe to keep me quiet!

But my anger was immediately counterbalanced with gratitude at being an American citizen. I realized that there were, after all, still parts of the world where women in my position were silenced or simply disappeared forever. But in this country, I had the right to speak. I thought of all the people who had given their lives to preserve this right and I felt a deep appreciation for their sacrifice. I might be in a church office, but I was also on American soil and I knew the time would come when I would speak. But for now, I just bit the inside of my mouth harder and answered that if that was the deal then he'd better keep his transcript.

The judge seemed surprised at my response and asked if I meant that I wouldn't promise not to talk. All I could mumble was that I couldn't make such a promise and that since I couldn't, I wouldn't. At least I was honest.

The judge and I glared at each other. I knew that he had the power to do whatever he wanted in his court, but he knew that he could not prevent me from talking about it once I left the Church's protective cocoon. He glanced at my advocate, but as Father Lory was sitting behind me, I was unaware of any responsive gesture, if in fact he made one.

Slowly, however, the judge began to turn the pages of the testimony I had sent to the tribunal in response to the questions in the blue folder. Then he asked me to place my hand on the Bible and to promise that I would tell the truth. I replied affirmatively, thinking it an odd question. It was, after all, my insisting on telling the truth that had caused all the trouble in the first place.

The judge began his questioning by asking if I had been happy as a child, particularly at boarding school. I sensed a suggestion that only an unhappy child from a hopelessly "dysfunctional" family would leave home for school as a teenager. I answered that everyone in my family had gone away to school and we had all done well there and afterward. I had in fact enjoyed my four years in the Virginia countryside and had made many good friends with whom I remained very close.

Most of the judge's questions seemed to search for problems that I might have encountered in my childhood, and he seemed to avoid questions whose answers might strengthen my case. For example, he never asked about the letters from Joe and his family, copies of which I had given to Father Lory. Nor did he mention the silver picture frame, engraved in Joe's handwriting expressing his joy at the birth of our children. To this day, I don't know if the judge read the letters or was even aware of the frame.

His questions then turned to the children. When he implied that I might have been reluctant to be a mother, I lost what little remaining patience I had. I answered more forcefully that in the first twenty months of marriage I had two children and I didn't see how two births in twenty months could be viewed as a bad production rate for either a Kennedy or a Catholic.

The judge seemed to find some humor in my response, although I had not meant to be funny. He smiled at Father Lory, relaxed a bit, and then asked if I wanted to ask anything.

I answered that I needed to know when we were going to discuss my side of the story. The judge answered that the defender of the bond would take care of my concerns. He would present my case.

I then asked when I would meet this defender, and he told me that I wouldn't. "But we're on the same side," I protested in perplexed amazement that I would never meet the defender of my marriage.

The judge told me not to worry and assured me that not only could the man do his job, but also that he had personally checked with him just to make sure. The judge explained that the defender of the bond would bring up points such as the fact that Joe and I had known each other for nine years before we married. Then he added, again almost parenthetically, that he was aware that we did not attend prenuptial classes.

I could see where this lack of prenuptial classes was heading and I quickly countered that we did have counseling before we married. The judge answered that he didn't think our counseling had been adequate. Then he added that we had talked mostly about where, meaning in what church, we were going to be married.

I smiled to myself. Not for what Joe and I had missed, but for what Joe might endure should the annulment be granted. Was I becoming vindictive after all? No, I was just searching for some humor in an otherwise bleak situation. My Catholic friends who had attended the courses Father O'Connor spoke of often joked at the irony of nuns and priests, many of whom lived in church housing, discussing sex and explaining the intricacies of mortgage payments and household finances.

If Father O'Connor had his way, however, there would be Joe, a forty-something father of teenage twins, who under American law had been married to his second wife for well over a year, a member of the Banking Committee of the United States Congress, a man whose family employed a bevy of talented professionals to handle its personal finances, a person not endowed with patience or a willingness to listen, who in order to remarry within his church would have to sit and at least pretend to pay attention as nuns and priests explained sex and mortgage payments.

There was, however, a more serious irony in Father O'Connor's comments. Although he was right when he observed that much of Joe's and my prenuptial counseling centered upon selecting the church in which we wanted to marry, he minimized the importance of those discussions. The decision to marry in a Catholic church, as opposed to the Episcopalian church where my family had attended services for years, was made only after lengthy talks with his priest and our minister and only because Joe cared so greatly that both the church and the service be Catholic.

Ironically, according to current canon law, unless the Catholic Church had granted us special permission to marry in my church, it would not have recognized the marriage and Joe would not need an annulment now to marry Beth in his own. To imply that after all these discussions either of us needed additional prenuptial counseling to grasp the significance of a Catholic wedding was difficult to believe.

My mind, however, did not dwell long on the image of Joe's second round of prenuptial counseling nor our choice of church. I resumed my questioning by asking if I would be allowed to read what the defender of the bond wrote. The judge answered that I would not. Then he added that my advocate would submit an opinion, too, but I would not be allowed to read that either.

The reality of my situation was now apparent. My marriage was to be defended in two papers that I would never see; one of them would be written by a man I would never be allowed to meet and the other by my advocate. Despite the fact that my advocate was supposed to represent me, I would not know what he wrote or even thought.

Nor would I ever know what was said by anyone during the hearing. Should an annulment be granted, I would only know that the grounds were "lack of due discretion," but I would not be told how the term applied to my marriage or even perhaps whose discretion—mine, Joe's, or both—was at issue. Nevertheless, I was still supposed to think of annulment as a "healing process."

Father O'Connor, perhaps sensing my concerns, noted that "their" people could do their job. He added that if they couldn't, the annulment process would have been over long ago and Joe would not have had to be married at his house in a civil ceremony. He then asked if I had anything else to say.

I replied somewhat sheepishly that I did. I explained that I had already asked Father Lory about this, but he wasn't sure why Father O'Connor had neither asked for information from the doctors I authorized the tribunal to talk with nor reviewed my medical history. Father O'Connor answered that the tribunal hadn't followed through with the review because I would not sign its medical release.

Since I thought it was important that Father O'Connor know why I had not given the tribunal permission to speak with the doctor it named on its release form, I told him that Father Lory and I had discussed the matter and come to an understanding. Father Lory had indicated that he accepted my reasons and I had agreed to provide the tribunal access to another highly respected psychiatrist, my hospital records, and my primary-care physician to ensure that the Church would have ample information concerning my mental health and any addictive tendencies I might have.

The judge reassured me that the tribunal was not looking for a diagnosis of my mental health. Nor did anyone think I was an addict. The tribunal just wanted to find out if there might have been an impediment that prevented me from having a true marriage. He then asked me to consider seeing one of their people.

When I asked somewhat skeptically who the tribunal's people were, he explained that they were all professionals. They worked in the counseling fields and they knew how to do their job. He added that the tribunal didn't use psychiatrists because they were too expensive. But he told me not to worry about cost anyway. The tribunal would pay for the evaluation.

I wanted to make sure that I understood what the judge was saying, so I summarized what I thought I had heard: I was supposed to meet a professional hired by the tribunal and talk to him for an hour or so. Then, based on what that person said about our conversation, a talk which would take place in 1994, the tribunal would determine to a "moral certainty" whether I had been capable of being married in 1979. The judge said that I had understood correctly.

I stressed that the doctor I had previously authorized the tribunal to speak with was probably better qualified than anyone to give the type of opinion they sought. And I had certainly spent far more than an hour talking with him. The judge concurred. We agreed that the tribunal would contact the doctor for whom I had signed the release, and in the meantime I would think about going to see one of its people.

Nevertheless, I remained confused about why I should see one of the tribunal's professionals and I voiced my concern to the judge. After all, the tribunal maintained that the burden of proving that the marriage was invalid rested on Joe, but it also wanted me to subject myself to some form of questioning that could only strengthen his case. Clearly, the tribunal did not have the proof it wanted or else it wouldn't be asking me to meet with one of its people. *I* didn't want this annulment. Even though I didn't think I had anything to hide, why should I do anything that might help the tribunal grant it?

For the first time since the tape recorder had begun running, my advocate spoke. He answered that even though what I said was in a narrow sense true, we were all in search of the truth. Indeed, I thought to myself, and you're supposed to be on my side.

Yet I knew I had to be careful. Even though I wanted to make sure I did not commit myself to what I considered a bogus practice, neither did I want to irritate the judge any more than I already had. I answered that I would indeed think about seeing one of their people. Then I asked about the schedule and explained that since I was planning on taking the children to Colorado in about two weeks for their spring vacation, I didn't want the tribunal to think I was not cooperating should they call and not be able to reach me at home.

Father O'Connor assured me that the trip shouldn't be a problem and explained that Joe needed to give his testimony and have the opportunity to read mine. In the cause of convenience, both of those things would probably happen in one day. I'd have a chance to review Joe's testimony if I wanted. Then, when the tribunal had everything, we'd both be asked if we wanted to add anything. After that, they'd hear the case and make a decision. The whole process would take about a year, he said.

The judge's summary of what remained of the process made me wary. I did not know, for example, whether there would be one judge or three. Or, if there were to be three, if I would ever meet the other two. More alarming, it seemed that not only would Father O'Connor alone control what the other two judges heard, but also that I would not be allowed to question what he told them. If, for example, he told them that the reason the tribunal did not have access to my medical records was because I would not sign the release, the other two judges might infer that I had something to hide or was being uncooperative. They would never know, unless Father O'Connor wanted them to, that I had very solid reasons for declining to sign the release, that I had written a long letter to my advocate explaining those reasons, and that Father Lory had accepted them.

In fact, as our discussion had just shown, Father O'Connor himself was either unaware of or chose to ignore my reasons for not signing the first release and the alternatives I had suggested that would still enable the tribunal to review my medical history. Furthermore, I, not my advocate whose job it was to represent me, pointed out that Father O'Connor was misinterpreting the significance of the unsigned release. In short, the way in which I had just seen the judge and my advocate interact gave me very little hope that my concerns would ever be expressed to those who were to rule on my case.

It was clear, however, that Father O'Connor considered the meet-

ing we were about to conclude as my official hearing, not a prelimi-
nary discussion as it had been described to me. I felt duped and I had
to fight an urge to simply walk out of what had become their courtroom. So I sat frozen to my seat, realizing that if I left, I would not
know how to complete the tribunal's inquiry.

I summarized my understanding of the next steps: I'd think about
seeing one of "their people" and they'd send the medical release I had
signed to the appropriate doctor. They had decided that they did not
need to review my hospital records nor talk with my primary physician, and that they'd contact me after the boys and I returned from
Colorado. The judge answered that my detailing of the process was
correct and we both stood up, shook hands, and politely said our
good-byes.

As I left the building, Father Lory hastily followed. Catching up to
me and waving a pair of fine leather gloves, he called, "Mrs. Kennedy,
Mrs. Kennedy, are these yours? They were found in the waiting area."

"No," I replied, "but thank you for checking." I couldn't help but
like Father Lory and even now, as angry as I was, I felt sorry for him.
It must be awful having me as his client. I wondered if he had
become a priest thinking he would be able to help people. I thought
of some of the gifted priests I had met in my community housing
work and how their dedication and ability had clearly made a positive
difference for so many people.

I hoped for Father Lory's sake that at other times he, too, was able
to do such work; but as far as my annulment case was concerned, he
wasn't helping. In fact, he was as much of a pawn on the annulment
chessboard as I was. What a waste of a kind human being, I thought,
as I stepped over the ice and climbed into my car.

I felt as if I were a time bomb about to explode as I pulled out of
the tribunal's driveway onto Lake Street. At the first intersection, I
narrowly avoided hitting an elderly women whose age and condition
combined with the ice made her crossing take considerably longer
than the time the light allowed. Feeling guilty about both my driving
and my self-absorption, I pulled over and I asked her if I could help.
The gratitude with which she welcomed my steadier hand to cross
the street served as my own reality check. By the time I reached
home, I knew I had to put my own anger at the tribunal in perspec-

tive. I had two hours in which to pull myself together before I picked up the children.

No problem, I thought. With all the snow and ice, I hadn't run in weeks. Even a short job would restore sanity. As soon as I touched my jogging shoes, our dog sensed that he, too, was about to be cured of his cabin fever and he began to bark and dance with gleeful expectation. The run, however, was not to be. Before I made it to the first corner, with my dog barking at me to hurry up, I had slipped three times. This is really stupid, I thought. End up in a cast and there goes the trip to Colorado. You'll be impossible, not to mention the boys.

This time I couldn't run from what was bothering me. I'd have to find another way to cope with my anger. It was hard to tell if I or our dog was more depressed as we returned to the house. I paced around the kitchen for a few minutes and then caught sight of the word processor. I sat down and stared at the Macintosh's smiling face looking back at me from the screen. Oh, I thought, at times like this I wouldn't mind being a computer, you'd just keep smiling, and for a moment I laughed at the absurdity of my situation.

Then I took a deep breath and asked myself what bothered me most about the annulment process. Months later, I would learn that the reasons for my anger had many dimensions. For now, though, my outrage was directed at the men who ran the tribunal. They presumably had no children of their own and obviously had never given birth to a child. They seemed completely oblivious to the importance many women, including myself, attach to being mothers. Yet they made moral judgments about the quality of a union that had produced and most often nurtured children. Slowly, my fingers began to touch the keyboard and I began to type.

To the men of the tribunal:
I dare you.
I dare you to give birth to a child.
I dare you to go through the months of waiting, wondering if everything will be all right.
I dare you to be at the delivery when the cries promise life.
I dare you to give up the safety of your job—health insurance, a pension, people to look after you.

I dare you to devote your day to others—not their spiritual
needs but their laundry, meals, and health care, not as
your job but in addition to your job.
I dare you to adjust to the life of a mother.
I dare you to be there when things go wrong.
Oh, you say, we're good in death.
Yes, I agree, but it's life I'm worried about.
Most of all, I dare you to look into my child's eyes.
I dare you to enjoy his smile and his humor.
Then I dare you to look me in the eye and swear on that
Bible of yours that my child was not the issue of a
sanctified union.
If you can do all that, then I guess you have the right God.
He will forgive you because perhaps you know not what you
do.
But don't ask the same from the rest of us.
For we do not pretend either to be God or to speak for Him.
We are just mothers, and when our children are attacked, it
is hard to forgive as God does.

There, that about summed it up. I felt better and in control of
myself again. I picked the children up at school and we went grocery
shopping. At dinner we talked about our spring trip and two weeks
later, the three of us left Boston for a much-needed vacation.

Colorado quickly worked its magic. Even as my college roommate
met us at the airport, the fresh air, clean snow, and brilliant sun and
sky began to erase the tension we all had been feeling. The tribunal
seemed far away, almost insignificant, and after ten days of exercise,
good friends, and time with my children I felt whole again. By the
time we returned to Boston, I was rested and prepared to follow
through with the Church's investigation.

While there was no correspondence from the tribunal in the large
pile of mail that had accumulated while we were away, there was an
envelope from the doctor for whom I had signed the release. It con-
tained three letters: The first was the medical release dated October
12, 1993, that the tribunal had sent to me almost six months earlier.
At that time, after explaining in writing that I had never had a profes-

sional relationship with the doctor to whom the release referred, I had signed the form and mailed it back to the tribunal, who in turn had received it on October 21, 1993. The second letter was a copy of the tribunal's letter to the doctor requesting information about me, dated March 1, 1994—the same day I met with Fathers O'Connor and Lory; and the third, the doctor's response to the tribunal's questions, dated March 21, 1994.

If the previous inquiries from the tribunal requesting information about my mental health seemed out of line, they paled in comparison to the March 1st letter. While beginning by correctly informing the doctor that Joe was requesting an annulment, the letter went on to say incorrectly that Joe had indicated that I had been in treatment with him. The Church apparently chose to ignore its own release which it had sent in the same envelope, the release on which I had noted specifically that I had never had a professional relationship with the doctor in question.

The Church also ignored all of my correspondence to Father Lory on this point, as well as what I had said to both Fathers Lory and O'Connor during our March 1st meeting. Furthermore, in defense of Joe, he never knew that I had even consulted with this doctor. To claim as the Church did that Joe had said I was in treatment with him was not only untrue but could only serve to increase the escalating hostility between us.

After misinforming the doctor, the letter went on to explain that the information would only be used in a "helpful manner," but avoided saying for whom it would be helpful. It referred to a list of questions to "guide the doctor in his response," but explained that it would be preferable if he would just send the records—records which I had explained several times never existed. The Church was interested, the letter stated, in our "probable maturity" and "psychological condition" at the time of the wedding. If the doctor did not know us at the time of the wedding, he was asked to draw "inferences."

What was most distressing about the letter was that even after Father O'Connor had assured me that they were not looking for a diagnosis, they asked for precisely that. "We are also interested in any long-term disorders. . . . An example would be 'a manic-depressive.'"

One of the questions was "What was your diagnosis of her?" Others were "What was your prognosis for her at the end of the treatment?" "Are you able to offer an hypothesis as to the origins of any psychological or emotional difficulties you observed in her? Please elaborate." "How early in life do you feel she manifested any symptoms of emotional or psychological difficulties?" "Would you offer an opinion as to her maturity level and state of mind when she contracted marriage with Joseph P. Kennedy on February 3, 1979?"

Reading this, I couldn't help but wonder what they asked if they were interested in a diagnosis. The letter concluded by explaining that while the Church realized this was an "unusual" request, it was being made as "one professional to another" and would only be used to the ultimate benefit of the doctor's client. It was signed by someone with the title of secretary to the tribunal and the signature was followed by two sets of initials. Later when I asked the doctor to whom the letter was written the significance of the initials, he explained that he often adds M.D.—medical doctor—when he signs professional correspondence. But, he added, in his fourteen years of practice he had never seen the initials the Church used to indicate that its "unusual" request was meant for "one professional to another." In short, he doubted the initials had any medical meaning.

Perhaps the kindest adjective to describe the tribunal's March 1st letter is sloppy. Not only did it relay false information, it contradicted in writing what Father O'Connor had told me during our meeting, namely that the Church was not looking for a diagnosis. In truth, had my children turned in such a sloppy piece of homework even in the fourth grade neither their teachers nor I would have accepted it. They would have been required to do it over and television would have been banned.

This letter, however, had not been written by fourth graders but by an institution full of learned men and women, experts in canon law who claim to be part of a process by which they can determine with "moral certainty" whether or not a marriage was valid. How can such a sloppy process determine anything to any degree of certainty, much less the sanctity of a marriage to a moral degree?

Fortunately for me, the third letter in the envelope, a copy of the doctor's response to the tribunal's letter, soothed any fears I might have had that men with straitjackets would shortly be at my door. On the contrary, the doctor referred to me as "thoughtful and mature," adjectives which certainly helped raise my by-now critically low level of self-esteem if not assuage the Church's concerns about my mental health. The doctor also informed the Church that he had never seen any indication that I had a "mental disorder or addiction" and had every reason to believe that I was a sensible and mature adult in 1979 when I married. He concluded his letter by summarizing his qualifications, which included affiliations with some of the country's most respected institutions as well as fourteen years of professional practice.

While I was grateful for the vote of confidence from the doctor, his letter could do little to restore my faith in the tribunal's integrity. From that time on, it was clear to me that the annulment process was bogus, and my heart went out to other women who perhaps did not know as honest or as accomplished a doctor as I did. And I could only imagine the power of such a process had I been raised a Catholic.

It was, in fact, a Catholic friend who laid it all out for me. As I handed her the March 1st letter she pulled back and then laughed. "You know," she said, "I know this sounds ridiculous, but for a moment I expected to see your fingers burn for touching it and I half expected mine to go up in flames as well. You don't understand the power the Church has over us, particularly women. They start when we're much too young to think for ourselves and the process continues. It gives the Church an enormous power."

"I know I don't really understand," I responded, "but I'm beginning to. From what the women who have written to me have said, the Church made them believe that their whole lives were in being wives and mothers. Then when they're too old to bear any more children and their marriages fall apart, the Church tells them they were never really married in the first place. The man they thought was their husband often remarries a younger woman who is more likely to have children, and the Church blesses the second union.

"In a religious sense, it's sort of like sending the brood mare to the glue factory when she can't have any more foals. Actually, in some ways it's worse. No one ever said the brood mare didn't exist, but that's what the Church is saying about the marriage when marriage was these women's lives. So even though these women are physically still alive and even still part of the Church, they have been stripped of their identities. Emotionally, they're dead."

"That's about it," my friend said. "Well, what are you going to do about it?"

"What *can* I do about it? The Church is going to do whatever it wants to anyway," I answered.

"You can write it all down. What you do with what you write isn't important right now. Just write," she replied.

And so I began.

8

A Certain Sadness

⊰━━━⊱

Once I decided to write about my annulment experiences, I felt it was crucial to learn more about those of some of the other women who had contacted me and if they were willing to record their stories as well. I was particularly interested in meeting Darlene, who had been married thirty-two years and was the mother of six children when the Church annulled her marriage. I telephoned her, and she invited me to her home in western Pennsylvania.

Darlene, an attractive, dark-haired woman in her late forties or early fifties, met me at the airport and we drove to her house about twenty minutes away. There is a small-town, homespun quality about many of the communities in western Pennsylvania, a part of the state that is very different from the Philadelphia area where I grew up. There is an abundance of rolling farmland. People seem friendlier than in a large city. They smile and take time to talk to you. Darlene's house is about ten years old, in immaculate condition, and nestled in a well-kept neighborhood. She lives with Jeff, a fit, pleasant man of medium build with brown hair and a welcoming smile. Jeff is meticulous about lawn care and it shows.

He gave me a warm hello and graciously showed me to my room. On the way, I noticed a playroom for the grandchildren. Darlene made some tea as I made myself comfortable in her tidy kitchen over-looking the backyard. When we began to talk, Jeff opted to watch television downstairs in the family room.

"This Christmas it will be four years," Darlene began. "As I look back it seems like a lifetime of trying to put my life together. You can't share your life with someone for thirty-two years and pretend it didn't mean anything. It makes it even more difficult to deal with when the Church says our marriage never existed. We had been through so many hard times together. My favorite song was 'Through the Years.' It was like I could see the light at the end of the tunnel. The six chil-dren would be grown and we could make up for the years we had lost being married so young."

Life was never easy for Darlene, yet she beat the odds and became not only a devoted wife and mother but also a talented and sensitive counselor in criminal justice. The eldest of three children, Darlene spent her early childhood in a rural town in Ohio not far from the West Virginia border. Her father suffered from a severe drinking problem and seldom worked. Yet he could also be kind. Darlene fondly remembers his buying her a horse and having a small diamond she had found on the side of the road made into a ring that she still wears today.

Nevertheless, his drinking took an enormous toll on the family. After Darlene finished eighth grade her parents divorced, and along with her mother and younger brother and sister she moved to a larger community in the eastern part of the state. Darlene found it difficult to adjust to her new home. Her mother worked as a presser in a Laundromat while she, a shy thirteen-year-old, attended the local high school.

In the late 1950s when Darlene was fifteen, her life changed dra-matically. Similar to millions of American teenagers, she met the love of her life after a football game. His name was Tom and as Darlene remembers he was tall, good-looking, and perhaps most important for her, was going to college. "I was on the top of the world when I met Tom," she remembered. "I was with some friends and he came over to where we were sitting. One of us remarked that two people we all knew had just become engaged and Tom turned to me and said something like, Well, we'll just have to get engaged, too."

Even at this first meeting, there were signs that Catholicism would be the dominant influence in their relationship. "After we met, I remember going for pizza. It was Friday," Darlene added with a smile, "and so because of the pepperoni topping, we had to wait until after midnight to eat it."

I must have looked confused because Darlene laughed and explained that "it was the 1950s. In those days Catholics did not eat meat on Fridays, and Tom has always been a very strong Catholic."

Darlene was not raised as a Catholic, but as a Protestant. Her family belonged to the First Christian Church, but attending church was not something they did together. In fact, Darlene remembered that as a young girl she used to walk alone to Sunday school. While Sunday school helped Darlene develop a strong sense of God, organized religion and specifically Catholicism became central to her life after she became involved with Tom; and both swept her off her feet simultaneously.

"I began going to Mass with him," she remembered, "and the service was so beautiful. At that time, Mass was in Latin. There was a kind of mystery about it, partly I guess because I couldn't understand what was being said. For me, it was really a religious experience. I thought I could feel the presence of God in the church. After the service, I usually had Sunday dinner at Tom's house and both his parents were always very nice to me. I felt secure and comfortable. Tom would be busy working on his car and I would just sit and watch him for hours."

Although Darlene and Tom began dating right after their first meeting, there were periods when Tom was at college in Georgia that they didn't see each other. In fact, in the early months of their relationship, Tom dated another woman while he was away. Invariably, however, when he came home, he and Darlene would resume seeing each other and soon their relationship deepened.

Darlene was in awe of Tom, who in addition to his physical attributes was dedicated, determined, and disciplined particularly about his religion, work, and education, qualities which enabled him to participate in a special college plan offered by his employer. Under the plan, Tom earned money by alternately working for three months in a roller bearing plant and then pursuing a degree in mechanical engineering for another three months as a full-time student.

For all of his dedication to discipline and Catholicism, Tom was also eighteen and he found Darlene, who was undeniably in love with him, irresistible. It was not long before the young couple found themselves in a not uncommon predicament in the 1950s. Darlene was pregnant and while abortion was not only illegal but also morally unacceptable to both of them, giving the baby up for adoption was an option. "Tom wanted to get married," Darlene explained. "I didn't know what to do. I would never have tried to force him into marriage. Marrying was his choice.

"Once we decided to get married," Darlene continued, "I knew I wanted to become Catholic as soon as I could; so I began taking the required instruction with our priest. I learned the prayers, the Hail Marys, and anything else the priest wanted me to learn, whatever it took. But we decided to get married before I finished my instruction."

Darlene and Tom married in a priest's rectory rather than the church itself because in those days Catholics were not generally permitted to marry someone of another faith in a regular church service. Darlene's mother as well as Tom's parents attended. After a brief ceremony, all returned to the groom's parents' house for wedding cake and then the newlyweds set off for their honeymoon to Niagara Falls.

In some respects, the honeymoon itself foreshadowed much of what was to become typical of the early years of the marriage. The car broke down and they never even saw the falls, but Darlene remembered the experience fondly and views what could have been a disappointing experience as a positive one. "I will never forget the people who owned the garage where we took our car. They were an older couple who acted like two lovebirds. We didn't have much money so they cooked for us and gave us a room right in their house. Unfortunately, by the time the car was fixed we had to head back home so Tom could go back to college, but because of their kindness we had a wonderful honeymoon."

Undeniably, the first years of marriage presented extraordinary challenges for both Darlene and Tom. Tom continued to attend college on the co-op plan, and when he returned after the first three-month semester, they moved in with his parents who had generously fixed up their attic for the growing family. Even with his parents' help, Tom worked three jobs just to make ends meet. By day he was a draftsman. In the evenings he sold cutlery and on the weekends he worked in a nursery that sold trees and shrubs. Such a schedule left little time for a home life.

Darlene, meanwhile, continued her instruction to become Catholic, attended to her younger siblings who lived nearby, and prepared for the birth of their first child. Soon a healthy daughter joined the family. Both families were joyful at the news and very supportive. Almost immediately, Tom planned the baptism, an event made all the more special since Darlene's instruction was now complete. Although today it would be unlikely for the Church to baptize someone who was presumed to have been previously baptized in a Protestant church, that was not the case in the 1950s. Thus, Darlene and her daughter were baptized simultaneously and Darlene confirmed immediately thereafter.

Darlene's acceptance into the Church could not have come at a better time, for during the next few years, she was to need all the emotional and spiritual support she could find. In fact, had the marriage ended at this time, there might well have been reasonable grounds for annulment.

The couple were young. Darlene was only sixteen and Tom eighteen, ages which although within the guidelines of canon law of at least fourteen for women and sixteen for men, certainly raise the possibility that either one or both of them might not have been sufficiently mature to marry. Additionally, they had known each other scarcely a year and were separated during much of that time.

More important, Darlene was pregnant and even though she might not have pressured Tom into marriage, it is difficult to believe that the pending birth of a child was not a factor in his decision. But the marriage did not end at this time. Rather, with the teachings of the Catholic Church as its guide, the marriage was to endure and blossom for the next thirty years.

Because of her Catholic beliefs, Darlene did not use birth control, and in 1959 she gave birth to their second child. With the birth of another baby the family outgrew the attic. Tom bought a trailer and for a short time they lived in a mobile park. Then, when Tom returned to college in Georgia, the family went with him, pulling their home behind them.

Darlene admits that she found it difficult caring for two babies

with the constant moving. Yet it was precisely in these times that
Catholicism seemed to grow in its significance for both Tom and Darlene, and it may well have been this focus that got the family through
the crises.

Soon there was a third child. The trailer was bursting at its sides
and some changes had to be made. Darlene and Tom not only faced
the challenge together, but also asked and received help from both
God and their families: Tom agreed to apply for a loan so that he
could complete his education more quickly. Darlene returned to
Ohio, lived with her mother, and worked in the kitchen at the local
hospital to help cover living expenses. Tom's mother took care of the
children.

After Tom graduated from college, he bought a car and headed for
California. The separation brought more difficulties for Darlene, but
she and Tom worked out their differences over the phone and soon
she and the three children joined him. Shortly thereafter, a fourth
daughter arrived. Darlene enjoyed California. In addition to regular
Sunday Mass, Tom became involved in other religious activities, one
of which was the cursillo movement. A cursillo is a three-day spiritual
retreat for lay men and women. During the retreat there are discussions on the importance of home, work, and community. The emphasis is on sharing, and participants experience the joy of being part of
what is considered to be a model Christian community. In contrast to
the monastic type of retreat that stresses solemn isolation, the cursillo emphasizes the importance of the group and is full of laughter
and music, particularly at mealtime.

The movement began on the island of Majorca during the Second
World War and later became an accepted part of the Spanish
Catholic Church. In 1957, the first cursillo in the United States was
held in Texas and in 1961, the first English-speaking cursillo took
place. Tom, in fact, was one of the earliest participants in an English-
speaking cursillo.

Since the 1960s, the movement has expanded throughout the
United States, to virtually every corner of the world, and particularly
to Central and South America. Unlike some other lay movements,
the cursillos have been able to adapt to changes within the mainstream Catholic Church and in fact seem to have anticipated if not
heralded many of those that have occurred since Vatican II.

Although Darlene was never as involved with cursillo as Tom, she attended prayer meetings and was supportive of Tom's participation. In fact, she thought the cursillos were making Tom a "nicer person" and she welcomed the greater sense of religious awareness in the house. Each night after supper, the family read the Bible.

Life in California was not, however, without its difficulties. The extended family had remained in Ohio, and the California job market was not as stable as Tom had hoped. When the opportunity arose to move back East, Tom accepted a job in Connecticut, which became home for a year. A fifth daughter was born and then partly in order to be closer to their families, Tom accepted a new job in Cincinnati, Ohio.

After five years of constant moving, life in Cincinnati brought a certain stability. It also brought what was perhaps the family's greatest challenge. "We were all driving home from South Carolina with Tom's brother," Darlene told me. "The five children were in the back of the station wagon and a car hit us head on. Tom hit the dashboard so hard his head left an imprint. I broke my jaw in three places and was given the last rites at the accident. At first we were all taken to the nearest hospital. Tom and the five children were all in one room. For a couple of days Tom didn't know if I was alive, and when he finally got up the nerve to ask, he was told I had been moved to Knoxville because of my jaw."

As usual, the family pulled together. Tom's father came down and stayed with Darlene while the rest of the family returned to Cincinnati when they were able. Once they were home, Tom's mother helped out with caring for both the children and Darlene, who could only drink through a straw. Slowly through several months, all recovered.

While life in Cincinnati undoubtedly brought the family closer together, the career opportunities were limited. When a major company offered Tom a more secure and challenging job in western Pennsylvania, the family moved again. Shortly after their arrival their sixth child, a son, was born. Western Pennsylvania remained home for the next twenty-two years of the marriage, and here, the family finally established roots.

I asked Darlene to describe how she held her family together during the ten-year odyssey that finally brought them to western Pennsylvania. While Tom may have been the helmsman, she had clearly been the one who kept the boat afloat. "I didn't think much about it," she began thoughtfully. "I was busy with cleaning, laundry, taking care of babies, and learning to cook. I had a Betty Crocker cookbook and Tom used to check off the recipes after I completed making one. I simply got through the day because that's what I needed to do. It was my life's work. I was raising a family and if that's what it took, I'd do it. I loved my children and I loved Tom. I just got everything done because that's what I was there to do."

As I listened to Darlene, I was impressed not only with her strength but also with how closely her beliefs and how she lived from day to day illustrate the writings of the well-respected priest and author Father John McKenzie. In his book *The Roman Catholic Church,* Father McKenzie explains that Catholics view faith as an "act of the mind" in which they accept something as true. He also notes that there is an element of mystery in Catholicism. Regardless of new discoveries in human knowledge, faith will always be a revelation of God and beyond man's understanding. As such, it will remain forever mysterious.

Father McKenzie explains that unlike Protestantism, which teaches that salvation is based largely on knowledge, Catholic salvation is based more on faith and works. A Catholic, he writes, attains salvation by "what he believes and by what he does." For Catholics, "faith is a total commitment to the truths which the Church teaches."

Darlene believed in Catholicism and lived by its rules. While a family counselor of another religion might have suggested that Darlene and Tom postpone having more children until Tom had completed college and family life was more stable, Catholic teachings said birth control was wrong; and so for them, using it was unthinkable. Rather, Darlene accepted each child as a gift from God to a marriage which He had blessed as a sacramental union. Catholicism told her that the sacrament brought an enormous, supernatural strength to marriage. Because Darlene trusted in the sacrament, she knew she could rely on the strength of God's love and grace; and so from somewhere deep within herself, she was always able to summon the resources necessary to nurture her growing brood.

Even now, as we sat in her kitchen more than thirty-five years after the birth of her first child, Darlene wasn't asking for praise for her accomplishments. As a matter of fact, while I was clearly in awe of what she had achieved, she seemed unaware of its magnitude. To her, she simply did "whatever it took." For Darlene, the way she lived and what she gave were merely acts of faith.

Once the family settled in western Pennsylvania, life became far more stable. Not surprisingly, the seed from which the family roots grew was the Catholic Church. "Our sixth child, a boy, was conceived that first night after we moved to western Pennsylvania," Darlene remembers. "Soon Tom resumed his work with the cursillo movement and also became a charismatic."

The charismatics, members of a movement which began in the 1960s, generally consider themselves Pentecostals. Unlike many Pentecostals, however, charismatics choose to retain membership in their institutional or mainline church, which for Tom was of course Catholic. Similar to most Pentecostals, charismatics define themselves through experiences as much as written doctrine and share many of the same beliefs. Both believe in baptism in the Holy Spirit, and participate in ecstatic worship and most in "speaking in tongues."

While Darlene was never completely comfortable with some of the charismatic practices—"I never felt right being so close to the altar" she explained—she was always supportive of Tom's interests and occasionally attended their meetings. She and Tom also found enjoyment and meaning in Marriage Encounter, a Church-sponsored retreat for married couples. Essentially one weekend a month, about thirty couples went on a retreat to discuss and work on their marriages.

"Sometimes," explained Darlene, "the discussions were general, such as talking about the joy of love letters in the sand. Other times participants led discussion groups or gave short talks. They were beautiful weekends and Tom and I always felt closer after we had gone to one." Tom and Darlene participated in Marriage Encounter for about five years, by which time both had become retreat leaders. In addition, Tom became a lay priest and Darlene taught classes to prepare parishioners for Confirmation.

With Catholicism as their guiding force, their lives blossomed in other ways as well. Tom was by now a successful engineer whose skills were not only in demand locally but also abroad. Darlene had long since mastered Betty Crocker and had become famous for her baking, and her holiday pies were the envy of the neighborhood.

But Darlene had mastered far more than baking. Her children were growing up and leaving the nest; yet they almost invariably returned for the holidays and not just for pie. Holidays had meaning at Darlene and Tom's house, and there was a closeness about the family that brought the children home. In the truest sense of the phrase, Darlene had become a "successful homemaker."

Indeed, it had been a long, hard road since Tom's car had broken down on the way to Niagara Falls for their honeymoon. Tom must have both understood and appreciated how much Darlene had given during those years, for it was his suggestion that they renew their wedding vows in honor of their twenty-fifth anniversary. As Darlene looked longingly into space, she told me softly, "We were finally going to have the wedding we had never been able to have."

"Wait a minute," I interrupted, slowly grasping the significance of what she has just told me. "Tom wanted to do what?"

"He wanted to renew our vows for our twenty-fifth anniversary, and so did I."

"And the Church went along with this?" I asked.

"Oh, yes." Darlene elaborated: "We had the service in the actual church this time. Remember, we weren't able to the first time because I wasn't Catholic yet. For our anniversary, a priest was there along with about two hundred and fifty of our friends. Some of our children read from the Bible. Then we had a big reception and afterward we went on a cruise for a second honeymoon."

"That wasn't really what I meant," I tried to explain. "I can see why the Church encourages people to renew their vows. What I don't understand is that given how you renewed your vows after twenty-five years, how can the Church then grant an annulment? Certainly you knew each other after all those years. Good heavens, you had six kids. Obviously you both understood what a Catholic marriage entailed. Tom was a lay priest and you taught Confirmation classes. By now, by anybody's rules, you were plenty old enough to marry. There was no reason to renew your vows unless both of you simply wanted to.

"Boy," I added, remembering what Father Curran had told *Prime Time*, "'There isn't a marriage in America we can't annul.' I guess that was certainly true in this case. But it still doesn't make it right."

"It also makes the annulment very hard to accept," added Darlene, her eyes welling with tears.

Darlene and I had been talking for several hours, and reliving her twenty-fifth anniversary had understandably been difficult for her. It seemed a good time to take a break, so I suggested we go for a walk around her neighborhood and she agreed.

It was early May and a beautiful weekend afternoon. Many of her neighbors were in their yards working on their well-kept lawns. The cul-de-sacs were alive with young children on their bikes. Indeed, Norman Rockwell's America seemed alive and well here. Community pride and family values were as evident as the spring daffodils.

Darlene was quiet for several minutes as we walked. Then she began thoughtfully, "You know, there was a time when I thought I'd write a book just about all we'd been through. People talk so much about family these days, but sometimes I think it's just talk. I tried so hard and we raised six children without relying on the government. Up until now, I believed that if you tried hard enough, you could make it work."

"But Darlene," I interrupted, "you *did* make it work. You not only raised six children, but you've gone on with your life. I still don't really understand how you made the transition from full-time home-maker to, for lack of a better phrase, 'career woman,' but you did it."

Darlene works with the district attorney's office and helps both witnesses and victims of violent crime such as robbery, assault, or rape. Sometimes her job merely requires that she explain how the court system works so that the individual is comfortable being a part of it. At other times, Darlene accompanies the witness or victim to court and provides the emotional support they need both to testify and to return to their daily lives afterward.

"Your work," I continued, "is very important to a lot of people. It helps them at a time they really need help. It really is remarkable. And you did it without ever really graduating from a regular high school."

"I earned a certificate that is equivalent to a high school diploma," Darlene explained in a matter-of-fact tone. "Then I began working at the center as a volunteer. After about a year or so, I had learned enough to become a paid employee. I have a wonderful boss. She has always been so supportive, particularly when everything fell apart.

She really got me through. But somehow, even with my job and Jeff, life doesn't have the meaning it had before it all fell apart and the annulment happened.

"It was all quite sudden," Darlene continued. "The girls were grown and had left home. Our son joined the army at eighteen. We didn't know it at the time, but he had also gotten married. Tom felt we should see a counselor because to him, things just weren't working out. We only went a few times when Tom announced that he wanted to leave. It seemed like my whole world had fallen apart. Our son left in November for the service and by Christmas, Tom was planning on leaving. I asked him to stay until after the holidays. Our thirty-second anniversary was December twenty-seventh. After we went out for dinner, Tom picked up his clothes and left."

Darlene was very open about her life falling apart after Tom's departure. "The weeks ahead were so confusing. . . . He moved into a house run by a priest for alcohol recovery. Tom did not have a drinking problem himself but he was to be in charge of the house and help with the prayer meetings. I remember sitting in front of the house at night just waiting for him to come out so we could talk, but I would end up crying and leaving. I heard Tom was dating so I filed for divorce.

"By then I had lost thirty pounds and I was angry, lonely, and hurt. A counselor told me that Tom said he didn't love me and that the counselor should 'fix me.' Tom wrote a letter to all the children about starting a 'new day' and how much happier I would be now. My world was falling apart and I couldn't do anything. Desperately, I tried to convince Tom to let a counselor help us. I wrote letters and tried talking about it, but finally, after many tears, I gave up. Tom didn't fight the divorce, so we divided everything and went our way. The only real thing I had was the memories of thirty-two years."

Several months after the divorce, Darlene began the painful process of putting her life back together. "After being home for thirty-two years and raising six children, I needed to move on. My children were all adults with their own families and for the first time I had a full-time job. Despite having an understanding boss, I knew how important it was to keep it together at work."

It was at work a short time later that she met Jeff. Jeff's wife had been killed by a drunk driver and he had come to the center where Darlene worked to participate in their victims' support program. Soon he and Darlene found that by confiding in each other, they could ease the pain of each other's loss. "We started dating," Darlene recalled, "but at the same time I was thinking Tom would want me back. Your heart can play so many tricks on you when you are hurting."

Darlene's openness about her feelings for Tom even after their civil divorce and despite the fact that both were dating others was significant. The Church is not supposed to consider annulling a marriage unless there is no possibility of reconciling the estranged couple. Civil divorce does not necessarily preclude reconciliation. Indeed, Darlene was working with a church counselor to examine this option as she continued moving ahead with her life.

The annulment letter, in fact, caught both the church counselor and Darlene by complete surprise. As she recalled, "I was living in a small basement apartment with a bedroom, bath, living room, and kitchen combined. I just stood there and screamed and cried. I was so upset because I knew if he was granted the annulment that would be the end of it all. I still couldn't accept the divorce, let alone the annulment. He wanted to end it all, and I wouldn't let him do this to the kids or me.

"As I set out to fight it," Darlene continued, "friends close to the Church said that he would be granted the annulment since he was so well known in the Church. I felt I had already lost because each time I met with the priest or advocate they tried to be gentle, but it seemed like no one was listening to me. Tom was preparing to get married in the Church as soon as the annulment was approved and I was hurt and numbed by it all. Even though I was dating Jeff at the time, he knew where my heart was. There were many times when I was crying on his shoulder.

"I was still going to a church counselor to try to make sense of everything. I was so up and down all the time that the counselor wanted me to get medicine because she was afraid of what I might do. I would love Tom and hate him at the same time. However, I refused the medicine because I wanted to be in control of my life and where I was going."

In addition to her counselor, the Church appointed an advocate to represent Darlene in the annulment process. Her advocate, a nun, was, however, of little help. "She seemed to be trying to talk me into the annulment," Darlene explained. "Even two of my children met with her to try and convince her that it just didn't seem right or fair to say the marriage didn't exist in the Church's eyes."

While Darlene's advocate was willing to meet with her children, she did not encourage Darlene to answer the questionnaire that would have given Darlene's views of the marriage. Nor did she ask Darlene to provide witnesses who could have supported her claim that the marriage was valid. In short, because Darlene was largely uninformed of her rights, she was unaware of how to formally and vigorously oppose the annulment. Indeed, as one of her daughters who spoke with the advocate later told me, "the advocate didn't really listen to what I had to say."

The annulment was granted in 1994 on the grounds of Tom's lack of due discretion. The Church found Tom incapable of ever establishing a true marriage with Darlene even though they had lived in a presumed state of matrimony for thirty-two years and their union had produced six children. The Archdiocese of Philadelphia confirmed the decision in a routine appeal.

The Church, however, imposed a restriction on Tom and prohibited him from remarrying until he received a favorable assessment from Catholic Social Services, a Church-sponsored service that provides counseling. The tribunal placed no such restrictions on Darlene. Apparently, the Church considered her fit to marry and she was now free to do so with the Church's blessing if she chose.

Some of Darlene's friends, and even to a certain extent her church counselor, tried to convince her that there were "positive aspects" to her annulment. Couldn't she accept it not only as a source of freedom but also one of vindication? After all, she was now free to marry, and it was also clear from the tribunal's findings that to the extent that personal shortcomings might have contributed to the failure of the marriage, the Church thought they were Tom's shortcomings, not hers.

Darlene, however, did not see it that way. To her, there was an enormous difference between saying their marriage ended and saying it never existed. For Darlene, the annulment was neither freedom nor vindication. "This was worse than death," she told me. How could the Church prove that she and Tom never had a true marriage?

"Part of me died when that annulment was granted. Yet," Darlene elaborated, "I knew I had to go on with my life. I had six children and eight grandchildren that needed me and I wanted to make a home for them. Jeff had been such a supportive, wonderful man through all this that I couldn't help but love him. We decided to buy a house together, and he let the children know that he would do anything in the world for me. He often says, 'I don't know how Tom could have ever let you go.' I still have difficult times and I know I still have a certain sadness about me; but I have moved on with my life between working, being a mom and grandma, and with Jeff, who is always there for me to lean on."

"Where do you think the sadness comes from?" I asked. "I sense it, too."

Darlene was silent for a moment and then she answered. "Part of it is because the Church didn't help save my marriage, even after all those years of my believing and working for it. The Church teaches you that marriage is forever, but it didn't help me when I needed help. The church counselor I'm working with now is a nice person, but the annulment has already gone through. The counselor's helping me now isn't the same thing.

"Another part of my sadness," she continued, "is that things just don't have the same meaning as they did before the annulment. I used to think the Church gave meaning to what I did, but I don't think that way now. It's not that I don't believe in God, because I still do. I just don't go to church anymore. I still have faith in God, just not the Church.

"In fact, I have a newfound image of God," Darlene continued. "When Tom's time comes and he goes before God on his day of judgment and God asks him, 'Did you love your wife as I love the Church?' I think God will mean the one he was married to for thirty-two years and the mother of his six children, not someone he married the second time around. What's more, when Tom stands before God and knows he has to tell the truth, I suspect he will speak of me as his wife, too. You see, I know God doesn't believe this annulment is right either. When Tom goes before Him, the truth will finally come out."

Darlene and I had been walking for some time. We were almost back at her house and a lovely spring evening was beginning to blanket the neighborhood. Considering we had only met in the morning, we had discussed a lot of things that weren't easy to talk about. We were both tired and as we walked in the front door, I smelled a delightful lasagna dinner that Darlene had prepared before we left and Jeff had put in the oven. I was in for a treat and it was time for some light-hearted conversation. We would be talking again of serious things the next day.

Typical of many American families, Tom and Darlene's adult children are constantly on the go: moving among cities, jobs, relationships, marriages, and others of life's transitions. Two daughters seem to have their father's gift for numbers and business. A third is a nurse, another a teacher. Three have children of their own. Tom and Darlene's son is married and will soon complete his service in the armed forces. Despite the constant state of flux in their lives, at least one child seems always to be living near their mother and two of the daughters, Tracy and Laura, were the ones who talked with me about the annulment of their parents' marriage.

"My parents' marriage wasn't perfect," Tracy began, "but there's nothing in Catholic teachings that says that means there was never a marriage. An annulment is an easy way out. People won't face up to the mistakes they made in the marriage if they can get around them by saying they were never married.

"The Church says annulment doesn't affect the children, but that's not true. Of course it does," she continued. "I have to admit I'm angry at my father. He told us one thing growing up about the right way to live and then he went and did the opposite. I've had it with the hypocrisy. I just want to live my own life now."

"It's all very hard to accept," Laura added. "We were such a Catholic family and I really don't see how the Church had a case. Yes, my parents were young when they married but they were together all those years and renewed their vows on their twenty-fifth anniversary. No one would have ever thought that the annulment was going to happen. My mother really hadn't even been able to deal with the divorce when it came about."

"I know," I interjected. "That's bothered me, too, because the

Church isn't suppose to consider annulment unless there is no hope of the couple's reconciling."

"I just know that it's very hard to accept annulment as church policy," Laura added. "I can see if a couple is married a short time, there might be grounds for one. But we were a normal and very Catholic family for thirty-two years. It seems as if an annulment is just an excuse for a divorce. It demeans marriage and everything the Church is supposed to stand for."

"Do you still go to church?" I asked.

"We go to Mass on Sundays," Laura answered. "I still believe and I think it's important for the children, but our house isn't as Catholic as my parents' was. I just hope my mother will get through this. I think she will, but there are still some hard times."

Once back in Boston, I found myself thinking about how lucky I was to have met Darlene and to have been able to talk with her daughters. As I thought about what they had told me, Laura's question about how the Church could have annulled her parents' marriage kept coming to mind. Later, after some additional research, I was to learn the answer to her question, an answer which made me angry.

Perhaps no other church publication reveals how far American tribunals are willing to go in order to grant annulments than the book of the same name by Lawrence Wrenn. There are five editions of *Annulments*. The first appeared in 1970 following Vatican II. The fifth appeared in 1988. All have been published by the Canon Law Society of America. *Annulments* is essentially a handbook for judges and others seeking justification to render a marriage invalid. My advocate recommended the book to help me understand the annulment process.

The 1988 edition is noteworthy not only because it is the most recent, but also because it bases much of its discussion of psychological and psychiatric grounds for annulment on what was at that time the most current information in the field of psychiatry, the *Diagnostic and Statistical Manual of Mental Disorders 111-R* (*DSM-111-R*). The *DSM-111-R* is published by the American Psychiatric Association and is used by mental health professionals to assist in making diagnoses. It is periodically updated to reflect current changes or new discoveries in the medical field. *DSM-111-R* is a revised edition of the third version and was published in 1987. A fourth edition, published in 1994, is more current but was not yet available when Wrenn completed his most recent edition of *Annulments.*

Wrenn devotes much of his discussion to a long list of ailments which could prove to be grounds for annulment. These include mental retardation, epilepsy, alcoholic disorder, identity disorder, personality disorder, anxiety disorder, mood disorder, and schizophrenia. In fairness, Wrenn does indeed base much of this material on the *DSM* and discusses it in a straightforward manner.

Then he gets crafty. As Wrenn explains, for centuries church law reflected the belief that marriage was forever. Spouses had a right to believe that their mates not only intended to live up to the obligations of marriage for a lifetime, but also that they had the capacity to do so. For example, if at the time of the marriage a person had no intention of being faithful, the marriage was invalid. What is more, even if a person had the intention to be faithful but was psychologically incapable of doing so, the marriage was invalid. At issue was the person's intent *and* capacity. A person's simple choice to have affairs was not grounds for annulment. What is more, the lack of either intent or capacity had to be proven to a moral certainty.

Wrenn points out that the right to perpetuity also applies to the marital conditions set forth at Vatican II, among them the right to an interpersonal relationship and sharing a covenant as opposed to a mere contract. He also correctly assumes that both parties must be able to make these commitments and have the ability to follow through with them at the time they marry. But then he correlates these rights with the psychological conditions discussed in the *DMS* and presents them in a format for judges or others looking for a rationale for annulment. In the process, Wrenn makes some extraordinary assumptions, assumptions which virtually assure that a judge can find justification to grant an annulment should he choose to do so.

Wrenn's approach stipulates four categories: severity, antecedence, perpetuity, and relativity. Severity describes the condition and indicates how the condition could impact an individual and a marriage. Sometimes the distinction between disorders is less than clear. Under mood disorders, for example, Wrenn discusses major mood disorders such as manic depression but also notes less-defined depressive disorders that simply involve periods of milder depression. Invariably, however, whatever the ailment or its severity, Wrenn determined that at the very least the condition could be a cause for annulment.

Antecedence is trickier. Here the tribunal tries to show that the condition existed or was present at the time of the wedding, thus rendering it invalid. But when there is no hard evidence supporting antecedence, Wrenn goes to great length to suggest that whatever the judge can find is probably sufficient. "The precise etiology of the mood disorder is not clear," Wrenn writes. "Perhaps hereditary, constitutional, biological, and psychological factors all play a part. It seems clear, however, that some kind of predisposition for the severe disorder certainly exists. Therefore, even when the first episode occurs after the marriage, antecedence may be presumed." I had to read this statement several times to see if I was interpreting it correctly. Finally, I could only ask, Since when are predisposition and existence the same?

Perpetuity offers yet another opportunity for the judge in search of an annulment. Again, under mood disorder, Wrenn notes that drugs can sometimes control the disorder, enabling the patient to live a normal life. However, he also notes, there is the possibility that the disorder could have destroyed a marriage before it could be controlled. In such a situation, the person would have not been capable of marriage because she was not capable of assuming its perpetual obligation. Thus, the marriage is invalid. Even though possibility is not the same as proof of a moral certainty, the degree of certainty on which annulments are supposed to be judged, a judge in these cases may, according to Wrenn, grant an annulment.

The fourth factor, relativity, enables the tribunal to annul a marriage on the grounds that at least one spouse was incapable of marriage while at the same time allowing the couple to remarry others. A rational reader might think that the person with serious or manic depression as described by Wrenn had a major problem, or at least one that would render him incapable of marriage, but not necessarily. Wrenn explains it may be that "the other party" is a "walking precipitating factor for the . . . disorder." In such cases, it is possible that the person could function in a marriage to someone else, just not with the spouse to whom he was married. In other words, the person was only relatively incapable of marriage and may marry again.

Depression is only one example of a condition that Wrenn discusses as grounds for annulment. But it is a good one, particularly as it demonstrates how open-ended the grounds for granting annulment have become in the United States. An estimated twenty-one million Americans experience depression each year, women twice as often as men. The elderly are particularly vulnerable, as are adolescents and young mothers. Are we supposed to believe that these young mothers are living in invalid marriages? Does the Church honestly think that elderly couples, some of whom have been married more than sixty years, were never truly married because in the twilight of their lives they have sought help for depression and possibly found relief in Prozac or a similar medication? Is the adolescent who has the courage to seek help for his feelings of despair possibly setting himself up to have his marriage annulled in future years?

Wrenn's analysis of annulment reminded me of an annual sailboat race we participated in as children. The boats were called Sunfish. They were small, with a single sail and a center board that could be raised with one hand and a tug. A child could rig and launch a Sunfish with relative ease. Each year there was a race through the slough, a winding, narrow passage between two lakes with shallow water, little wind, and lots of weeds and mud. The point was to get through the slough and it didn't matter how. The general rules of sailing did not apply. You could swim your boat, splash your opponents, whatever it took. There was never sufficient wind to move the boats fast enough for the race to be dangerous. The point was to get from one lake to the other and have fun. No one took it too seriously.

Wrenn navigates the waters of annulment much as we sailed those of the slough. He will find a way to an annulment and it doesn't matter how. Rules and even common sense are suspended. Whatever became of the marital vow "through sickness and in health"? Are we as rational human beings really supposed to go along with this nonsense? Are we really supposed to view annulment as an act of compassion on the part of the Church and one that is undertaken in the name of God?

The differences between Wrenn's race and ours should be as obvious as the similarities. Even as children we were fair-minded enough to admit that the rules of sailing were suspended. Other than perhaps wanting to show who could get the muddiest, we were not out to prove anything. Everyone had fun and no one was in danger of being hurt. The same cannot be said for Wrenn's race to annulment. The Church has broadened its rules to such an extent that it has virtually suspended them, yet it does not admit to doing so.

With such an open path to annulment, however, it should not be surprising that the tribunal could have found something in Tom's past to justify its granting one. After all, no one would hold it accountable for its decision. What is more, by its ruling that Tom's rather than Darlene's lack of due discretion was at issue, he would be able to re-marry with the Church's blessing and she would, in a sense, be exon-erated for their failed marriage. Viewed within the context of Wrenn's widely accepted work, the tribunal not only followed standard proce-dure, but also lived up to the Church's mandate of providing com-passion to a divorced Catholic without compromising its historical opposition to divorce.

When I finished reading Wrenn's analysis of annulment I was angry. I could not fathom how the psychiatric community could pro-vide data that could so blithely be used to justify annulment. My instincts told me that Wrenn's conclusions could only be a mis-representation of *DSM-111-R,* and so I borrowed a copy from a friend who was also a doctor. As I had suspected, a review of *DSM-111-R* gave a very different picture than Wrenn's discussion. For starters, the manual specifically notes that its classifications do not apply to family or other interpersonal relationships. What is a mar-riage if not a family or an interpersonal relationship?

DSM-111-R also explains that while its classifications refer to "physical" and "mental" disorders separately, these terms are not meant to imply that mental disorders are unrelated to physical or bio-logical factors. However, perhaps because the only physical limitation recognized under canon law that invalidates a marriage is impotency, Wrenn regards all of the disorders discussed in the manual as primar-ily "mental," thus enabling a tribunal to have a much greater selection from which to choose a justification for annulling a marriage.

What is more, in large black type not unlike the warning on a cigarette pack, the *DSM-111-R* cautions the reader about misuse of its manual. It begins by noting that its classifications should be used only as a primary step in evaluation, and that additional information about the person should also be applied. Wrenn, however, deletes any such caution from his own analysis.

In addition, the manual is not to be used by persons lacking specialized professional training. Again, Wrenn seems to overlook this warning by enabling tribunals to render judgment based on *DSM-111-R*'s classifications with or without the assistance of professional analysis.

Perhaps most astonishing is that the manual not only cautions that it is to be used only in clinical or research settings, but also notes *specifically* that it is not to be used in making legal determinations. When I read this warning, I couldn't believe its implication. The same church that had boasted to me that its annulment process rested on a legal system dating back to the twelfth century was basing annulment cases on a manual that specifically warned readers not to use it for legal purposes.

After reading Wrenn's work and reviewing *DSM-111-R*, I felt a deep compassion for Darlene's daughters who could not grasp how the Church could have betrayed their mother. I was also fearful that Darlene would not be able to overcome the effects of such deception. Even though I remained in awe of what she had accomplished in her life, Darlene seemed to think her accomplishments were insignificant. I was troubled by her sadness. As she so acutely observed about herself, "I have a certain sadness about me. . . . My life doesn't have the meaning it had before the annulment."

Her sadness, of course, is understandable. It was the Church that had given her life meaning and had guided her through all those difficult times, and it was this same church that had abandoned her in her hour of greatest need. With her faith in her church shattered, Darlene had at least temporarily lost the essence of meaning itself.

I suspected, however, that her loss was only temporary. Darlene was not only aware of what she had lost, but she was also willing to talk about it. More important, perhaps, while she might have lost her faith in the Church, her faith in God remained strong. As her daughter Laura so aptly put it, "I think when she gets more confidence in herself, the sadness will go and the rest will come. I hope that will happen with her working and getting out more."

It seemed somehow appropriate that Darlene's daughters had greater confidence in their mother than she did in herself. It was a testament to how much she gave to them even if it meant denying herself some of the nurturing she needed. Up until now, Darlene had lived within the boundaries of traditional Catholicism and its conventions, which stress that a woman's role as wife and mother is to give to others and think of herself, if at all, only after she has cared for her family.

It is ironic that while her church was not there for Darlene in her time of need, her work required that she be there for others at just that time. If Laura was right, then her mother's work would be the catalyst that encouraged her to find new meaning. As Darlene moved on from the shattered remains of her faith to one that was more encompassing and which celebrated who she is, she would find new meaning to replace what she had lost.

As I continued to think of Darlene, a feeling came over me that time would prove Laura right. Her mother would not only get through this, but would emerge a stronger person. Surprisingly, for a moment at least, my own anger at the Church vanished. In fact, I felt sad for this most powerful of institutions, for in losing Darlene, the Church had lost another of its most dedicated champions.

9

A WAY OF BEING

◆━━━◆

The feelings of betrayal that Darlene had experienced as the result of her annulment made me wonder about those of Terry, who had also written to me when my case became public. Terry was from the Chicago area and in some respects her story was similar to others. She was a lifelong Catholic and the mother of three children. She had been married for more than twenty years when her marriage failed and she filed for divorce. Then her husband had sought and subsequently received an annulment. Now, she wished that she had opposed the petition with more vigor, but at the time she had assumed that the Church would never annul her marriage.

There was an urgency in her letter, however, that made it different from the others I had received. While Deirdre had also told me that my feelings about annulment mirrored her own and that she was relieved to find she was not alone, Terry told me that we needed to bring national attention to the abuse inherent in the annulment proceedings. She concluded her letter by telling me that her prayers were with me and my children.

I wrote Terry to thank her for her words of encouragement, and put her letter in a safe place. As the months passed and I learned more about annulment, I came to see that Terry had been right. Not only did the Church's policy seem wrong, but it became increasingly clear to me that it was unlikely that anything would ever be done to address the injustices unless those who had experienced annulment broke their collective silence. But before I could include Terry's views in my story, I needed to know more about her and her case. When I phoned her to ask if we could meet, she invited me to stay with her for a weekend in her home in Chicago.

Like that of Boston, the Archdiocese of Chicago is intertwined with social services and politics. An estimated two and a third million Catholics live within the archdiocese's roughly fourteen-hundred-square-mile area, and its boundaries include the city of Chicago as well as Cook and Lake counties. Approximately eight hundred Catholic institutions operate within its jurisdiction, including over three hundred parishes, about two hundred and eighty elementary schools, almost fifty high schools, six colleges or universities, and three seminaries. The archdiocese's school system is the largest parochial system and the eleventh largest school system of any kind in the United States.

Nor are its activities limited to education. There are twenty Catholic hospitals located within its boundaries and its major charitable organization, Catholic Charities, is the largest private social services agency in the Midwest. In 1995 alone, Catholic Charities served an estimated half a million people. In addition to services, the archdiocese provides approximately twenty thousand jobs in its parishes, schools, charities, seminaries, cemeteries, and pastoral centers.

Terry's life was very much a part of the world of the Chicago archdiocese. She grew up in a working-class neighborhood referred to by the name of its parish. Her mother worked for a department store before she married and returned to her job when Terry was in the eighth grade. Her father worked for a local utility. Terry's mother made sure they attended Mass every Sunday and that her only child received an appropriate Catholic upbringing. While Terry's early education was in public schools, she attended high school and college in Chicago's parochial system.

Yet Terry's childhood experiences with the Church went beyond religion and education. She grew up emotionally aware of the repercussions of the Church's stand against divorce. Her father had been married, fathered a son, and divorced before he fell in love with and married Terry's mother in a civil ceremony. "I have a half brother fifteen years older than I," she explained. "My father tried for years to get an annulment, but because of lack of funds or whatever reason the Church gave at the time, his request was always denied.

"After twenty years of marriage to my mother, he finally made peace with the Church. He and my mother went to confession and promised to live as brother and sister. That was in the early 1960s. It was the only way at that time that he could be assured of having a Catholic burial. He and my mother lived as brother and sister for about ten years until he died. It was a very high price to pay for their religion."

Terry met her future husband, John, at a local dance in the midsixties. He was in his early twenties and an apprentice in the construction industry. She was twenty-one and taught elementary school for the archdiocese. "John was of medium build, about five feet ten, with blond hair and blue eyes. "Looking back, I think he was a dead ringer for Robert Redford," Terry remembers with a smile. "He came over and asked me to dance. Oddly, what I remember most was his overcoat. It was the same type that the Jesuits wore at the seminary, and as I discovered, that's where he had gotten it when he was a student there. We talked about religion a lot. Later I learned that John was from a large and very religious Catholic family. His entire education had been in Catholic schools, and after two years in the seminary he dropped out and began working in the construction industry. He believed strongly in the Church's teachings of right and wrong and the importance of the family."

John also knew of the pain that can be caused by the Church's unwavering opposition to divorce. One of his sisters, the mother of ten children, had married a man who physically abused her. While the Church granted her permission to live apart from her husband and she obtained a civil divorce, the Church did not recognize the civil decree. Under church law she remained married. She was never permitted to remarry, and church custom frowned upon her even associating with men. What's more, her parents saw that church policies were enforced and forbid their daughter to date or even socialize with men.

"That was the 1950s and before I met John," Terry explained. "His sister wouldn't have dared go against her parents' or the Church's wishes. So with the exception of her children and later grandchildren, she has lived alone ever since. I found it odd that when John and I first talked about his sister's situation, he didn't seem to have more compassion for his sister. He agreed that she needed to be divorced because of the abuse. But he also thought her life was what her life was and nothing would ever fix it. I think he saw it a matter of faith. You accepted what the Church told you and that was that.

"On our first date," Terry recalls, "John took me to a very nice restaurant and we talked about religion again. From then on we dated heavily. In a funny way, from the very beginning I thought John was a better person than I was. Part of it may have had to do with the fact that the Church never recognized my parents' marriage. Even though the Church says that doesn't make a difference for a child, when religion is as strong an influence in your life as it was in mine, it does mean something. I felt a bit inferior to other people because of it."

It was the 1960s when Terry and John fell in love, a period of profound unrest in America. As was the case for many young men, the draft and the Vietnam War loomed over John's horizon. "Soon we began talking of marriage," Terry explained, "but as something we'd do in the future after he returned from the service."

Around Christmas, John was inducted into the army and assigned to a base in the Southeast. John called Terry often and went to visit him when he was on leave. "I was teaching at the time and I found a novena to Saint Jude, the Patron Saint of Hopeless Cases. We didn't think of ourselves as hopeless," Terry explained, "but we were both worried about the possibility of John's being sent to Vietnam and since that was a problem we could do nothing about, in that sense we were hopeless. Every evening at six o'clock the two of us prayed to Saint Jude. Our prayers made us feel very close even though John was far away."

Soon John was transferred to a base not far from Chicago, and he decided there was no reason to postpone their wedding. Terry concurred. "He was very insistent and everything seemed right," she recalled. "We were happy. We shared a deep commitment to religion and family. He was stationed close enough to Chicago that it was easy to plan a wedding. When we met with the priest, the Church was so much a part of both of our lives that we already knew what Catholic marriage was about. The priest didn't have to give us a lot of counseling."

In June, John was given weekend leave and he and Terry were married. "It was a regular church wedding with a big reception. Our rings were engraved with our initials and those of Saint Jude. That was John's idea, and engraving a saint's initials on our rings made them and our prayers to him more meaningful.

"Later John's mother told me that for fifteen minutes before the service, he stood before a statue of Saint Joseph and prayed that he would be as good a husband as Joseph had been to the Blessed Mother. Everything was as it should have been; but since he only had the weekend off, we didn't go on a honeymoon. John returned to the base and I stayed at home with my parents for about a month and a half until I joined him.

"We had a good life. I taught at the parochial school. We lived off the base in a little duplex that the army subsidized. Because we lived off base, John's being in the army wasn't much different from a regular job. We had good friends and often went out to dinner. Most of the other wives didn't work although one was an army nurse. I became pregnant in October of that year and in August of the next year our first child, a son, was born. We were very happy as new parents, and one of John's sisters came down for the baby's baptism.

"The following year, we moved back to Chicago. For a few months we lived with my parents while we looked for a house, and then we moved into our own. It was small, but we worked hard fixing it up. John worked in construction. I took care of my son, and on days that I could find child care, I was a substitute teacher for the archdiocese. In short, we had a normal life and Catholicism was its center. We both taught for the archdiocese on Saturdays and on Sundays we always went to Mass. Everything we did was in accordance with church law."

Not long after John and Terry had settled in their new house, Terry met a man who would influence the course of her life. "He was a former classmate of John's who was studying to be a priest," Terry recalled. "He came for dinner one night and from then on he was a regular visitor. Soon he became a major presence in our family, and after he was ordained as Father Francis, his influence grew. Eventually his word became law for us.

"He and other former classmates of John's who had entered the priesthood would also come over for dinner. Sometimes we would go out, but invariably we would talk about religion. I was the only woman in the group, which looking back may have been a little strange, but they were very enjoyable evenings."

Terry's life was the Church and she was content. During the week, when not attending to her child, she taught for the archdiocese. On Saturdays both she and John led religion classes; Sundays they went to Mass as a family. On nights when they socialized, they usually did so with several priests, and their closest family friend had become a priest himself.

Around Christmas, however, a crisis occurred and Terry experienced the power, but from her perspective not the compassion, of her husband's religious beliefs. She suffered a miscarriage. Although neither her doctor nor the hospital where she was treated were Catholic, both were highly respected. As Terry remembers the incident, after tests had revealed that her hormone level was no longer consistent with pregnancy, her doctor prescribed medication to help her system adjust to the miscarriage. The doctor then explained to John that he might need to perform surgery to ensure Terry's full recovery. John, however, maintained there was no proof that the baby had died and forbid the doctor to take any action that might harm the unborn child.

Terry went home without surgery but took the medication. Soon she began to hemorrhage. "I was terrified. I literally thought I was going to bleed to death. But John kept saying that Father Francis had told him that the child should be baptized and so he kept blessing the blood on the floor rather than taking me back to the hospital. Fortunately, he finally agreed to take me to the hospital. The operation was performed around midnight two days before Christmas, and the next day I was discharged."

Understandably, Terry was exhausted when she returned home. "I did the best I could for my son, who was now an excited two-year-old waiting for Santa Claus. I got everything ready for Christmas Day and then I just wanted to stay home, rest, and be with him. But John wouldn't hear of it. It didn't matter how I felt. He just said it was Christmas and we were going to Mass. So I said okay, I would go, but after Mass I needed to rest. I told him that I would do the best I could making dinner for the three of us, but afterward I would need to lie down.

"When dinner was over, my parents came over for a very short time," Terry continued. "After they left, I started to get ready to go to bed, and John told me we were going to his parents' house. I tried to explain how tired and sick I was, but it didn't matter. John just repeated that this was Christmas Day and since we always went to his parents on Christmas Day, I would go. There was no choice. I was handed my coat and purse and told to get myself together.

"Once we arrived at his parents' house, it became clear to me that only they knew I had lost the baby. Other family members kept congratulating me on my pregnancy, and I couldn't help but think that for some reason John was punishing me for the miscarriage. I realized that the only way anyone would know I had lost the baby was if I told them. So I explained as gently as I could what had happened. The whole situation was very puzzling and painful for me. It was as though John thought I had offended his religion and the miscarriage was my fault. It really felt as if I was being punished."

It is Terry's understanding and a fact confirmed by several priests that at the time of her miscarriage, church policy stated that neither the child nor the mother was to be sacrificed to save the other. However, such a policy would not have been relevant to Terry's case. The baby was not due until July and it was December when Terry began bleeding profusely. "It wasn't a question of my hanging on a little longer," Terry recalls with sorrow in her voice even after all these years, "or using medical technology to save a premature baby. I simply miscarried. It happens."

Terry was understandably confused and hurt by what she experienced as both her husband's and her priest's unwillingness or inability to provide compassion, support, and love at a time when she needed help. Yet she remained nonjudgmental. "Even though I was terrified, I had faith that everything would be okay," she explained. "I lost the baby and that was hard. But I accepted that and went on. I didn't dwell on what either John or Father Francis might have done differently. I wanted to be a good Catholic wife and so I tried harder."

Terry's account of her miscarriage and its aftermath were so powerful that I thought it important to hear Father Francis's and John's recollections of the tragedy. Once I was back in Boston, I contacted them. Father Francis declined to comment on any aspects of Terry and John's marriage and annulment, but John, while understandably wary of sharing the details of such a personal tragedy with a stranger, was willing to discuss the incident in general terms. He explained that even though the miscarriage had occurred more than twenty-five years before we spoke, he was relatively sure that he had never considered the possibility that the surgery could have been the equivalent of taking the baby's life. Nor could he remember discussing the case with Father Francis. He assured me that while he had been upset by the miscarriage, he had not blamed Terry, and while he wasn't surprised to learn that losing the baby had affected Terry more severely than it had him, he attributed her feelings of abandonment to the lack of communication between them rather than any misinterpretation of church policy on his part.

Regardless of how differently Terry and John experienced her miscarriage, their faith brought them and their marriage through the crisis. In the early 1970s, they moved to a larger house in a Chicago suburb. Almost immediately Terry and John became active in the Church. Terry taught religion classes. John did free construction for the Church, participated in some of the lighthearted plays the parish produced, and became a member of a new church initiative which trained laypeople to assist the priest during communion.

John enjoyed his new role in the Church and told Terry that once she was through with her childrearing responsibilities, perhaps she too could participate. From all outward appearances, the family appeared to be flourishing. Soon a daughter, Joan, was born and although the pregnancy was difficult, both Terry and John were delighted at the new addition. Father Francis, their closest family friend as well as their priest, baptized the new baby in a spirit of Christian warmth and love.

But the joy of Joan's birth was dampened by the death of Terry's father. In addition, Terry soon learned that she was pregnant again and it seemed to her as though John offered little if any comfort or support. "He was an hour and a half late to pick me up for my father's wake. I didn't want my mother to be there alone when they brought my father's casket in, but she was. I don't think John cared. Father Francis performed the Mass, but it was clear to me that John was not going to be there for either me or my family. At this point I honestly thought about leaving him, and sometimes I think I would have if I hadn't been pregnant. I would have moved in with my mother, but I thought three children would be too much for her.

"On the other hand," Terry continued, "even when I look back at all the pain he put me through, I realize how much I really loved this man. I know that in the beginning there was mutual love and commitment. With that kind of love, you think the hard times are just temporary and that somehow you'll pull through together. It's what marriage is about and it's part of what I believe in. So I decided that I would try harder to live up to my Catholic faith."

Their third child, another son, was born about a year after Joan. He was three to four weeks premature, and Terry was so weak that she and the baby both spent ten days in the hospital. "When I got home," Terry recalled, "my health began to deteriorate. I had two babies and a first grader to take care of and was getting less than three hours of sleep a night. John was no help."

Rather, John decided that he wanted to take courses that would enable him to become a lay deacon, a position that enables married people to perform some priestly duties such as baptism and certain types of counseling. "When I told John that I needed him to help at home," Terry explained, "he said that if I didn't support his being a deacon, I would be denying him his role in the Church. So I told him to go ahead. I think," Terry continued, "his becoming a lay deacon was a way to withdraw further from me and the children yet still hold on to the family he thought he should have. Using the Church as a reason or excuse to do it made it not only all right but even noble."

Meanwhile, Terry's health continued its downward slide. Eventually she was so anemic that her doctor warned her against becoming pregnant and told her she must use some form of birth control. "I told John," Terry related cautiously, "what the doctor had said. His only response was that he always knew that one day I would compromise his soul. Then he added that there was no way he would either use birth control or allow me to, and that if I got pregnant, I would just have to suffer the consequences. I was so upset by what appeared to be his lack of concern for my well-being that I turned to Father Francis for help. I told him that I didn't understand why John was acting the way he was. After all, I had given him three children. I had been pregnant four times in six years. It wasn't as if I wasn't a good Catholic wife. All I was asking for was some time to get my health back.

"When I told Father Francis what John had said about my compromising his soul, he seemed as shocked as I was. He came for dinner, and a heated argument followed over whether I had the right to say no. John said that I was there for him, that I could never say no. His view was that church law said if he wanted sex, then I had to have it. I couldn't say no. I can remember Father Francis looking at him and saying very strongly, 'She can say no whenever she wants.'"

After Father Francis's reprimand, John became less demanding, and for the next couple of years Terry and John lived in relative harmony. Once again it seemed to Terry as if her faith in her church and God's grace, evident in this instance through Father Francis's support, had brought her family through another crisis. "I didn't use birth control," Terry recalled. "I counted the days and was lucky. I was also becoming more independent. The children were getting older. I could get a full night's sleep and life was more manageable. John worked all the time and was making a lot of money, which helped. He never complained about the bills, so I basically ran the house and cared for the children and he did what he wanted.

"On Friday and Saturday nights we would go out for dinner, usually with our neighbors. It became a regular thing. The Church was still the center of our lives. When there was a problem in our relationship, I felt it was because I wasn't a good Catholic wife and if our marriage were to fail it would be my fault. From the time the children were infants they went to Mass every Sunday. I would sit in the pew with the two babies and my daughter, and after John distributed communion he would join us."

"A good Catholic wife" was a phrase that Terry used often and she later explained that to her the phrase epitomized how she thought John expected her to behave. "It meant that I should do as I was told. I was meant to take care of everything, be submissive, and keep quiet. So I tried harder at home, but basically, even though he paid the bills, I was becoming a single parent. The way I saw it, he didn't seem to care what his children were doing. He was seldom there, and in the late 1970s he began taking courses to earn another professional degree."

The stress of trying to be "a good Catholic wife" took its toll on Terry. That summer she broke down both physically and psychologically. "I just couldn't handle it all anymore," Terry confided. "I felt trapped and it wasn't just affecting me, it was also hurting my children, and that was killing me. I was diagnosed as being clinically depressed." Terry was admitted to a hospital, placed on medication, and given counseling to help her learn how to deal with her life. Her breakdown and subsequent recovery marked a turning point and afterward she began to take more control of her life.

Terry's newfound strength could not have come at a better time. Soon after John completed his courses, the family learned he would need surgery. "It was a very severe situation and not even the doctors were sure how bad it was," Terry explained. "While I didn't notice at the time, John was home even less in the six or eight months before his operation. I was too busy making plans to take care of him when he came home from the hospital. It was odd in a way. He had caused me so much pain, but when I learned he was sick, I prayed he'd be okay. I was ready to take care of him regardless of what happened.

"We scheduled his surgery for September, after the children had returned to school, and that morning my daughter and I went to be with him at the hospital. Right before they took him into the operating room and in front of the doctor and nurse, he held up two fingers and said to me, 'I have something to tell you. I have two girlfriends. They're downstairs. They're coming to see me after the surgery.' Then he went to sleep. I was shocked. My daughter started to cry, and the doctor was standing there with his mouth wide open.

"When the surgery was over," Terry recalled with some pain, "I was allowed upstairs to see him. I was waiting for him to return from the recovery room and as I was leaning against the supply cart in the hall, I kept telling myself, 'This man has just told me he has two girlfriends and I'm standing here with my heart in my stomach hoping he's okay.' Well, he was okay. When he was wheeled in, he asked me if he was going to be all right. I told him that he was, and then he faded back to sleep.

"The next morning when I came to see him, he repeated his question and again I told him he'd be fine. Suddenly he became cocky. He told me to go home, that people would be coming to visit him and he didn't need a whole lot of company right now. So I decided he shouldn't have any. I went down to the desk and told them that my husband was extremely ill and shouldn't have any visitors except for me and our daughter. Then I went to the switchboard and told them to cut off all phone calls."

That year brought another setback for Terry. Father Francis wrote her to tell her that he was also ill and would require hospitalization. "It seemed as if everything was falling apart at the same time," Terry recalled. "I hadn't really thought about why we hadn't heard from Father Francis even though John was sick. I was too busy just trying to hold everything together. I wished him a speedy and complete recovery and assured him that he would again be able to resume his role as a priest."

Terry knew she was facing a big decision and with Father Francis also ill, it was one she had to make on her own. Her husband had admitted that he was involved with two other women. In a couple of weeks this man would be returning home for a six-week recovery period during which time Terry would have to care for him—a lot to ask of any marriage.

Both Terry and the marriage rose to the occasion. While John would not discuss her concerns about their marriage, he nevertheless promised a new start. "I thought he was trying," Terry admitted. "After he was well, I kept track of him and he was where he was supposed to be. So I thought he really was trying to make things work."

For a while it looked as if it would be a year of second chances. Father Francis resumed his duties as a priest, and in in the spring Terry and John took a trip together. "John promised it would be a second honeymoon," Terry remembered. "He even said he'd buy me a new wedding ring."

The honeymoon never happened. Although the trip lasted two weeks, John was on the phone a lot and according to Terry refused to say whom he was calling. "They weren't numbers I recognized. When the plane landed at the Chicago airport," Terry recalled, "I knew it was over. I got off the plane and told him so. It took me until the fall to get him out of the house, but I never let up. I couldn't live this lie anymore."

In the late 1980s Terry and John divorced. About two weeks before the divorce became final, John phoned her to say that he was involved with another woman, who was Catholic and had never been married. He then explained that they planned to be married and he had already spoken with Father Francis about getting an annulment.

"I didn't know how to respond to him," Terry remembered. "I had no idea he would go through with something like this. I realize that there was a lot missing from the marriage, but I never thought it didn't exist. To this day, I do not think he truly believed it either. I think he was looking for a way to hurt me and to make it all right for him to remarry . . . he could never justify anything he did in his life unless it was okay with the Church. In his way of dealing with life, you don't fix things, you just erase them. He was looking to erase a marriage that had lasted more than twenty years and, to be honest, I don't think he ever thought that the annulment would affect the children, that it would hurt them as well as hurt me.

"After I talked with him I was distraught," Terry continued. "I cried a lot, and the children asked me what was wrong. When I told them, they said that he'd never go through with it. But the next time John and I spoke he told me that he was going ahead. He then added that during the course of our twenty-three-and-a-half-year marriage, he had never loved me one day.

"I couldn't believe what he said. So I asked him, 'You mean to say that for twenty-three and a half years you lived with me, we had three children, and you never loved me one day?' And he repeated his answer: 'I never loved you one day,' and then added, 'and that's what I'm going to tell the Church.' "

Terry was devastated at what John had told her, and the next morning she called Father Francis. "Even though I hadn't heard from him since his own illness, I assumed he would help us. After all, the children were involved too. It wasn't just me," Terry recalled. "I asked him point-blank what he was doing about it. Was it possible for John to get one? Father Francis replied that absolutely it was possible. Then he told me, 'It's a done deal.' Those were his very words: 'a done deal.'

"He said that there was no sense in my fighting it or even in filling out a form. It was going to happen, and it didn't matter what I said or did and it didn't matter what anyone else said or did. His final remark was that I had better resign myself to the fact because John had the right to fall in love and marry again. He was going to get an annulment and marry in the Church, and he would perform the ceremony."

Even though Terry felt completely betrayed by this priest who for so many years had been a part of her family, she found the courage to push on for answers. She asked Father Francis how he could do such a thing. Didn't he realize how an annulment would hurt the children? He had baptized two of them and given First Communion to all three. Yet now he seemed willing to abandon them without so much as a backward glance just so their father could remarry in the Church. Father Francis was unmoved by Terry's appeal. "He turned to me," Terry said almost in a whisper, "and his words were, 'They aren't babies anymore and they'd better grow up.' "

Terry hung up the phone in complete despair and tried to prepare for the onslaught of the Church's official notification that would surely follow. Yet for months she heard nothing. Six months later, she called the archdiocese and was told that while her former husband had inquired about annulment, he had not filed any paperwork.

Then in September, a friend called Terry and told her that John had asked her to fill out papers for the archdiocese. Even though the Church had not notified Terry of the impending investigation, John had given their names as witnesses and the Church was asking her and her husband questions about Terry's marriage. Terry's friend had returned the questionnaires to the Church unanswered and explained that neither she nor her husband approved of the annulment and they would not participate in the investigation.

A short time later, another couple contacted Terry and explained that the archdiocese had asked them to be witnesses as well. Like Terry's other friends, they had refused to answer the Church's questions.

While the archdiocese continued to keep Terry in the dark, it nevertheless must have told John of his friends' unwillingness to cooperate. Soon John was on the phone trying to convince the couple to change their minds. Terry's friends held firm, however, explaining to John that they thought the annulment was wrong.

About this same time, Terry finally received official notification that her former husband was seeking an annulment. As had mine and those of most of the other women who had spoken to me about their annulments, the notice stated that the grounds were lack of due discretion at the time of the marriage. Terry also received a pamphlet similar to the one I had that described the annulment process and the rules that needed to be followed.

As she was reading the material, she noticed a stipulation that a priest who had listened to confession from either or both parties should not participate in an annulment investigation. Terry wondered how Father Francis could be involved, given the fact that he had listened to her confession, and she assumed, though she was not positive, John's as well. Terry phoned him with her concerns, concerns which he brushed off with the words, "Oh well, they don't care about that."

Terry answered the archdiocese's initial questions about her marriage with one statement in which she explained that she had married in good faith and in love and that she did not think there was any reason an annulment could be granted. Later the tribunal would claim that this explanation was her testimony.

A short time later, two of Terry's physicians, a general practitioner and a therapist whom she had seen when she had suffered her breakdown, phoned her. Apparently the archdiocese had sent both doctors a list of questions, some of a highly personal nature. While John had signed a release allowing the doctors to provide the information, his signature was irrelevant. Terry, not he, had been the patient. Her confidentiality, not her former husband's, was at stake and only she could authorize her doctors to provide the information. Even though both doctors knew and followed the laws covering doctor and patient confidentiality and refused the Church's request for information, the incident raises ethical questions.

When Terry called the archdiocese with her concerns, that spokesperson told her that there was nothing wrong with the request and that the Church routinely sent out such letters. Terry emphasized that she had not given permission for her doctors to release the information, permission that is required by law. The spokesperson held firm, saying only that there was nothing wrong with the practice and that it was routine policy.

Terry never learned who if anyone John finally persuaded to be witnesses. All she knows is that the two couples who had told her of the

Church's request for their views on the marriage refused to cooperate. When she called and asked the archdiocese who the consenting witnesses had been, she was told that in such cases the petitioner keeps sending them names until someone responds, but the spokesperson would say neither who had responded in her case nor when.

About two weeks before the final papers arrived, the tribunal wrote Terry and said that sufficient information to render a decision had been obtained and that if she had any additional evidence, she should present it at this time. As Terry recalled, "I gave up. I couldn't see that there was anything more I could do."

The Church notified Terry that it had granted John's request for the annulment. Although its original notification indicated that it planned to judge the case on the grounds of "lack of due discretion at the time of the marriage," the final declaration failed to indicate either if those were the grounds on which the case had been decided, or whose discretion if anyone's was found to be wanting.

Neither Terry nor John was restricted from entering another marriage. Thus, the Church must have assumed either that whatever had prevented them for having a true marriage had been "fixed" or that the defect that had affected each or both of them was only relative to the other and would not be of consequence in a subsequent marriage. For Terry, however, the grounds were irrelevant. The Church's ruling was devastating.

"It was a Saturday afternoon when the papers arrived," Terry remarked slowly. "I opened the envelope and believe me, it took me three hours to get myself to completely read through them. I can't describe the feeling I had. When they say that people have a broken heart, I always thought, oh well, that's just a saying. But a physical feeling went through my chest. A weight, a pain went through my entire body when I knew those papers were there. I have only felt like that twice in my life," she continued. "One time was when John was in the army. He was leaving and we thought he might be going to Vietnam. I was at the airport and when he went to get on the plane, I felt that pain. I remember it to this day, and that was almost thirty years ago.

"The other time," she recalled, "was when they were going to close the casket at my father's funeral. I went to put my hand on his arm. I knew I would never see him again and the loss was unbelievable. It was that same pain and it too went through my entire body. I felt such sorrow.

"When I finally got myself to read through those papers, that same pain was there. It was as if twenty-three years of my life had been erased. I had no accounting for them. They were never there as far as the Church was concerned. It was like taking a person and throwing them away. All I can say is it's just the ultimate deceit, the ultimate deceit, for someone to lie before God just so he can stand up in a tuxedo and marry a woman in a white dress in church. Was it worth throwing four people away? His children have not spoken to him in almost five years. Is it worth throwing his three children away? I can't imagine what he was thinking, and I can't imagine what Father Francis was thinking when he helped him. I can't believe he would help him do this. He knew my children since they were babies. It really is the ultimate deceit.

"For more than twenty years this man took my life and turned it upside down in the name of a church to which he purported to be so dedicated. I tried the very best I could to be a good wife. I loved him when I married him. I had every intention of staying married to him my entire life. What makes me so angry about this annulment is that the Church has let him put forth this lie and made what he did okay.

"I think the pope has lost total control over the Church in the United States. I don't know if he doesn't know what's going on or if he's turning his back on it. I regret not having fought harder, but I believed that no right-thinking panel of clergy would believe what my former husband had told them. I worry sometimes when I see what is going on in the Church today. It's different from when I grew up. Today parishes and schools in Chicago are being shut, not because they aren't needed, but because they don't bring in enough money, and huge new ones are being built in the more affluent suburbs. The emphasis used to be on helping people. Now it's on the bottom line.

"Yet I still feel that the Catholic Church is the church where I belong. I was brought up Catholic. I remember what I was taught as a child. I remember what I was taught in high school, and none of the things that happened to me or my children were based on church teachings. For me, God and religion are about a way of being. I really believe that God smiles upon the gentle, on those who mean no harm, people who help others, and those who are not always looking out for themselves or for ways to make money. The Church has betrayed me, but I look at it as members of the Church that have betrayed me, rather than the Church itself. I plan to remain active in the Church and so do my children. My son will be married in a Catholic service, but his father will not be there. Their father betrayed everything they were taught when he lied to get an annulment, but they will have worked the betrayal out for themselves."

While John does not think he betrayed anyone by receiving an annulment, he is deeply saddened by the fact that it has left him estranged from his children. "I have lost my children and every day I pray for a reconciliation," he explained. "Asking for an annulment was very hard for me and I never took it lightly. It required a great deal of soul-searching, but I thought it was the right thing to do. I had fallen in love with a wonderful woman who was Catholic and had never been married. If I hadn't been able to get an annulment, I think we would have let God be our judge. But I felt I had to apply and complete the process.

"I also think there was justification for an annulment. The Church never told us the grounds on which it decided the case, and I won't comment about Terry, but we were both twenty-one when we married. I had been in the seminary and then the army and there was the possibility that I would be sent to Vietnam. I knew Terry for three weeks when we became engaged and we were married four months later. Don't you think it's possible that I wasn't mature enough to be married?" John asked somewhat rhetorically.

John's reasons for wanting to be remarried in the Church are understandable and his concerns that the annulment may have forever severed his relationship with his children are valid. Patrick and Michael discussed their views on their parents' marriage and the annulment with me. "My mother, brother, and sister had become dependent upon me to maintain the house since I was thirteen or fourteen," Patrick began. "My father and I were never very close. By the time of the divorce he had virtually left my mother and three dependent children very vulnerable. I was, in high school, thinking that I might have to get a full-time job just to make sure that we could eat and have a place to live, but I was intent on going to college and I didn't want to give up that dream.

"I went with my mother to court to see her through the divorce. I felt responsible since I had pushed her to proceed with filing the divorce papers. He was seeing other women before he was divorced and continuing with his antics through the day the divorce was final. That day in the courtroom was something I will never forget. To see the ease with which the legal system can dissolve twenty-three years of marriage is quite astonishing.

"I helped my mother do what she had to do. On the train ride home from downtown Chicago," he continued, "I looked out the window at the Chicago Housing Authority housing projects and I felt secure that my mother had a house. I won a scholarship to college. My brother, sister, and I have good educations and solid careers and we did all of it without any help from my father. Every day that goes by, things happen that reassure me that what we did was the best thing.

"Even though the divorce was hard on my mother, the annulment was much more devastating. I tried to console her by assuring her that it could never go through. How could it?" he asked. "It was so ridiculous—a marriage that lasted more than twenty years and three children. And now none of this was supposed to exist. I was dead wrong. The annulment went through and I was left confused about how the Church worked. This was wrong. I was forced to go to religion classes and taught to believe that marriage was final. Marriage is supposed to be a one-shot deal, especially in the Church. Why is this no longer true?

"When I confronted my father about the annulment, he told me to seek counseling with a priest to understand that it wasn't that way anymore. I couldn't believe his rationalization for what he was doing," Patrick continued. "I told him that despite what he was going to do, God would know the truth. The truth is that they were married in front of God and had three children. Where is the dispute that this marriage ever existed? I cannot find any, although I may be biased as a product of the 'pseudo-marriage.' I told him that if he continued with the annulment I would consider him dead to me . . . I haven't spoken to him since . . . I don't intend to speak to him either. I don't feel angry or desire revenge. I just want to go on with my life without his interference."

Listening to Patrick, it is hard to believe that the Church views annulment as a process to help families heal. How different the story might have been had the Church helped Patrick's father confront the mistakes he made in his marriage rather than deny that he was ever married. Patrick is clear that he will be married in the Church and that he doesn't find fault with the sacrament or the religious beliefs for marriage even though he thinks that the sacrament has been diminished in the eyes of Catholics by annulment.

"I have always found," Patrick explained, "that I believe marriage to be a once-in-a-lifetime choice. Two different people choose to be together to share everything in life with the security that your partner will always be there for you without exception. I think a lot of people don't form the trust with their spouse that creates security . . . We all look for the what's-in-it-for-me. I think that is just the way we ultimately look at everything. The only what's-in-it-for-me that can survive in marriage is the knowledge that you can depend on your wife or husband . . . In addition to this trust, there must be respect. This respect has to be second only to the respect one pays to God.

"I still believe God is our ultimate judge. Matrimony is a sacrament. It has been designated as a sacrament to indicate its importance in our spiritual growth in the Church. Through this sacrament, we should become closer to God, much like all of the other six sacraments. Annulments contradict this dogma of the Catholic faith. Sacraments serve as milestones in our life in the Church. Annulment seeks to destroy these milestones and our faith in the Church as a source of spiritual guidance.

"If," Patrick continued, "the Church changes its stance on what is right and wrong when it is convenient or when money is involved, how is the Church like the Rock that Peter sought to create? I am not surprised by many of the controversies that engulf the Church presently. The Church does not stand on moral principles or the Scripture when it is not popular or convenient. Religion is supposed to be timeless and unswaying with respect to society, but the Church fluctuates much like the government does to popular opinion."

By the term "Church," Patrick explained that he means "the American hierarchy of the Catholic Faith." Like others who have been involved with annulments, he questions if "the Vatican and the Holy Father condone the Annulment of the Holy Sacrament of Matrimony."

Terry's younger son Michael shares his brother's view of their parents' annulment as well as a commitment to his faith. "I am very angry with my father for what he has done. He tries to explain that his new wife had never been married and he wanted her to have a Catholic wedding. My answer to that is that she ought to have married someone else. My father had his chance and he blew it.

"To me," Michael continued, "the Church created annulments simply to accommodate an important Catholic somewhere along the Church's history, one who had the money to persuade the Church to implement the policy. This does not tell me that the Catholic religion is bad, but that someone made a bad decision in the name of all Catholics. I do not choose to turn away from the Catholic religion and I do not choose to stop attending the Catholic church. Instead, I pray to God that He forgive my father for what he did to my mother and her family by annulling her marriage. This hurt me a great deal and I don't understand how it can be allowed.

"I suppose the only way I can solve this is to bear in mind that the true basis of faith is between the person and God, and God is always watching. If it is a sin to annul a marriage, then eventually the sinner will face the consequences. All I can do is continue to try to be a good Catholic and do what I know is right. I don't believe in annulment and I won't have a marriage annulled.

"I believe that what my father sought was a divorce, not an annulment. But since the Church does not grant divorce, he took what he could get, although I believe he lied to get it and that is wrong. If he believes that a true marriage never existed, then he went before God and lied at the altar. If he believes that it did exist, then he paid a lot of money to lie now. Either way, I believe he committed a sin. I am hurt by it, but I believe he will be hurt more."

Michael sees faith as a relationship to God rather than to the institution of the Church. Terry too sees a distinction between faith in the Church as an institution and faith in God and her Catholicism. While her faith in the institution has been shattered, her belief in God and in Catholicism has remained strong. As she so succinctly put it, "For me, God and religion are about a way of being."

Terry is working again in a local school, a job which she likes because it encourages her to continue learning and broaden her horizons while helping young people to do the same. She has been able to recapture the joys of life as well as her compassion and ability to reach out to others. Recently she helped Patrick plan his wedding.

As I left Terry's house for my flight back to Boston, I realized why her letter had stuck with me those many months. Part of the reason was her awareness that what had happened to her was part of a larger web of deceit that should be stopped. But there was much more than that. Terry's story showed me that the sheer power of Catholicism can still control the everyday life of a true believer much as it did the lives of Charles and Nicole in the 1600s.

Terry also showed me that the power of believing could be both supportive and undermining. Of course, I had encountered numerous examples of this duality in books, but Terry had lived these contradictions in a modern world. The power of her belief in the sanctity of marriage and God's grace helped her to raise three extraordinary children under very difficult circumstances. It also enabled her to come to John's aid when he needed her despite her feeling that he had betrayed her, and it was the power of her beliefs that enabled her to show compassion to Father Francis when he became ill.

On the other hand, Terry had been hurt by the power of her faith in the Church. Had she not believed so strongly in Catholicism and its teachings, she would not have been so shattered when her husband, Father Francis, and her church betrayed her. But even when betrayed, Terry refused to let the strength of those more powerful than she dictate her conscience. Rather, she held firm to her own belief in the sanctity of her marriage and the importance of telling the truth. It was these beliefs and her children, whose lives she saw as being God's supreme gift to a marriage He had blessed, which pulled her through the worst crisis in her life.

In my mind I kept hearing Terry's voice saying, "I wish I had fought harder." It was the same sentiment that I had heard from Deirdre, Barbara, and Darlene. I didn't know how any of them could have done more than they did, but I knew I should take their words to heart and do precisely that. Suddenly, I realized that my annulment wasn't about me at all. Rather, as Terry had written well over a year before, it was about an abuse of power and a perverse practice that needed to be revealed for what they were.

10

FATHER DOYLE

◁———▷

My conversations with Darlene, Terry, and their families heightened my anxiety about my own annulment. The spring, summer, and much of the fall of 1994 had passed without so much as a word from the tribunal. Despite the outward calm, the mere sound of the doorbell could set off a churning in my stomach. Subconsciously, I was anticipating another letter from the tribunal, similar to the one I had received the previous Easter.

I spent much of my time during these months searching for people and material to help prevent what I now feared was inevitable—a favorable ruling for Joe. I began by reviewing some of the letters I had previously received. Several were from a woman named Ida who lived in Oregon. Ida had been one of the first people to contact me, but at the time I hadn't really understood the implications of what she had written. Her typed letter listed case after case, each with a corresponding number. Across the top of the page and in red ink she had written by hand, "the Rota, the Rota."

At the time, I had no idea what "the Rota" meant and in fact I thought she was referring to the plumbing company. After reading *Scandal in the Assembly*, however, I understood she was referring to the Vatican court in Rome that rules on annulments. Still, I couldn't fathom what the Rota would have to do with my case. After all, my advocate had explained that only if the tribunal and the appeals court disagreed as to whether a marriage was valid was the case then sent to the Vatican.

Several months later, Ida sent me more material, including a clipping that told of a man from Boise, Idaho, who had the annulment of his marriage overturned by the Rota. Curious about how this had happened, I found Ida's phone number and called her. She told me that anyone could appeal to the Rota. She and the man from Boise had, and both their annulments were overturned.

When I asked Ida about the discrepancy between the tribunal's explanation of the appeal process and her own experience, as well as that of the man from Boise, she was adamant: the tribunal was wrong. I would need to be strong, this seventy-something fireball explained to me, but it was my obligation to defend my marriage, not just for me but also for my children. She and others would pray for me. I didn't know quite what to make of Ida. I certainly needed and welcomed all the prayers I could get, but I couldn't imagine how I would appeal my case to Rome.

Then an unexpected and unrelated church incident led me to the person who would alter the direction of my case. A former priest had been extradited from Minnesota to stand trial in Massachusetts for the purported sexual abuse of young boys. Even though as many as twenty years had passed since the alleged incidents, the victims' powerful testimonies were carried on the evening news. As I watched the report on television, I saw victim after victim, all now grown men, tell how their lives had been shattered by this man whom as children they had been taught to trust. As a mother of two boys who were roughly the same age as these men had been at the time they were abused, I found the stories all the more horrifying.

But it wasn't these men's pain that prevented me from changing the channel. Rather, it was their courage and my own growing awareness that as much as there were people both inside and outside the Church who denied that such a scandal could ever happen, there were also those who sought to bring the truth to light so that others would not suffer as these men had.

I became convinced that there must be people, even a network of people, involved with this case who had both the moral courage to say that what was alleged to have happened in fact did, and a knowledge of the law that enabled them to bring those responsible to justice. If I could find someone within that network who thought that the annulment process was also morally wrong, then perhaps we, too, could use the law to rid annulment of its pain and injustice.

As do many news stories that run for more than several days, this one began to generate its own unofficial version. Invariably, as people discussed the case among themselves, a lawyer's name surfaced. After a few calls to friends and some digging, I learned where he worked, phoned him, and asked if he would be willing to talk with me. He graciously agreed and a short time later I met him in his office in downtown Boston. He ushered me into a conference area and told me I could "speak freely." In case I missed the significance or perhaps the double meaning of what he had said, he added that not only would he hold in confidence whatever I told him, but that also he would not charge me for his work.

I suspect my relief was evident, and I began telling him about my case and what other women had told me about theirs. As fast as I could talk, I told him that the judge in my case had said that he would only allow me to have a copy of the transcript of my so-called hearing if I promised never to tell anyone what had happened in the room. I told him how the Church had tried to obtain women's medical records without their permission, and of Ida who had appealed her case to Rome.

He didn't seem surprised by what I had to say, and I sensed he had heard far worse. He simply explained that in America a church is given enormous latitude owing to our constitutional separation of church and state. A church can establish its own rules, and unless someone can prove it has violated a civil law, there is very little that can be done through civil procedures. What is more, even in cases such as child abuse, which is a clear violation of law, it can take years to bring the evidence to light.

For cases such as mine where the evidence is less conclusive, it would be even more difficult to work through a civil procedure. Nevertheless, he was not convinced that the annulment of my own marriage was a done deal. The Church, he explained, is supposed to follow its own laws and he knew someone who could help me work within their system. If I wanted, he would contact him. This man was a priest, had a doctorate in canon law, and had been an enormous help in cases of child abuse. He also lived in Florida.

I laughed when I heard where the priest lived. "That's probably good," I replied. I suspected that in some regards, the farther away he lived the better. I doubted that anyone in Boston would be willing to stick his neck out for me on this one. I told him that I'd very much appreciate the priest's help and thanked him for his. I left his office feeling better, but not knowing what to expect. A short time later, I received a letter from Father Doyle.

The short biography which Father Doyle enclosed with his letter offering his help not only indicated that he had a doctorate in canon law, but also that he had written more about religion than I had ever read. He had directed one of the Church's projects on marriage and subsequently edited *Marriage Studies,* the series which I had previously found helpful. He was also a licensed pilot with an instrument rating, a winner of an award for moral courage in government and business, a captain in the United States Air Force, a member of the Titanic Historical Society, and a member of numerous canon law societies.

I telephoned Father Doyle to explain the details of my case. He told me he sympathized with my situation and would be happy to give me advice, but that he would not be able to come to Boston or present my case before the tribunal. I told him that I understood these limitations and I reiterated how grateful and relieved I was to have his help. We agreed that I would call him again as soon as I'd heard from the tribunal.

Although I felt much better knowing I had Father Doyle to advise me, I became increasingly anxious that I had not heard from the tribunal. Then one crisp fall day a friend phoned and said only, "He's been sighted." My mind was not on the annulment at that moment, and I assumed she was referring to a red-tailed hawk that had been visiting a neighborhood park. "You saw him?" I responded. "Isn't he beautiful? Imagine a red-tailed hawk so close to the city."

My friend, however, wasn't interested in hawks. "Are you nuts?" she asked. "I'm not talking about birds." She continued, "I'm talking about Joe. He was sighted leaving the tribunal. He's up to something."

My stomach began churning and I replied, "Do you think they'd dare just give him the annulment without telling me? They said they'd get back to me, but that was almost nine months ago. People can have babies in less time than that. Even by their own rules, they're not finished with their process."

"What they do and what they're supposed to do aren't necessarily the same thing," my informer reminded me. "You'd better find out what's going on."

On November 11th, with my friend's advice and with Deirdre's then year-old warning to put everything in writing echoing in my mind, I wrote to my advocate. I told Father Lory that I hoped he had enjoyed a pleasant eight or so months and expressed some surprise that I hadn't heard from him. Then I didn't know what to write. I was ambivalent about how outspoken I should be about my case, particularly about my efforts in its defense. After careful thought, I decided it was best to be direct. After all, when this process was over, I didn't want anyone at the tribunal to be able to say "She never told us" or "If she had only said . . ."

I told Father Lory that the psychiatrist had sent me copies of the letters the tribunal had sent to him and that I was confused by the reference to me as the doctor's client. I had gone to great lengths to explain both orally and in writing that I had never had a professional relationship with the doctor in question.

I explained that I was miffed by what appeared to be a discrepancy between what the letters asked for and what the judge told me the tribunal wanted to learn about me. I pointed out that even after the judge had told me that the tribunal was not interested in a diagnosis, the letter asked for precisely that, and that even after the judge told me that no one was suggesting I was an addict, the tribunal asked if I had any problems of this nature.

Then I told Father Lory that during the past months I had been gathering information that I thought might help my own case and that I had also met with other people who had attempted, often unsuccessfully, to defend their own marriages. I even told him about some of the books I had been reading, including the pope's recently released book, *Crossing the Threshold of Hope.*

Next, I asked some general questions about how the tribunal defines mental illness. I asked how its members distinguish between physical and mental illness, noting that although the line between the two seems fuzzy, it appears that only mental illness constitutes grounds for annulment, and I asked him what the Church meant by "physical," "mental," "emotional," and "psychological."

Without revealing Ida's identity, I told Father Lory that I had read an appeal to the Sacred Roman Rota which had been written in 1984. The appeal, I explained, referred to "natural law" and said that the parties in an annulment must be given the possibility of defending their case—a right that consists of two elements: the right to argue and the right to be heard in court.

"I do not see," my letter continued, "how if I am never allowed to be in court when my case is presented and not allowed to read even your brief, not to mention that of the defender of the bond, that I have the right to defense."

Even though I had no idea how I would appeal, I thought that if Ida had done it, I, too, would find a way. So I told Father Lory that should the annulment be granted on the tribunal level, I planned to appeal to the Rota as did "this brave lady in the 1984 case."

Finally, I brought up the issue of the tribunal's timing. I explained that since providing them with the information they asked for was both emotionally difficult and time-consuming, I did not think I would be able to work with them effectively during the Thanksgiving and Christmas holiday season. Furthermore, I was sure that neither I nor the Church wanted the children upset during another religious holiday. "To be blunt," I wrote, "particularly since nothing has happened in seven months, I assume your time is somewhat flexible and you will be able to spare my family a repeat of Easter 1993." I ended my letter by thanking Father Lory for his support.

To his credit, Father Lory wrote me back within the week. He assured me that my case was still proceeding "just like many others." He answered my questions concerning the distinction between physical, mental, emotional, and psychological by giving a brief definition of each: "physical means the body, mental means the mind, emotional means the emotions or affective dimension, and psychological means the psyche." He then explained that as he was not a mental health professional he could not comment on my examples of mental or emotional or physical problems. Rather, he reiterated what he had told me before: that the tribunal does not do diagnoses nor is a marriage judged in the abstract.

While Father Lory's answers didn't shed any light on my questions, in retrospect I probably shouldn't have expected them to. I was looking for simple answers to complicated questions and there weren't any. Rather, as I thought more about what he had said, I saw how his brief responses illustrated portions of Professor Donahue's discussion of the annulment process that I had read earlier in the *Michigan Law Review*. Neither Father Lory nor the tribunal was going to be pinned down or even discuss in any depth questions about mental disorders.

Rather, both would claim to leave that to the professionals. Having also read both Wrenn's work entitled *Annulments* and *DSM-111-R*, however, I couldn't help but wonder about both the degree and the manner in which professionals would really be used in my case. For me, the enormous flexibility that Wrenn gave tribunals to use mental disorders as grounds for annulment was in itself cause for concern.

Father Lory concluded by telling me that he had informed the judge of my concerns about the calendar and by wishing me a happy Thanksgiving. I felt somewhat relieved by his letter. Even though he had ignored the issues I had raised about the tribunal's inquiry to the psychiatrist, at least the Church had not simply given Joe his annulment without my knowledge. Nor would the holidays be interrupted by another epistle from the tribunal. I breathed a sigh of relief.

But I was wrong. While Thanksgiving came and went without a hitch, on December 7th, Pearl Harbor Day, the tribunal dropped its holiday bomb. Father Lory wrote to ask me to make an appointment with a doctor affiliated with the tribunal, who worked about an hour north of Boston. The letter noted his name, address, and phone number. I was to contact him and make the necessary arrangements directly and then let Father Lory know if I was going to continue to cooperate with their investigation.

I was irritated at the tribunal's letter. Not only had I already explained to Father Lory that the holidays were a difficult time, but a highly respected psychiatrist had already answered their questions regarding my mental health. Yet even though I couldn't see what could possibly be gained by picking at old wounds during the Christmas season, I was reluctant to just say no to the tribunal.

I phoned Father Doyle for advice and told him that since I had already had a psychiatrist answer the tribunal's questions, I didn't see why I should go to another doctor. I also asked him if there were any value in having additional mental health professionals write to the tribunal on my behalf. Father Doyle told me that additional letters couldn't hurt and that particularly as a psychiatrist had already provided information to the tribunal, he thought that I was well within my rights to decline meeting with the tribunal's expert, and he added that it was probably in my best interest to do so. He cautioned, however, that as I was under no obligation to meet with its expert, neither was the tribunal required to accept the testimony of those I asked to write on my behalf.

Following Father Doyle's advice, I contacted a second psychiatrist and a psychologist who knew me. I explained that the tribunal was looking for evidence that I was incapable of marriage in 1979 and had asked me to meet with a doctor. The doctor, I continued, would talk with me for an hour or so and then make some kind of determination. Since I was suspicious of both the doctor and the process, I was hoping to avoid seeing the psychologist by having them write letters to the tribunal attesting to my mental and emotional stability, presuming of course that each thought I was in fact stable.

As was the case with every mental health expert I spoke with about this matter, my friends questioned if anyone could make assumptions about someone's state of mind based on a meeting that occurred sixteen years after the time under study, but both agreed to help with the understanding that as I wasn't a client, they could not give a formal evaluation. Both felt confident, however, based on what they had seen of me over a period of years, particularly those difficult ones when my marriage was failing and I was trying to adjust to the demands of being a single parent, that they could tell the tribunal that in their professional opinion I was balanced and capable of marriage.

Then the psychologist asked me in a matter-of-fact way for the name of the doctor affiliated with the tribunal. When I told her, she paused and then said, "That's odd. I have a manual here that lists all the licensed psychologists in the state and I don't see his name. I'll check when I get to the office and call you back. It might take a day or so."

I thanked her and as I hung up the phone, I thought how lucky I was to be able to talk to Father Doyle as well as to have friends in the mental health profession. I thought about how much harder it must have been for the people who endured their annulments alone.

I knew I had to answer Father Lory's letter, which I now referred to as the Pearl Harbor bomb, but I kept putting it off. I knew I should be honest and tell the tribunal that I was seeking additional outside help, but I didn't want to. I was afraid they'd intervene and sabotage my support although I didn't know how. I also knew that I should give them some response to their request that I see another doctor; but until I heard their reasons why they wanted me to, I didn't want to commit myself. I even cleaned the boys' closets and washed the dog to postpone the inevitable. Finally, I sat down and as I began to write, the words came slowly.

"I received your letter of December 7, 1994, which asked me to undergo an evaluation with a psychologist," I began. "While I'm sure your request was made in good faith, I cannot give you an answer at this time. As I tried to explain in my November letter, the Christmas holidays are extremely hectic for me as they are for most families and perhaps partially because I am a single parent, I often find them emotionally charged and tricky. It is important that I focus all of my energy on providing an enjoyable and meaningful Christmas for my children, something I cannot do if I am reliving the failures of my marriage or helping uncover evidence that in 1979 I was unfit to marry their father . . ."

Several days later, the psychologist who had written to the tribunal on my behalf phoned. She apologized for not having called me back sooner, but there had been the holidays and it had taken longer than she anticipated to find out why the tribunal's doctor had not been listed in her manual. The reason, however, was simple. He wasn't a psychologist, but a social worker. Then she asked me to read her the letter that the tribunal had sent asking me to contact him. Sure enough, the letter did not refer to him as a psychologist but as a "psychological consultant." He was a doctor only insofar as he held a doctorate, or Ph.D., in sociology.

"What," I asked, "is a psychological consultant?"

"Beats me," she answered.

"You know, the people at the tribunal may not have said he was a psychologist but they certainly led me to believe he was," I told her. "In all my letters to Father Lory, I referred to him as such and no one at the tribunal ever corrected me or clarified the situation. It's hard to imagine that they actually expect me to believe that a social worker, even one with clinical experience, could speak with me for an hour or so in 1995 and determine to a moral certainty whether I was fit to marry in 1979. How dumb do they think I am? Is he even qualified to make psychological evaluations, and are evaluations different from diagnoses?"

"I suspect they just never thought anyone would check," my friend answered. "I'm not sure what his qualifications are. I don't know what they mean by psychological consultant or the value of an evaluation completed by a consultant. Why don't you ask the tribunal?"

My friend then raised her primary concern about the way in which the tribunal used professionals. She explained that it wasn't so much the qualifications of a social worker versus those of a psychologist or even a psychiatrist—all three have qualifications to provide counseling to someone seeking it, and in some instances, the social worker might prove to be the most beneficial for the client. However, none of the three—social worker, psychologist, or psychiatrist—regardless of how qualified in their fields, could meet someone for an hour or so and determine much of anything about what a person's state of mind was like over a decade ago, much less their capacity for marriage. Professional qualifications are relevant only because the Church implies that there are psychological grounds to justify its actions and it is questionable if social workers are licensed to do professional psychological evaluations. "But," she concluded, "it's the process itself that isn't valid. It isn't medicine. It's a hoax, period."

I was working on my letter to the tribunal when I received one from them. On February 8th, the judge wrote to tell me that it appeared that all available testimony had been submitted. Therefore, a decree had been issued which granted both parties twenty-one working days to say whether or not either wanted to provide additional evidence. The judge also explained that there was a possibility of my viewing some of the evidence and if I wanted to do so, I must notify him within fifteen working days.

The letter then said that any review would be at the approval of the tribunal, "within the confines of Church law," and conducted in the tribunal office. The judge concluded by telling me that if they did not hear from me within their time frame, they would presume that I had no further evidence. He added that I would of course be informed of "additional developments" in my case.

Clearly, the tribunal had moved ahead without answering any of my questions about its "doctor." I presumed—correctly, I would later learn—that Joe had met with the doctor, and from the tribunal's perspective provided sufficient information. How I would have loved to have been a fly on the wall for that meeting!

I wrote the judge immediately and told him that I wanted to review the evidence and to provide additional information. I informed him of when I was going to be away with the children for their spring vacation and noted that I would not be available for Easter week either. I reminded him that I had already told the tribunal, in two letters, that I had additional information to present to the tribunal. Given the fact of these letters, I was surprised that he thought that "all the testimony available has been obtained."

Finally, I came to the main point of my letter—their doctor. Since I thought this might well be my last chance to raise these issues, I was direct. I explained that the judge must know that their doctor was not a psychologist. "What exactly is a 'psychological consultant'?" I asked. "What are his qualifications? Is he licensed? If so, as what? And in what capacity?

"I have been waiting, I thought, patiently and politely, for two months for answers. It appears, however, that the tribunal now plans to skip this evaluation. Am I correct? Please explain."

I wrote that since I was taking their study seriously, I hoped that I would be given the time and support necessary to respond to his inquiries appropriately. I concluded by thanking him for his consideration, and sent my letter by certified mail. Then I phoned Father Doyle.

As usual, Father Doyle's voice was very calming. He also had good advice. "Forget about Boston," he told me. "Go through their process as best you can; but remember, if they give Joe an annulment in Boston you can appeal to the Rota in Rome. It's that simple."

Father Doyle then explained that if the tribunal ruled favorably for

Joe, I need not wait for the Boston-based appeals court to make a decision. Instead, I could appeal directly to Rome as, in the words of canon law, "the court of second instance." Furthermore, even if I chose to follow through with the local appeals process and even if it, too, ruled in favor of Joe, I still had the right to appeal the decision to Rome.

The Rota in Rome—I could appeal to Rome. Ida had been right all along, and the tribunal had perhaps unintentionally misled me by saying that only in the event of a disagreement between the tribunal and the appeals court is a case sent to Rome. Neither Rome nor the Rota seemed far away anymore. "Forget about Boston—Rome, Rome, Rome." In fact, I said "Rome" so often that even our parrot, who hadn't learned a new word in at least a dozen years, began mumbling something that sounded like Rome.

It would be some time, however, before I would complete the process for the Boston tribunal. In early March, I received another letter from the judge. He told me that if I wanted to review selected materials from my case, a review he would permit only in the presence of my advocate, then I should contact his office and schedule an appointment. He explained that ecclesiastical law provided certain "safeguards" to ensure confidentiality, and he enclosed an agreement that I would be required to sign should I wish to pursue the review. Then he made it clear that if he did not hear from me within thirty days, the case would go forward to judgment.

He addressed the issues I had raised about the doctor by telling me to discuss them with my advocate, although I doubt he could have been unaware that I had tried repeatedly to do just that. He concluded his letter by telling me that I had had ample time to submit whatever evidence I wanted and that if I wanted to submit additional testimony, I must do so immediately. The case, he made clear, would proceed within the legal time frame.

The judge's implication that I was delaying his process infuriated me, but I remained calm. Rome, I kept saying to myself, Rome. I sat down and wrote the judge a peaceful letter, one that was devoid of anger. Then I called the tribunal to arrange for my review and followed up my call with a letter.

On March 10th, Father Lory wrote to confirm my appointment.

He also enclosed a map showing the tribunal's location and two additional sheets: the tribunal's "Testimony Review Policy" and its "Permission for Review" form. The Testimony Review Policy listed eight criteria. I had to meet these requirements in order to be allowed to read the documents the judge had selected for me to review. First, I had to make the request to the tribunal in writing within the time limit it had established. I had done that.

Second, before I would be allowed to begin my review, I would be required to sign a statement saying that I understood that the only reason I was being allowed to see the selected evidence was to enable me to present a better defense before the ecclesiastical court. I also had to agree that I would keep the information I "gleaned" from the review in strictest confidence and not use it for any other purpose than that intended in ecclesiastical law.

I found this second requirement contradictory. Virtually everyone familiar with tribunal proceedings who had been willing to talk with me openly had said that the public discussion my letter to *Time* had sparked had been my best defense. Without it, the tribunal most likely would have given Joe his annulment long ago.

Nevertheless, I didn't see that I had anything to lose by signing the tribunal's form. Based on what the judge had already told me, I was virtually certain that the only "evidence" he was going to allow me to see was Joe's testimony. The truth was, even without their requiring me to sign their form, I doubted I would have felt comfortable publicly discussing what Joe had testified. I wasn't ready to talk about the sordid details that invariably encompass any failed marriage, ours included.

Joe might have convinced himself that our marriage had never been sacred, but he hadn't convinced me. Unless and until the Church annulled it, I would continue to treat our marriage accordingly. I signed the tribunal's form and filed it so that I would know where to find it when I went to their office.

The third requirement was to make an appointment for the party to come to the tribunal. I had done that.

The fourth was that the tribunal would stipulate what portion of the testimony I would be allowed to review. Under no circumstances would I be allowed to review the testimony of a witness who requested confidentiality. Even though I could find no specific reference limiting my review in the material the tribunal had sent, the judge had already suggested that I would only be allowed to review Joe's testimony.

The fifth requirement was that I provide "photographic proof" of my identity when I arrived for my appointment. No problem: I had a driver's license and I'd have it with me anyway.

The sixth criterion was that a member of the tribunal staff would be present while I conducted my review. I assumed this would be Father Lory.

The seventh requirement was that my review had to be completed at one sitting. I would not be allowed subsequent or repeated reviews of the same testimony. I looked at my calendar and crossed off the morning and half the afternoon of March 28th. That should be ample time, I was sure.

The final stipulation explained that although I would be permitted to take notes, I would not be permitted to copy any of the testimony. I had assumed such a restriction.

That was it. I filed the tribunal's Testimony Review Policy with the form I had signed promising to keep whatever I reviewed confidential.

I was ready. The boys and I would enjoy spring break, and when we returned I would again face the tribunal.

11

THE ROAD TO ROME

◆━━━◆

I t was a little before ten on March 28th when I arrived at the tribunal to review Joe's testimony. The tribunal was crowded that morning, although I never learned why. The receptionist greeted me warmly, ushered me into a small office, and told me that Father Lory would be with me shortly.

I couldn't help but notice how quickly we made our way through the waiting room and into the office. It was as if she were afraid to leave me on my own where I might talk with some of the other women who were waiting. I felt a bit as if I were a leper, sure to infect people with my ideas. I didn't know whether to feel grateful for the privacy or angry at my isolation.

Father Lory arrived a short time later. I told him that I had brought a copy of the boys' baby picture that Joe had put in a silver frame and given me for Christmas shortly after their birth. It was the same photograph I had shown Father Lory almost two years earlier. Now I explained to him that I thought the picture itself was as significant as the engraving in Joe's handwriting.

He then handed me Joe's testimony. When I asked him if I could take notes, he suggested that we discuss any points I thought needed clarification and that he would summarize what I said in writing.

190

What he wrote would later be submitted to the judge as my response to Joe's testimony. I told Father Lory that while I had no objection to his taking notes, I nevertheless wanted time to think about my comments and to type them myself before I submitted them as my formal response to Joe's sworn statement.

Father Lory agreed to my request and since he was not prepared to give me a copy of his notes to take home, he allowed me to take my own, adding that he was concerned that I not spend too much time on my rebuttal. I thanked him for his concern and assured him that my time wasn't that important.

Because I signed the tribunal's form promising to keep Joe's testimony confidential as a condition of being allowed to read it, I will continue to honor that agreement. Suffice it to say, I disagreed with virtually everything Joe said. Father Lory and I discussed these disagreements for well over an hour in what was a cordial meeting.

After we discussed Joe's testimony, Father Lory no longer took notes and our conversation became more general. I mentioned that one of the things bothering me was that annulments discouraged people from accepting responsibility for their actions. The Church says no one is to blame and that the marriage itself never existed rather than admitting that people made mistakes and the marriage failed.

I gathered from what Father Lory had told me that this investigation was no longer focused on my psychological fitness, but rather on proving Joe's lack of due discretion. This change, however, did not make me feel better. To me, neither of us suffered from a lack of due discretion at the time of our marriage. Rather, we both entered into it fully aware, capable, and intent on having it last a lifetime. Nor did either of us suffer from psychic incapacity. For a number of years the marriage had worked. It had survived numerous tests, and it had produced twin sons in an atmosphere full of joy, caring, and Christian love.

Then priorities changed, but they changed not because of fate or God or an invalid marriage, but because at least one of us freely chose a different path with a different set of values, and the other either could not or would not follow. Whatever mistakes were made, we made them.

Father Lory listened to me and said that other people would have made different choices. He noted that some would have even left Congress if that's what it took to save a marriage.

I conceded that might be true, but then added that just because some people might quit a job to save a marriage didn't mean that someone who wouldn't or didn't make the decision to quit wasn't capable of doing so. Unless there was legitimate proof of psychological incapacity, it must be presumed that a person who failed to take action to save a marriage was capable of doing so but didn't want to. No one ties such a person down. No one forces them to stay at the job. Rather, they make the choice of their own free will. Further, their making such a choice doesn't necessarily mean that they were never married.

Father Lory did not answer my objections directly. Rather, he repeated his implication that it was Joe's rather than my lack of due discretion that had become the focus of the tribunal's inquiry. Even though the intent of these comments might have been to appease me, they in fact made me suspicious. Virtually every woman who had discussed her annulment with me had been told something similar by the tribunal at some time during the process. The patterns were similar: the former husband applied for an annulment; the tribunal sought to uncover personal information about the former wife, sometimes in an ethically questionable manner; the investigation then focused on the former husband. The annulment was usually granted, and if so, the former wife was almost always told that the grounds were her former husband's lack of due discretion.

Even in cases such as Barbara Zimmerman's, where the former husband was told that other factors were the basis for the decision, the tribunal led the former wife to believe that the grounds were her husband's shortcomings. Perhaps the tribunal thought that citing such grounds as a basis for their decision would be easier on the former wife. The tribunal would give the petitioner his annulment, but tell the former wife it was because of his defect, not hers. In a way, the tribunal was "splitting the difference," or reaching a solution to an impasse which was meant to make both parties feel as if they won something, or at least hadn't lost everything.

Neither the other former wives nor I considered such rulings reasonable. For starters, I never claimed that our marriage had failed merely because of choices Joe had made. I made choices, too, choices for which only I could and should be held responsible. I asked Father Lory if what he was really saying was that anyone in politics or any demanding job could always get an annulment. After all, it seemed that the only important criterion was that they be divorced.

Father Lory answered that maybe they shouldn't have married. I found his answer ironic and pointed out that the Church not only allowed but encouraged such people to marry, not just once but a second time and sometimes even repeatedly. It was the Church, I noted, that ruled that the previous marriage had never existed and blessed the new one.

Wouldn't it be easier, I asked, and definitely less hypocritical, particularly for long-term marriages that brought children into the world, if the Church just said, "Look, folks, you get one crack at a sanctified marriage. If you blow it, you blow it. But if you face up to your mistakes and straighten out, we'll recognize your new marriage as valid. After a while, once you've shown us that you've really straightened out, we'll let you go to confession and take communion.

"In short, we'll forgive you. We'll welcome you back. We'll recognize your new marriage as valid, but we won't say your first marriage never existed. Nor will we accept divorce and because we won't, we will draw a distinction between valid marriages and those which are both valid and sacramental. Because you were married before, we will regard your new marriage as valid but not sacramental."

I asked Father Lory if the Church didn't already recognize a distinction between sacramental and valid marriages. I pointed out that I have plenty of Catholic friends who have Jewish spouses and vice versa. Their marriages are valid but not sacramental, the Catholic spouse may participate in the sacraments, and everyone seems happy enough with the arrangement.

Father Lory conceded that the Church makes a distinction between sacramental and valid marriages when at least one of the parties has not been baptized as a Christian. He also noted that the Orthodox Church essentially handles the remarriage of its members as I had suggested the Roman Catholic Church might, but he added that the Roman Catholic Church has different rules.

I sensed that I had pressed Father Lory about as far as I could or

wanted to. He was, after all, a Catholic priest and even though I
sensed that he wouldn't mind if the Church changed its policy
toward remarriage among its divorced members, I wasn't going to put
him on the spot by asking.

I told him that it would take me a week or so to complete my rebuttal to Joe's testimony and he said that would be fine. I thanked
him for his help and as I left his office, we wished each other well. I
had no ax to grind with Father Lory. Rather, I would do exactly as
Father Doyle told me: I would go through the process in Boston as
best I could and I would be ready to appeal to Rome should the tribunal here grant Joe his annulment. "Rome, Rome," I said to myself
as I walked to my car.

Responding to Joe's testimony was one of the last formal tasks I
was to complete for the Boston tribunal and in some respects it was
the most difficult. I found myself defending not only myself but also
my family from outrageous fabrications about my upbringing and
character. Even though I had told Father Lory that I thought I could
complete the job in a week, I spent well over two weeks thinking,
writing, and redrafting. In addition to countering Joe's charges, I
needed to address certain issues regarding his witnesses.

Although the judge had forbid me to read any of the witnesses' testimonies, he had allowed Father Lory to reveal their identities. One
was a family member who had recently issued a public statement that
he himself had sought professional treatment for alcohol abuse.
While I made it clear that I applauded his decision to confront his
problem and seek professional help, I questioned if he was a reliable
witness at the time he testified, particularly considering the sensitivity of the questions he was asked.

Joe's second witness was one of his childhood friends who had for-
merly worked as a member of his staff and was now a lobbyist on
Capitol Hill. I explained the obvious conflict of interest inherent in
this arrangement. While lobbyists' giving gifts to congressmen was a
well-established and now regulated practice, help with procuring an
annulment did not officially qualify as a gift. But what greater gift
could anyone give Joe, I asked, than help with his annulment?

The third witness constituted a greater conflict of interest and
even perhaps violations of both civil and canon law. He was our civil

attorney and had assisted both Joe and me as a couple and individually prior to, during, and subsequent to the divorce. His work had covered a wide range of issues, including the divorce and even provision for the children in the event of one of our deaths. I had first learned that he had testified not from Father Lory but from the lawyer himself almost two years earlier. At the time, I had told him that I objected to his serving as a witness and I had told the tribunal this as well. Now I reiterated my objections in a formal statement to the tribunal.

Finally, there was the issue of the tribunal's "doctor." No one had yet explained to me how a social worker, even one with clinical experience, could determine to a moral certainty whether either Joe or I was capable of marriage in 1979 based on a meeting in 1995. Nor had anyone defined the tribunal's term "psychological consultant," answered my questions concerning his abilities to perform a psychological evaluation, or explained if and how an evaluation differs from a diagnosis. I told the tribunal that I was now formally objecting to their "doctor's" medical credentials and to his qualifications.

My response to Joe's testimony ran about three thousand words. Before sending it back to the tribunal, I wanted Father Doyle to read it and suggest changes that might improve it. I sent the draft to him in Florida and while I waited for his comments, I prepared the last piece of evidence I wanted to present. Lest anyone at the tribunal again imply that either of us was less than joyful at the time of our marriage, the wedding pictures would set them straight.

It was hard for me to look at these pictures, and my eyes welled more than once before I finished. Particularly moving was a photograph of Joe and me inside the church at the altar with his family's priest. Here we stood saying our vows before family and friends in a ceremony that Joe now claimed had no religious significance. Both of us looked younger and I looked considerably thinner as well. More to the point, we both looked happy, full of hope and love. How dare he or anyone else suggest otherwise? I had the pictures copied and set them aside to include with my soon-to-be-finished statement.

There was one final question I needed to answer, not for the tribunal but for myself. It was the same question Joe had asked me over the phone almost two years earlier. Chris Wallace had explored the issue during our interview and many of Joe's friends, usually in an attempt to win me over, had asked it: Why did I care so much? Why did it matter? Why couldn't I just go along with the annulment? After all, I wasn't Catholic.

As I thought about the question, I realized that even though my reasons for opposing the annulment had remained constant during the two years that I had been defending my marriage, the factors influencing my thinking had broadened. I was still, as I had told Joe, concerned for the boys, but not for their legitimacy. I had always known the boys' legitimacy was protected by American law. I was still concerned that the children know that their birth was the result of great love, commitment, true happiness, and a Christian marriage rather than a nonexistent union. They should never have to question that their lives brought immeasurable joy to both of their parents, and neither their father nor his church would ever be able to convince me otherwise.

But there were other reasons I had to fight Joe's request for annulment. In her book *The Critical Years,* Professor Sharon Parks discusses how a person's faith evolves as he matures but retains its essential purpose of giving life its meaning. In her introduction, she recounts a conversation between two professors talking at a gathering of faculty and students initiating the new academic year. In the course of their talk, one asked the other a hypothetical and thought-provoking question: What do you think would be the worst thing that could ever happen to your son?

The second professor thought for a moment. For him this academic year was different from others. This year his son had left home for his first year of college. He was on his own for the first time in his life and his father was aware of both the opportunities and the pitfalls that life might throw his way.

The father paused and then answered that the worst tragedy that could befall his son would be for his life to lose its sense of meaning. As I read the professor's response I thought how true, but also how mind-bogglingly simple and also complicated. How in today's world does a child gain a sense of meaning, a sense of sacredness that can evolve as he matures and yet last a lifetime? How can a parent guide and encourage such development in his child? Can society and the community in general be partners in this effort?

In less complicated times, even in the world in which I grew up, the terms "meaning" and "sacred" had religious connotations. Indeed, while it may have been our parents' responsibility to take us to church, it was primarily the Church itself that instilled "meaning" in our young minds and taught us that some things are sacred. Yet while religion may have been the primary vehicle to teach us to distinguish right from wrong, moral development was also reinforced by the larger community.

Most educational institutions were not afraid to speak of morals, and indeed some institutions of higher learning proudly traced their origins back to religion. By and large, our parents and we as children trusted the institutions and individuals that were so much a part of our lives: government, business, the health profession, law enforcement, and our churches. For most who worked hard and followed the rules, job security in the growth period that followed the Second World War was almost a given, and if a person should lose his job, society provided a safety net to help the family through the hard times.

Today, many of my generation bemoan the loss of community as we knew it. The school, the church, the neighbors, the family doctor, the police, banks, and stores all contributed to a physical environment that many felt a part of. Indeed, while many of us complained about it at the time, most of us experienced a sense of belonging to the community in which we lived.

Granted, for many in my generation much of that world has either fallen apart or changed dramatically. For most of us life is now more complicated and answers far harder to come by than when we were young.

Yet despite our own doubts, many of us who have become parents hope that our children will somehow be spared the uncertainty that we have endured. Like the professor, we hope our children's lives will always have meaning. But if we found the world we inherited confusing, what about the one in which we are raising our children? Where will they find meaning? What and whom will they be able to trust? It was in fact one of my children who best described the differences between the world in which I grew up and the one in which he and his brother will come of age.

Not unlike most young boys who play football, or as it turned out most of America, my children closely followed the Simpson case. He

had been one of their heroes. At the beginning of the trial they like
many others were convinced of his innocence. "Of course he didn't
do it, Mom. He's 'The Juice.'" As one completely ignorant of football, the significance of "The Juice" eluded me, yet I could tell by the
tone of my children's voices that "The Juice" had an almost sacred
meaning. As the case progressed, I was careful to let the children talk
of it on their own terms. I never asked if they thought "The Juice"
was innocent or guilty. Nor did they reveal their thoughts on the
matter to me.

Rather, after the verdict, one of my sons said, "Mom, the trouble is
no one could trust anyone. People who were married didn't trust each
other. People couldn't trust the police. How could anyone tell who
was telling the truth? We weren't on the jury. We didn't hear all the
facts and we didn't grow up black in L.A. either. Without trust nothing works. Everything just broke down."

My son had rendered me silent. For a moment I thought he must
be repeating something he had heard elsewhere, but there was too
much feeling in his voice. While I was in awe of his ability at age
fourteen to grasp the importance of truth and trust, I was also fearful
for his future. Did he see a forever racially divided America where it
was a given that some groups had more reason to trust than others?
Whom or what did he think he could trust? Did he think he could
trust me? Did his valid skepticism about the judicial system pervade
his own beliefs about the world in general? Was I doing all I could to
ensure that his life would have meaning and trust? Would it be
enough?

For many of us, religion provides a basis from which meaning and
trust can grow, a trust lacking in the world of business, politics, and
our consumer-oriented culture. The renewed thirst that many Americans have for spiritual guidance, meaning, and trust in their lives
makes the Church's annulment practices even more tragic. Just when
Americans seem more open to religious guidance, the Catholic
Church seems unwilling to respond to their needs.

As Barbara Zimmerman's son Stephen explained, the people who
dismiss the significance of the religious right miss the point. The
point is that people need spiritual guidance and the mainstream
churches have abdicated their responsibility to provide it. The re-

ligious right has moved into the vacuum. So have the Pentecostals, whose expanding membership, coming largely from disillusioned Catholics, has made it the fastest-growing faction in the Christian world.

Stephen's point is well taken. How can I encourage my own child who clearly understands the importance of truth and trust on both the individual and community level to believe in an institution that creates a dishonest process to declare marriages invalid?

I cannot. As Deirdre's mother told her long ago in Ireland, it is a mother's responsibility to provide moral education for her children. If I wanted my children to learn the importance of truth and develop their own sense of trust, then it was paramount that I show them by example that I had the strength to stand up for principles that I felt were sacred—even if it meant publicly disagreeing with a powerful institution and their father.

If my children saw that lying before God about their conception and birth was not only unacceptable for me but that I cared enough to do something about it, then I could hope that as adults they, too, would understand the importance of living a life based on truth. Despite the complexity and contradictions in the world they would inherit, they would know how to trust, how to determine right from wrong, and the value of truth. In short, they would have the tools to develop lives with meaning. To me, that reason alone was enough to justify opposing an annulment.

Much of my opposition came down to lying. The lying inherent in the annulment process hit me on many levels. I would not, as I told Chris Wallace, "lie before God." In her book *Lying,* Sissela Bok notes that many of the great religious writers have taken strong stands against the practice. In fact, Professor Bok begins her introduction with words from Saint Augustine: "When regard for truth has been broken down or even slightly weakened, all things will remain doubtful."

Saint Augustine lived from 354 to 430 and is thought by many Catholics as well as Protestants to be the founder of Christian theology. He defined lying as saying something contrary to what was in one's heart with the intent to deceive another. Saint Augustine believed that God gave man the ability to speak so that he could communicate with his fellow man, not deceive him. To him, lying was contrary to the purpose of the God-given ability to speak and was therefore a sin. Yet even though all lies were sins, Saint Augustine thought there were degrees of lies and he divided them into eight categories, the least offensive being those which hurt no one but saved another from physical harm and the worst being lies spoken in the name of religion.

Augustine's prohibition against all lying constituted a moral high ground, but it was hard for most people to live up to it. After eight hundred years, another great thinker, who was to become one of the principal saints of the Catholic Church, dealt with the thorny issue of lying. Using Augustine's ranking of various types of lies as a basis, Thomas Aquinas developed a new three-tier hierarchy for lies, a hierarchy the Church still uses today. Helpful lies are the least serious, lies told in jest are in a middle category, and malicious lies are the worst. While all lies remain sins, only lies told to harm someone are mortal sins.

With Aquinas's tier as its guide, the pardoning of the more minor sins became a principal function for the Church and raised new questions. Was it acceptable to tell lies and then be pardoned? Could the liar do so repeatedly and even perhaps plan his lies with the knowledge or hope of a pardon?

The issue of lying and the question of whether, when, and how it is acceptable has continued to be debated, and not only by theologians and philosophers. As Professor Bok explains, virtually all professions struggle with the question of what constitutes not just legal but also ethical misbehavior. She notes further that in 1978 when she first published her book, there was far less public discussion of lying and its implications than in 1989 when she published a second edition. Americans, it seems, have a renewed and growing interest in ethics, no doubt due in part to our increasing lack of trust in our institutions and in one another.

While the renewed interest in moral and ethical behavior grows, it is noteworthy that despite the hundreds of years that the issue of lying has been debated, at least one theme has remained constant. Since the days of Saint Augustine, the worst lies have been those associated with religion or those committed in God's name.

Somehow even when I received the archdiocese's letter in 1993, I knew this to be true, but now I understood why. I was being asked to lie in the name of religion. It did not matter if I were Catholic or Protestant; after all, even though at the time I had no specific knowledge of Saint Augustine's writings, my religious training had grown from his theological root. I wondered even then how the Church could justify its actions. I wondered what Joe told himself and our children.

Had annulment proponents convinced themselves that the annulment process was honest? Did they see annulment as an acceptable lie that helped those who wished to remarry and hurt no one? Were they really oblivious to the harm the lie of annulment brought to families and former spouses who believed the marriage to be valid? Or was the whole process acceptable because after it was over, everyone could go to confession and be forgiven for their lies?

I knew I would never know the answers to these questions. But I could find no justification for myself to lie. In fact, I saw annulment as the worst kind of lie and I saw it as one from which, if I went along, I would never recover. Lying takes its toll not only on those the lie deceives but also on its perpetrator. The liar gives up a piece of himself, a piece of what it means to be human, a piece of his soul.

Divorce is hard. The children and I had lost a lot when we moved out of their father's house. But for all that the divorce had cost, I had never denied what I believed to be true and because I had not, I had a seed from which to rebuild my life and my family, a process that was well under way at the time of that fateful Easter dinner.

Still, I knew there was more at stake with annulment. This I had learned from the women who had told me of their journeys. On one level, there was the issue of the women themselves and what gave meaning to their lives. It was a hard concept to explain, especially to men, at least most of the ones I knew. I ended up relying on an analogy with which I thought men would more readily identify—the importance of a career.

Imagine for a moment, I told one of Joe's ambassadors who was doing his best to coax me into submission, that Congress passed a law that changed the way votes are counted in presidential elections. Assume for a moment that these ways of counting, if valid in 1960, would have given Nixon the small percentage he needed to win the election.

Now Congress makes this law retroactive and annuls Kennedy's presidency. What's worse, anyone with any sense knows the way these people are counting the votes may not be honest, but those who count are not accountable to anyone, so the tally stands unquestioned. The annulment does not alter the legal ramifications of the Kennedy presidency. Congress doesn't take away any pensions, health insurance, or other benefits that his family may have gained from his years of service. The Nuclear Test Ban Treaty remains valid. It's just that he was never president as we now view the presidency. He just thought he was.

Joe's ambassador points out the obvious: that Kennedy gave his life for his country and the presidency. It would be unthinkable to take it away. Precisely, I answered. I doubt the Kennedys would go along with it. I doubt Joe would accept anyone's saying his father only thought he was attorney general either. But that is what annulment does. These women gave their lives to marriage and motherhood with no less dedication than Joe's uncle gave his to the presidency, and without getting Air Force One, marching bands, or the White House in the bargain. Even though men would never be expected to remain silent while an institution erased what they had done with their lives, that is exactly what the Church and others expected of these women.

Annulment, in fact, hits a deeper level of the soul by calling into question the essence of what it means to be human. Humans are the only species that has the ability and responsibility to seek truth and to determine right from wrong. As I thought about this, a television program that I had watched a year or so ago kept coming to mind. The show was about Henry VIII, and I remembered that at the time it had seemed fitting that as annulment sought to prove that a marriage never happened, what was perhaps history's most famous annulment never happened either. Now after my own experiences with annulment, it seemed even more appropriate that this four-hundred-year-old true story should illustrate both the meaning and the timelessness of humanity so well.

In 1501, Catherine of Aragon, the daughter of King Ferdinand and Queen Isabella of Spain, was betrothed to Arthur, eldest son of King

Henry VII of England. Arthur died in 1502 at age sixteen and it was agreed that Catherine would marry his younger brother, also named Henry. The elder Henry, however, kept delaying his son's marriage because he was having difficulties getting along with Catherine's relatives, who were some of the most powerful people in Europe. It was not until 1509, after the king's death and a papal dispensation waiving a church law that would have prevented Henry from marrying his brother's widow, that the marriage took place. Henry became king and Catherine his queen.

Most historians are not kind to Henry VIII. He is usually depicted as an obese man who chased women and ordered that his wives be beheaded. But in recent years, *Masterpiece Theatre* took issue with this depiction. In its well-received made-for-television series *The Six Wives of Henry VIII*, Henry, at least in his younger years, was an attractive, religious, and learned man, committed to the arts, his people, and England. He is also shown to be deeply in love with Catherine, whose intellect matched his own. She helped him rule England and bore him six children, although only their daughter Mary survived infancy.

But then trouble started. Henry became obsessed with having a son and a male heir. He began to question if maybe there wasn't something immoral or illegal about his marriage, and if God was punishing him by taking his children. Assurances that the papal dispensation would have taken care of such problems, if in fact there were any, did nothing to calm his anxiety. Nor were his anxieties solely a matter of conscience. He had become infatuated with a younger woman whom he wanted to make his wife.

Henry saw a solution to his problem. He reasoned that there was a possibility that the pope should not have granted the dispensation and that his marriage to Catherine was therefore invalid. So he would ask the pope to annul his marriage and once this was done, he would marry the other woman. The only hitch was that Catherine refused to agree that she was not his lawful wife.

At first, Henry offered her enticements to change her mind. She could live wherever she wanted and in the style to which she had become accustomed. Their daughter Mary would still be regarded as his legitimate heir. Or, if she preferred, since church law would permit Henry to take another wife were Catherine to answer God's calling and enter a convent, she could choose the religious path. But Catherine would not budge and Henry decided to try the case before an English court.

Catherine, however, declared that an English court had no jurisdiction over her marriage and demanded that the case be tried in Rome. Yet Henry proceeded, and not surprisingly his court found his first marriage invalid. The other woman, then pregnant, became his bride and turmoil took over England.

The pope recalled the case to Rome, essentially nullifying any action taken by Henry's court. Henry decided to play hardball. Catherine was shipped off to inferior lodgings and her household staff and budget were cut severely. Most painful, her daughter, whom Henry declared illegitimate, was taken from her. Still Catherine held firm. Finally, in 1534 the pope condemned Henry's second marriage and declared Catherine the king's lawful wife. Chaos ensued as Henry broke from the Catholic Church. Monks were tortured. Monasteries were burned. Many prominent leaders who sided with Catherine were sent to prison and some, including Sir Thomas More, one of the finest thinkers of the day and author of the famed work *Utopia*, were beheaded.

In *Masterpiece Theatre*'s dramatic conclusion, Catherine was on her deathbed and aware of the suffering her tough stance had brought to those she loved. Slowly she asked her friend, the Spanish ambassador, if what she had done was wrong. "No," he assured her, "you followed your conscience when no one else did."

"Conscience and love," Catherine added, "and that can't be wrong, can it? Can it?"

"Never, never," he told the dying woman.

Seconds after Catherine's passing, her lady-in-waiting stepped from her mistress's deathbed to confirm what the ambassador had said. "Was she wrong?" she, too, asked.

The ambassador sighed and answered that when Catherine came to England her ship encountered storms and was nearly lost. "When a storm strikes," he explained, "it sometimes happens that everyone on board runs about from side to side trying to save themselves. There is no hand at the wheel. The ship yaws to and fro with every gust and every wave. And then some hand more determined than the

others grips the wheel and turns the ship into the wind and holds it
there. Perhaps this course drives it upon the rocks. But though the
ship may be broke, some fragments of it remain."

"Our queen," he continued, "when danger threatened, turned her
ship's head into the wind and held it upon the only course she knew,
the course of truth. It struck upon the rocks of passion and circum-
stance and all aboard perished: herself, the king she loved, her
friends, the other woman, the Church, even Spain, perhaps all perished. But they did not disappear without a trace as they might otherwise have done. Some spars and timbers of that ship remained to
show . . ."

"To show?" inquired the lady-in-waiting.

". . . that there were human beings there and that they cared profoundly about the terms on which they lived and died. Europe sun-
dered. A kingdom nearly plunged into revolution. The power of the
Catholic Church weakened forever. And yet it was such a little thing.
She wouldn't say that she wasn't married when she was. She would
not say it."

The image of this brave woman standing up for principle and truth
and prevailing against those far more powerful than she is very appealing. Such an image, however, does not tell the complete story,
and to its credit *Masterpiece Theatre* was quick to explain that the
pope's decision was not just high-minded.

Henry began annulment proceedings in 1527 and it was not until
1534 that the pope made his final decree. It did not take the pope
seven years to interpret canon law. Rather, he was waiting to see what
happened on the battlefields. As long as France, with or without England, was equal to or stronger than the Holy Roman Empire, the pope
was willing to let Henry have his way.

Only when the Holy Roman Empire, which included Spain and
was led by Charles V, defeated the French did the pope's tolerance
for Henry wane. Charles V was not only Europe's most militarily
powerful Catholic, but also Catherine's nephew. It was too risky even
for a pope to provoke him. If he had to choose between the two leaders, it was better to offend Henry than Charles. The pope denied
Henry his divorce. Henry broke with Rome, and the Church remains
divided to this day.

While the political and historical ramifications of Henry and Catherine's story are self-evident, the moral and social implications inherent in annulment are equally significant. Having to grapple with what is true is what makes us people and distinguishes us from animals. Man alone has the ability and the responsibility to discuss and distinguish truth from falsehood. How an individual views and lives truth affects more than his own life. It affects the community and the larger society in which he resides.

Truth and the trust which evolves from it endure. They give meaning to our lives and they enable us to function as human beings and in communities both large and small. What we tell one another and our children about truth and what we show them by our actions are an awesome responsibility, but one which by virtue of our humanity we must accept.

For these reasons I cared about the annulment.

I was still thinking about the ramifications of annulment when I received a letter from Father Doyle. While he thought my testimony addressed the points I wanted to make, he suggested that I add two additional points and then have it notarized, preferably by a priest, before submitting it to the tribunal.

First, he suggested that I address the issue of the medical expert a little differently than I had. While I had asked the tribunal to clarify the qualifications of its "doctor," Father Doyle suggested that I specifically request that the case be submitted to a medical expert in the event that the tribunal had not already planned to do so. He also suggested that I ask the tribunal to inform me of both the identity and the qualifications of this expert. Father Doyle explained that my request for a medical review by an expert whose identity and qualifications were known would strengthen my case in an appeal more than if I merely implied that the "doctor" the tribunal wanted me to see was unqualified to make psychological evaluations.

He also suggested that I notify the tribunal that I would like to review the brief that my advocate was to prepare on my case. Then he gave me the name of a fellow priest at the seminary near the tribunal who he thought would be willing to notarize my statement. After adding Father Doyle's suggestions to my statement, I called his friend and we arranged to meet the following Friday.

When I arrived at the seminary, however, I found that no one would open the door or even speak to me. I was sure that the word must be out on me or that I was in the wrong place. I was about to give up and head home when Father Doyle's colleague arrived. He explained that the reason for the locked doors and the silence was that it was Good Friday, a day when the seminary along with the tribunal and many church offices are closed and seminary residents take a vow of silence. While it was okay for the two of us to speak to each other, residents were not going to say casual hellos as we passed, so I should not be offended by their silence.

I was grateful for both his explanation and his help. He notarized my testimony and we wished each other a pleasant holiday. As I walked to my car, I realized that it was again Easter weekend, the second anniversary of the tribunal's notifying me that Joe had requested an annulment. How right Joe had been. As he had predicted, I had spent much of the past two years "wallowing in ecclesiastical law," and the truth was I would probably never be free of its hold.

Yet even as I put the finishing touches on my statement, I reassured myself that although my fight had been painful, it had been time well spent. I thought of the women I had met and what they had taught me during the past two years that I could never have learned from books.

Deirdre was the first to warn me to be wary of the tribunal, but of far greater significance, she had shown me that by holding to her own moral truth, she had been able to give her daughters the gift of faith—in God, in life, and in themselves. What's more, she had done so with such grace and lack of bitterness that she would forever be an inspiration.

Pat had shown me the importance of humor, perhaps particularly when dealing with the Church. But because she was also willing to share her vulnerability, she had taught me much more. Pat was honest enough to admit that despite her efforts to free herself from the Church, it would always have a hold on her. This wasn't rational, and at first that was troublesome to someone raised as a Protestant such as I had been. But I had learned from Pat that it was the way it was, and I had grown from her teaching. Because of Pat I now had the insight and the honesty to realize that this church of which I was not even a member had a hold on me as well.

Barbara showed me that despite the worst kind of betrayal, if a person is honest and has the courage to take risks, she can always begin again. Even if it means discovering a new life in a different part of the country, if someone is willing to trust, a new start is always possible. This, too, comes from faith, albeit a different kind than the Church teaches young girls.

Ida, the gutsy elderly lady from Portland who had appealed her case to the Roman Rota and had her annulment overturned, showed me that neither self-pity nor passivity has any place in defending a marriage. Ida demonstrated the importance of perseverance, particularly when the odds are heavily against you, and for me she became the personification of moral courage.

From Darlene, I gained an appreciation for the enormous strength that the act of believing imparts to the human spirit and the power of resilience. Darlene is a survivor, and as I came to know her better I grew to appreciate her quiet strength.

Terry's story showed me a sinister side to the power of believing, a sad but important lesson. Yet because she did not waver from her own beliefs, Terry instilled a powerful sense of faith and determination in her children. It was her children that brought her through her crisis and are the core of her new life. They are testaments to her faith.

As I thought about these women, a phrase from *Masterpiece Theatre* kept coming to mind. When Catherine's lady-in-waiting asked the ambassador what her mistress's stand against annulment had shown, he answered, ". . . that there were human beings there and that they cared profoundly about the terms on which they lived and died." This was the one common thread we all shared. Despite our different backgrounds, none of the women who had told me of their annulments, nor I, nor a queen of England living four hundred years before us was willing to say we had not been married when we believed we had been. None of us was willing to lie, because we all cared profoundly about "the terms on which we lived and died" and we cared deeply about the world we passed on to our children.

As I took my statement to the post office to be sent by certified mail, I realized that my work with the Boston tribunal was more than likely complete. I kept reassuring myself, however, that regardless of what action the Boston tribunal took, the annulment was not a foregone conclusion. If the tribunal granted Joe his annulment here, I would appeal directly to Rome.

Now it was time to put annulment aside, go home, and prepare for another Easter.

EPILOGUE

———◇———

After I sent my comments concerning Joe's testimony to Father O'Connor, I enjoyed another Easter with my family and then settled in for the Boston tribunal's decision. Since most annulment cases are decided within a year and it had been two years since the tribunal began investigating my marriage, I anticipated that I would be informed within a month or so.

But spring passed and summer gave way to fall. We celebrated Thanksgiving. Even Pearl Harbor Day and the first anniversary of the tribunal's asking me to see their "doctor" went by. In fact, it wasn't until February of 1996 that I heard anything about my case. This time, however, the messenger was Joe and the unlikely setting one of our sons' hockey games.

In retrospect, I suppose I should have known something was up. Between periods Joe brought me a cup of coffee and my surprise must have been evident, as another mother standing next to me remarked, "You look like you think he put a bug in it." I laughed in recognition of my paranoia and thanked Joe. The last period went by quickly and ended with a win. Our son's team was jubilant and the spirit was contagious. As our son headed for the shower and I for my car, I told Joe to have a nice weekend. But he stopped me and asked if we could talk for a moment in private. I looked around at the crowd and couldn't see how, but before I could answer he had begun to speak.

He explained that the tribunal had told him that they had found grounds to grant an annulment, but were worried that I might cause some kind of "trouble." He wanted my word that I wouldn't. I answered that I didn't know what he meant by "trouble." I also said that even though I hadn't heard anything from the tribunal about our case, I had already told them that in the event they granted the annulment, I wanted to appeal the case to Rome.

Joe looked both angry and hurt and asked me why. I explained that it was important to me that our children know they were the offspring of a real marriage, not some mishap. And what was more, since I had been drawn into the process of defending our marriage, I had met some very brave and good women who had been betrayed by their church. I didn't see annulment as just being about our marriage anymore. I saw it as a gross injustice that had to be faced.

Joe answered that there was injustice throughout the world and added that people came to him daily with horrible stories. He than asked me if I couldn't find another cause. His reference to my defending our marriage as a cause made me angry and I had to struggle to express my feelings calmly.

I took a deep breath and replied that as a congressman of course he was told of injustices. It was part of his job. And granted, my life wasn't as exciting nor my work as important as his, but I did the best I could in the work that I did. I didn't need a cause to make my life meaningful, nor was I looking for one. In fact this "cause," as he referred to it, had literally landed on my doorstep and was the result of an investigation he had initiated.

Joe answered that he understood what I had told him, but then he asked if I couldn't see how unfair the situation was. He pointed out that even though Beth hadn't done anything wrong, now she couldn't even go to confession.

I simply answered that what Joe said might well be true, but Beth also knew when she decided to marry him that he was a divorced man with two children. And she also knew that if she did marry him, according to church law she would be unable to go to confession or

participate in communion. I explained that while I had no problem
with the Church's declaring that our marriage was over and recog-
nizing his and Beth's, our union and the children from it would
always be part of who he was and should not be denied. I also said
that I agreed completely with his point that the entire system was
unfair and that was why I refused to go along with it. I told him that I
couldn't understand why he insisted on being part of something
which seemed so morally flawed, and I suspected that if the powerful
such as he were to refuse to be part of such a corrupt process, it
would change—slowly, to be sure, but it would change.

Joe didn't answer me. By now our son had caught up with us and
was clearly uncomfortable at hearing what was escalating into an argument between his parents. A cease-fire was called for. "Just think
about it," Joe told me.

"I will," I answered, wondering if he was really oblivious to how
much I had already thought about annulment since I had received
the tribunal's notice almost three years before. As I walked to my car,
I began to wonder how Joe had learned that the tribunal had reached
a decision. No one had said a word to me. A feeling of uneasiness
came over me as I remembered how Deirdre's former husband
had been told of the annulment of their marriage and she had been
kept in the dark because, the tribunal was later to explain, of a typing
backlog.

On Monday, I telephoned Father O'Connor and he gave me a different interpretation of the events surrounding the annulment than
Joe had related. The tribunal had not contacted Joe, but Joe had
called Father O'Connor to inquire about the status of the case. He
had explained to Joe that while the judges in Boston felt there were
grounds for an annulment, the defender of the bond thought that if
one were granted there would be grounds to appeal the case to Rome
and he anticipated that the judges in Rome would regard Joe's request less favorably than those in Boston. Therefore, because the defender of the bond had voiced such strong concerns, the tribunal had
asked Joe if he wanted to withdraw his petition and they were waiting
for him to respond to their inquiry.

One thing was clear: both Joe and the judge seemed wary of
Rome. I reminded the judge that in the event of an affirmative ruling
and regardless of the views of the defender of the bond, I wanted the

case appealed to the Rota. I then asked how long Joe had to decide if he wanted to withdraw his petition. The judge said I should know the outcome of my case in a couple of weeks. The prospect made me both nervous and relieved.

Yet despite the judge's reassurance, I heard nothing, and by fall the tribunal's stony silence began to make me wary. An uneasy feeling came over me that the tribunal must have allowed Joe to submit additional evidence which I had neither been allowed to see nor to defend and was now judging the case on the basis of this new information.

Then unexpectedly, on October 23rd, almost a year and a half since the Good Friday that I had mailed my comments on Joe's testimony back to the tribunal and on the third anniversary of Joe and Beth's civil wedding, Father O'Connor in his role as judge wrote to inform me that the tribunal had granted Joe the annulment he had sought. While the official statement did not cite grounds for the ruling, the accompanying letter stated that the tribunal had reached its decision based on the petitioner's lack of due discretion. In other words, at the time of our marriage Joe had suffered from a lack of due discretion of such magnitude that he was incapable of marriage and therefore our union had never been valid.

The notice put me in a mild state of shock. While I had anticipated that in the end the tribunal would grant Joe's request, I was surprised that it had decided the case on the basis of his lack of discretion. None of Father O'Connor's questions to me nor any of the evidence presented in the case had implied that Joe lacked qualities necessary for marriage. The focus had always been on my shortcomings.

In my last meeting with Father Lory, I had mentioned how our discussion seemed to have shifted from me to Joe, but the emphasis had been on whether Joe had been willing to take certain actions that might have saved our marriage, not on whether he was able to do so. This change in the case's focus to Joe's lack of discretion further convinced me that the tribunal had gathered new information which it had neither allowed me to see nor to comment upon but had nevertheless used as the basis of its judgment.

In retrospect, I suppose I shouldn't have been too surprised at the tribunal's ruling. Most of the cases I knew of had been decided on the basis of the petitioner's lack of due discretion. I remembered how Deirdre and I had laughed as she told me of her former husband who, according to the Church, had suffered from a lack of due discretion of such magnitude that even in his thirties he was incapable of marriage, and yet he was a respected physician and had lived in a presumed union for more than twenty years and was the father of three children. I recalled how her eyes had twinkled at the absurdity of the ruling as she noted that when this same man wanted to remarry, the Church found that this terrible malady had vanished, and how she and I had agreed that maybe Joe was right. Maybe it was all just gobbledygook.

The contrast between what the Church alleged were Joe's personal shortcomings and his professional accomplishments was as odd as in the case of Deirdre's former husband. The timing of the judge's letter to me underscored the paradox: October 23rd was not only Joe and Beth's anniversary but also the homestretch for the 1996 national election. Joe was running for reelection to the United States House of Representatives. While few people in Massachusetts, including me, even knew the name of his opponent, the lack of serious opposition had not dissuaded this campaign from mounting a massive million-dollar advertising blitz on television. The spots were very effective, portraying Joe as strong yet thoughtful, appropriately vulnerable and empathetic particularly with children and the elderly. While they neglected to mention that Joe was running for Congress, they made it very clear that he was a man with vision, depth, and solid family values—the very man to lead us into the twenty-first century.

A few hours after the annulment decision arrived, I turned on the television to catch the evening news and the irony of the tribunal's decision became obvious. While Joe's promising image pervaded our kitchen and assured me that he was the man to guide our future, in my hand I held the letter from the Archdiocese of Boston asserting with moral certainty that this same man had suffered from a lack of due discretion so severe as to invalidate our marriage. Which Joe was the real Joe? Could both be? Was annulment gobbledygook, or politics, or both?

Looking back, I realize that there was a humorous side to my situation just as there had been to Deirdre's, but at the time I was consumed with anger at the tribunal's decision and the injustices inherent in the annulment process. That evening I had to struggle to remain calm and patient with the children. I didn't like myself when I was that way.

In the morning, I tried to call Father Doyle but couldn't reach him. Then I phoned a friend who was gifted at working with people who looked at the same problem but saw it so differently that it tore them apart—the way the annulment had torn apart Joe's and my ability to parent together. I summarized my situation for her and pointed out that I couldn't understand why in the eleventh hour Joe had decided to describe himself as the one lacking discretion. It seemed to me that he was taking an enormous risk.

"Well," she remarked, "Joe may not have figured that the Church would tell you how it reached its decision or he may not have known that the tribunal was going to 'put it on him,' so to speak. Either way, he's probably counting on your discretion."

"He's counting on a lot," I answered. "Particularly considering he was the one who launched a three-and-a-half-year investigation that tried to prove I didn't have any discretion."

"Do me a favor," she continued. "Don't send anything back to the tribunal before running it past a canon lawyer. This is supposed to be a legal proceeding and even if the process here in Boston seems flawed, hopefully the one in Rome won't be. Right now you're too emotional. That's understandable, but emotions don't help these situations."

I knew my friend was right. I thanked her for her insight and sat down and wrote a response to the tribunal's notice which I then faxed to Father Doyle to review. "Dear Father O'Connor," my draft began. "In reference to your letter of October 23rd and in accordance with canon law, I am appealing your affirmative decision to the Rota as the Court of Second Instance. I assume that your office will follow the necessary procedures to ensure that my case receives the Rota's consideration which canon law provides and that I will be kept informed of its progress."

Father Doyle called me back a short time later to tell me that I had worded my appeal appropriately. He noted that after I sent the appeal, the archdiocese would be required by law to forward my case to Rome. I retyped my letter and sent it to the tribunal by certified mail, relieved that my work with the Boston tribunal was now over.

But a day or so later Father Lory left a message on my answering machine asking me to call him. When I did, he told me that he assumed I had received notice of the decision and asked me what I wanted to do. I told him that I thought the case had been a travesty of justice from the beginning and that I had already informed the tribunal of my intention to appeal the case to the Rota.

Father Lory didn't sound particularly surprised. He answered that the tribunal had not yet received my appeal, and we agreed that it was appropriate that my concerns about the judicial process be reviewed in Rome. He then asked if I wanted to read the judge's decision. I said I did, and we set a time for November 12th.

A few days later Father Lory wrote me to confirm our meeting and enclosed a form essentially identical to the one that the tribunal had insisted that I sign in order to review Joe's testimony over a year and a half before. It stated that unless I was using the information I had "gleaned" from my review to defend my case before the ecclesiastical court, I was to hold it in confidence. In addition, Father Lory told me to send a check for $850 made payable to the Archdiocese of Boston to cover the cost of the appeal.

I wasn't surprised that the tribunal wanted me to sign a form promising confidentiality, although I wondered how legally it could enforce the requirement. If it made my reading the judge's decision contingent upon signing the form, then I would be signing under duress, and one of the justifications for granting an annulment was the premise that an agreement signed under duress was not valid. I also wondered what legal system the tribunal could use to sanction me were I to violate its confidentiality. Throughout its investigation of my marriage, the tribunal had maintained that its actions had no bearing on civil law. If that were in fact true, I didn't see how it could use a civil court to enforce its requirement. Nor did I see that the tribunal could treat me or my case any worse than it already had. Since I wasn't Catholic, it couldn't excommunicate me for publicly defending my marriage.

Then it dawned on me. I doubted that had I been raised Catholic I would be questioning the legality of the tribunal's actions. In fact, the Church had never informed any of the women who had talked with with me about their annulments of her legal rights. Only Ida had known that she had the right to appeal to Rome, and she had learned this from her own research. Everyone else—albeit reluctantly—accepted what their tribunals told them about the process. Largely because of their upbringing as loyal Catholics, they had been unwilling to question their church's authority.

The tribunal's request that I send the Archdiocese of Boston a check for $850 took me by surprise. The Church had always maintained that the petitioner covered the charges associated with the annulment that it did not subsidize and had stressed how affordable these charges were. Indeed, the brochure the tribunal had sent me in April of 1993 informing me of Joe's request for an annulment noted that the petitioner would pay a $300 fee. I also remembered a judge from a New York tribunal proudly telling Chris Wallace during his *Prime Time* interview that Americans could obtain an annulment for less than the price of a camcorder. I thought to myself how odd it is that it costs almost three times more to defend a marriage than to procure an annulment, yet the Church simultaneously maintains that its judicial procedures favor the sancity of marriage.

I called Father Doyle to voice my concerns and ask for his advice. He told me neither to sign the form nor to send the archdiocese a check. He assured me that the tribunal had no right to force me to sign a document under duress and that canon law was clear: the tribunal had to forward the appeal to Rome regardless of whether or not I paid the archdiocese.

As grateful as I was for Father Doyle's support, I was also nervous about defying Father Lory's orders. I remembered that Ida had told me I would have to be strong to appeal, but I hadn't even really begun the process and I already felt weak. The holidays were coming and I certainly didn't have an extra $850 to send to the tribunal. On the other hand, I didn't want to jeopardize my case and even if paying the archdiocese meant that I'd have to cut back on Christmas, I knew the boys would understand.

On a deeper level, of course, my objection to the tribunal's insistence that I send a check wasn't about money but about trust. Father Doyle had never misled me, whereas the tribunal had, repeatedly and deliberately. I decided that I would follow Ida's advice and try to be strong. I would put my trust in Father Doyle and I would meet with

Father Lory without either signing the tribunal's form or sending a check.

At our meeting I explained that I could not sign the tribunal's form requiring confidentiality because I planned to discuss the statement with Father Doyle. Father Lory said that he considered my talking with a priest who was also a canon lawyer to be within the parameters of defending my case before an ecclesiastical court and not a violation of the agreement. I wondered just how encompassing the phrase "defending a case before an ecclesiastical court" was intended to be. After all, if speaking to friends about the judge's decision helped one retain one's emotional balance, would doing so not be considered helping to defend one's marriage before the court? How could someone defend her marriage if she had an nervous breakdown and was perhaps even hospitalized? I though it best to keep these specific questions to myself and just noted to Father Lory that based on what he had said, it seemed as if the tribunal had a rather flexible interpretation of the phrase. The truth was that I knew that regardless of what the judge's statement said, it would not be the law that would keep me quiet.

Suffice it to say that the statement more than lived up to all of my negative expectations and was very difficult to discuss rationally with Father Lory. We decided not to dwell on specific points and concurred that my concerns would best be addressed in Rome.

Next we discussed the tribunal's demand that I send the archdiocese a check for $850. I explained that Father Doyle had told me not to pay the fee. I asked why it wasn't Joe's responsibility. Father Lory answered that it was the person making the appeal who was responsible for the cost. Then he seemed to hedge. He added that if I couldn't pay the fee, the case would be appealed anyway. The process, he explained, had already begun, but I should be aware that my unwillingness to finance the appeal might be interpreted by the judges in Rome to mean that I did not care as much about my case's outcome as if I had agreed to cover the cost.

I found his statement strange. Judges were supposed to review the case according to legal principles. If or how much someone paid should not be relevant. Besides, the check was to be made payable to the Archdiocese of Boston. How would the judges in Rome even know if or how much I had paid for the appeal?

Father Lory then handed me a copy of a 1993 memo from the archbishop of Baltimore which outlined the procedures for cases submitted to the Rota. The memo referred to the tribunal in the United States forwarding a $750–850 stipend to the Rota and stated that parties who could not afford the fee could apply for "gratuitous patronage." The implications of the memo for my case were not immediately clear to me and I didn't know whom or what to believe.

Once I was home, my anger at the judge's decision surfaced. I sat down at the word processor and banged out a three-thousand-word response, which I then faxed to Father Doyle. He called me a few days later and suggested that I send a shorter and "less emotional" reply to the tribunal. He then faxed me his suggested changes.

"Rather," my revised edition began, "than refer to specific points in the section dealing with the justification for the decision, suffice it to say that I challenge the accuracy of many of the conclusions drawn by the judge. I believe these are based on an inaccurate reading of the evidence or a selective reading and willful misinterpretation of the evidence."

I then explained that on principle I could not pay the $850. I noted that my former husband, whose income was vastly greater than mine, had initiated the case and was also interested in obtaining a decision favorable to him. In addition, the defender of the bond concurred with my view that the case should be appealed to Rome. "For these reasons," my letter continued, "I cannot contribute to this process. . . . I trust that either my former husband will pay the appeal charge to ensure that the investigation he initiated reaches its rightful conclusion or that the Rota will arrange to handle this case *pro bono*."

Father Lory replied to my letter on December 11th. He explained that although the petitioner is required to pay the court-assessed fee in the process of first instance, when a party chooses to appeal the decision it is the party making the appeal who is responsible for the cost. Since I was asking for the appeal, I was therefore responsible for the fee. He reiterated his demand that I forward a check for $850. This time, however, he told me to make the check payable to the Roman Rota so that the tribunal "may proceed with preparation of the Acts and forward them to Rome."

I faxed Father Lory's letter to Father Doyle. A few days later Father Doyle called me and stressed what he had told me before. The tribunal was required by canon law to forward the appeal to Rome. I should not send a check. I knew Father Doyle was right.

My mind flashed back to Terry and our meeting in Chicago so many months before when she told me that my fight wasn't just about my own annulment; it was a stand against a perverse practice and an abuse of power that had to be revealed for what it was. I knew she was right too. Why then, if I knew that both Terry and Father Doyle were right, was I still so afraid to defy the tribunal?

I asked myself this question repeatedly. Slowly I realized that on a more profound level, I was afraid for my children's future. Even though I wasn't a Catholic and even though I had never promised to raise my children as Catholics, I had always welcomed and joined with the Church to promote their moral and spiritual development. Because of this partnership and perhaps partly because I felt more at ease in Joe's church than he did in mine, as a family we had spent far more time in Catholic settings than in Episcopalian. Even after our divorce, I thought that my partnership with the Church would continue, and I assumed that in the event one of our children experienced a moral or spiritual crisis, as a family we would turn to the Catholic Church for help. Regardless of Joe's and my personal differences, because we both trusted the Church to look out for our children's moral and spiritual well-being, we would always be able to put our disagreements aside and work with the Church as parents.

The annulment process had changed all that. The tribunal was morally bankrupt and should not be subsidized by a respondent defending a marriage. It was also part of the Church and as such it had shattered my faith in the institution's ability and even willingness to be a beacon of hope and trust in times of moral or spiritual need. My defying the tribunal's demand for a check was a recognition of these truths and of the source of my fear.

Now I knew what I had to write to Father Lory. But I was still afraid. As I sat frozen at the word processor, I caught sight of Pope John Paul II's book *Crossing the Threshold of Hope*, which had been on my desk for well over a year. On the back cover, in what I presume was a facsimile of His Holiness's handwriting were he to have written in English, there was the phrase "Be not afraid." Then I understood. If my faith in the Church were to be restored, it would be in Rome.

My obligation was to appeal to the Rota in a way that reflected my own moral beliefs. The rest I would have to leave to faith that the teachings of the universal Church would prevail.

Four days before Christmas and feeling a newfound strength, I wrote to Father Lory. I told him that I found his letter of December 11th troubling because it contradicted much of what he had told me during our meeting and differed from the written material he had given me pertaining to the appeal process. I referred to the 1993 memo from the archbishop of Baltimore stating that the tribunal in the United States was to send a stipend of $750–850 to the Rota and that no other fees were requested or required. The memo also noted that parties unable to sustain the stipend could apply for *pro bono* services.

The archbishop's reference to "parties" clearly implied that both Joe's and my ability to cover the fee should be at issue. Joe was after all a party in the case. His income was significantly greater than mine and he had begun the process. I noted the archbishop's memo did not say that the respondent or the person seeking the appeal was obligated to pay its cost. I pointed out that my case had been a travesty of justice from the beginning and noted that I believed too strongly in the "teachings of the Church regarding marriage to subsidize a process that made a mockery of the sacrament by extorting funds from those less able to pay . . . while assisting far wealthier petitioners in destroying a Church-sanctified bond.

"The Boston tribunal," my letter concluded, "is required by canon law to forward my case to the Rota. I insist that the law be followed."

As I mailed my letter, I wondered if I would hear from the tribunal again. In a way it didn't matter anymore. Father Doyle's counseling ensured that my appeal was based on moral principle. Now I would try, as Ida had told me, to be strong. Most of all I would heed the advice of His Holiness. As my appeal began its journey to Rome, I would try hard not to be afraid.

GLOSSARY

The following is a list of terms as used in *Shattered Faith*.

Advocate: An expert in canon law employed by the tribunal to represent the petitioner and the former spouse during the Church's investigation.

Annulment: An official ruling by the Catholic Church that a marriage, though thought to be valid, was in fact defective from the beginning and therefore never existed.

Canon law: The legal system of the Catholic Church.

Defender of the bond: An expert in canon law who works for the tribunal and defends the marriage during the Church's investigation.

Expert witness: A person trained in counseling and/or the mental health profession who provides the tribunal with information about the couple and their marriage.

Lying: Saint Augustine defined lying as saying something one knows to be false with the intent of deceiving another. In *Shattered Faith,* however, lying is more generally defined to include either saying or doing something in order to deceive or to give a false impression, presenting false information with the intention of deceiving, and conveying a false image or impression in order to deceive.

Petitioner: The person seeking an annulment.

Respondent: The former spouse of the petitioner.

Rome: The city in Italy in which the Vatican is located. In *Shattered Faith,* the word "Rome" is used only in reference to the annulment process and is therefore synonymous with the terms "the Vatican" and "the Rota."

The Rota: The church court that hears annulment cases in the Vatican. As referenced in *Shattered Faith,* the Rota may be best understood as playing a role analogous to that of the United States Supreme Court in the American system of civil law.

Tribunal: The church court that initially hears the majority of annulment cases.

Vatican: The official residence of the pope. The word may also refer to the government of the Roman Catholic Church.

Vatican City: An independent papal state within Rome.

Witness: A person who provides the tribunal with information about the couple and the marriage under investigation.

ACKNOWLEDGMENTS

My thanks to everyone who helped make this book a reality: the strangers who encouraged me to "hang in there"; the women who shared their stories; the scholars, lawyers, and doctors who patiently explained what appeared to be inexplicable; and my family and friends who on occasion put me up and invariably put up with me. I would particularly like to thank Chip and Terry Carstensen, Ellie and Tom Crosby, Charles Donahue, Thomas Doyle, Linda Healey, Judy Katz, Kristen Kuehnle, Eric MacLeish, Sara Mattes, Phil Mayfield, Terry Monroe, Elaine Noble, Francine Pillemer, Ben, Susie, Ru, and Sheila Rauch, Bob Riskind, Margaret Scott, and Rhoda Weyer.

SUGGESTED READING AND
BIBLIOGRAPHY

Alesandro, John A., ed. *Marriage Studies: Reflections in Canon Law and Theology.* Vol. 4. Washington, D.C.: Canon Law Society of America, 1990.

American Psychiatric Association. *Diagnostic and Statistical Manual of Mental Disorders.* 3rd ed., rev. Washington, D.C.: APA, 1987.

Bennett, William J. *The Book of Virtues: A Treasury of Great Moral Stories.* New York: Simon & Schuster, 1993.

Bennett, William J. *The De-Valuing of America: The Fight for Our Culture and Our Children.* New York: Simon & Schuster, Touchstone Books, 1994.

Bennett, William J. *Moral Compass: Stories for a Life's Journey.* New York: Simon & Schuster, 1995.

Bok, Sissela. *Lying: Moral Choice in Public and Private Life.* New York: Vintage Books, 1989.

Brown, Ralph. *Marriage Annulments in the Catholic Church.* 3rd ed. Bury St. Edmonds, Suffolk: Kevin Mayhew, 1990.

Brundage, James A. *Law, Sex, and Christian Society in Medieval Europe.* Chicago: University of Chicago Press, 1987.

Buchanan, James M. *Ethics and Economic Progress.* Norman: University of Oklahoma Press, 1994.

Canon Law Society of America. *Code of Canon Law: Latin-English Edition*. Washington, D.C.: Canon Law Society of America, 1983.

Cox, Harvey Gallagher. *Fire from Heaven: The Rise of Pentecostal Spirituality and the Reshaping of Religion in the Twenty-First Century*. Reading, Mass.: Addison-Wesley, 1995.

Curran, Charles. *New Perspectives in Moral Theology*. Notre Dame, Ind.: University of Notre Dame Press, 1976.

Curran, Charles E. *Faithful Dissent*. Kansas City, Mo.: Sheed & Ward, 1986.

Curran, Charles E. *The Church and Morality: An Ecumenical and Catholic Approach*. Minneapolis: Fortress Press, 1993.

Daloz, Laurent A. Parks, Cheryl H. Keon, James P. Keen, and Sharon Daloz Parks. *Common Fire: Lives of Commitment in a Complex World*. Boston: Beacon Press, 1996.

Donahue, Charles, Jr. "Comparative Reflections of the 'New Matrimonial Jurisprudence' of the Roman Catholic Church." *Michigan Law Review* 75, nos. 5–6 (April–May 1977).

Doyle, Thomas P., ed. *Marriage Studies: Reflections in Canon Law and Theology*. 3 vols. Washington, D.C.: Canon Law Society of America, 1980–1985.

Fay, Martha. *Do Children Need Religion? How Parents Are Thinking About the Big Question*. New York: Pantheon Books, 1993.

Gilligan, Carol. *In a Different Voice*. Cambridge, Mass.: Harvard University Press, 1982.

Girzone, Joseph F. *Joshua: A Parable for Today*. 1983. Reprint. New York: Doubleday, 1994.

Glendon, Mary Ann. *Abortion and Divorce in Western Law*. Cambridge, Mass.: Harvard University Press, 1987.

John Paul II. *Crossing the Threshold of Hope*. New York: Alfred A. Knopf, 1994.

Kelleher, Stephen J. *Divorce and Remarriage for Catholics?* Garden City, N.Y.: Doubleday, 1973.

McKenzie, John L. *The Roman Catholic Church*. New York: Image Books, 1971.

McDonough, Elizabeth, O.P.J.C.D. *Religion in the 1983 Code: New Approaches to the New Law*. Chicago: Franciscan Herald Press, 1985.

Noonan, John T., Jr. *The Power to Dissolve: Lawyers and Marriage in the Courts of the Roman Curia.* Cambridge, Mass.: Harvard University Press, Belknap Press, 1972.

Parks, Sharon. *The Critical Years: The Young Adult Search for a Faith to Live By.* San Francisco: Harper & Row, 1986.

Robinson, Geoffrey. *Marriage, Divorce, and Nullity.* London: Chapman, 1985.

Schulman, Michael. *Bringing Up a Moral Child: Teaching Your Child to Be Kind, Just, and Responsible.* New York: Doubleday, Main Street, 1994.

Shriver, Donald. *An Ethic for Enemies: Forgiveness in Politics.* New York: Oxford University Press, 1995.

United States Catholic Conference. *Catechism of the Catholic Church.* Chicago: Thomas More, 1994.

West, Morris L., and Robert Francis. *Scandal in the Assembly: A Bill of Complaints and a Proposal for Reform in the Matrimonial Laws and Tribunals of the Roman Catholic Church.* New York: Morrow, 1970.

Wrenn, Lawrence G. *Annulments.* 5th ed. Washington, D.C.: Canon Law Society of America, 1988.

INDEX